Population *and* Poverty

Current Status & Future Approaches

Population *and* Poverty

Current Status & Future Approaches

M. Walter

ADHYAYAN

Adhyayan Publishers & Distributors

Delhi-110094

Published by
ADHYAYAN PUBLISHERS & DISTRIBUTORS
L-9 B, Street No. 42, Sadatpur Extension
Delhi-110094
Ph. : 011-22191282, Fax : 011-22199182
E-mail : adhyayanpublishers@yahoo.com

Population *and* Poverty : Current Status & Future Approaches

Ist Edition : 2004
ISBN—81-89161-14-8

Printed in India

Published by Harish Chandra Yadav for Adhyayan Publishers & Distributors, Laser Typesetting at Himanshu Printers and Printed at Roshan Offset Press, Delhi.

PREFACE

Today, the population increase in Asia & Pacific region have led the world in identifying problems related to rapid population growth. Apart from rapit population growth Asia has also made an excellent progress over the past 30 years and we must maintain the momentum. On the other hand, Asia is also a home to the majority of the world's poorest peoples living in poverty. This new emerging issue has major remification for the countries of the Asian and Pacific region, which still do not have systems of social protection in place.

Growth can actually increase income, inequality and widen the gap between rich & poor. To reduce extreme poverty, social envestment is needed to expand opportunities, capabilities and participation so that people can climb out of poverty. Over the past decade, East Asian countries have halved the proportion of people living in extreme poverty from 28 to 14 per cent, on a dollar or less per day. During the same period, South Asia, which is the home for nearly half the world's poor, has seen a modest drop from 44 to 40 per cent.

Through this book the editor has tried to provide an over all view on global issue of poverty and problems related to increasing population and its impact on developmental issues at micro as well as macro level, including the valuable contributions from social scientists, planners and administrators to present a more comprehensive view on the subject.

It is expected that students, teachers researchers, administrators, policy planners and professionals from different streams of disciplines would find this book informative and useful.

The Editor is also very grateful to Sri Harish Chandra Yadav of Adhyayan Publishers & Distributors, New Delhi for taking keen interest in publishing it in very short time.

M. Walter
Editor

Contents

1

Population and Poverty Challenges for Asia and the Pacific

Over the past decade, East Asia has halved the proportion of people living in extreme poverty on a dollar or less per day, from 28 to 14 per cent. During the same period, South Asia, where nearly half the world's poor live, has seen a more modest drop: from 44 to 40 per cent. While part of East Asia's success can be attributed to good economic policies, economic growth is by on means a magic potion. In fact, growth can actually increase income inequality and widen the gap between rich and poor. To reduce extreme poverty, social investment is needed to expand opportunities, capabilities, and participation so that people can climb out of poverty.

To achieve the millennium development goals, poor people must be empowered to take steps to improve their lives, and Governments must assist them by ensuring that they can obtain the services they need these services include universal access to reproductive health and primary education, as world leaders agreed in 1994 at the International Conference on Population and Development held at Cairo.

While great progress has been achieved in the Asian and Pacific region over the past few decades, we must now actively maintain the momentum. Combating widespread poverty and illiteracy, gender discrimination, growing demands in urban areas, environmental degradation and the spread of HIV/AIDS require greater political commitment and financial support. Unless these issues, and the challenges presented by a large youth population and growing numbers of older persons, are tackled with leadership and vision, there is a danger that the gains achieved so far may be reversed.

Although five years have passed since the economic crisis of 1997, most East and South-East Asian countries are still recovering and the social sector needs to be further strengthened.

Since 1969, the United Nations Population Fund, in close collaboration with ESCAP and other partners, has helped countries to plan and expand their population and family planning activities and operationalize their reproductive health services, with an emphasis on national capacity-building. As a result the region now has considerable institutional capacity and expertise to undertake research on important population and policy issues. UNFPA has also been extensively supporting projects that improve the status of women by promoting programmes that improver their education, income and employment opportunities and address gender discrimination and violence.

Although wide variations exist in the Asian and Pacific region, significant progress has been achieved in the social sector, particularly in reproductive health, over the last decade. Better medical facilities and improvements in health and nutrition have resulted in declines in fertility and mortality rates. In the past two decades, the Asian economies have shown a rapid decline in average population growth rates. Yet, Asia still accounts for almost half the world's annual population increase because of the large existing population base and there is still a large unmet need for family planning in most countries.

As a human rights and development priority, everyone should have voluntary access to reproductive health information and services, including family planning.

Population and poverty

We now have solid evidence, based on new research, that work towards population goals help to reduce poverty at both household and national levels.

At the national level, it is becoming increasingly clear that slower population growth encourages overall economic growth. Evidence also suggests that successful emerging economies almost always have favourable demographics.

Since 1970, developing countries with lower fertility and slower population growth have seen higher productivity, more savings and more productive investment. They have registered faster economic growth. Investments in health and education, and gender equality are vital to this effect. Family plainning programmes and population assistance were responsible for almost one third of the global decline in fertility from 1972 to 1994. These social investments attack poverty directly and empower individuals, especially women. They enable choice.

Given a real choice, poor people in developing countries have smaller families than their parents did. This downturn in fertility at the micro level translates within a generation into potential economic growth at the macro level, in the form of a large group of working-age-people supporting relatively fewer older and younger dependants.

Demographic opportunity

This "demographic window" opens only once and will close as populations age and older dependants increase in number. When other policies are supportive, the opportunity can allow dramatic progress as was seen in the "Asian tigers" of the 1980s and 1990s. while the proportion of their working-age populations started to increase as late as the mid-1970s the pace of change was extremely rapid up to the early 1990s. The relative growth of the working-age populations in these countries will continue for another decade. These countries made the supporting investments in health and education early in the development process, and created a framework for more open markets and social participation.

South Asia will reach its peak ratio of working-age to dependant-age between 2015 and 2025 and therefore social investments are needed now to lay the groundwork for transformation.

While investments in health and education help to boost individual and family well-being and economic growth, lack of investment and access to these vital social services has the opposite effect. Poor health diminishes personal capacity, lowers productivity and reduces earnings. Furthemore, a high prevalence of disease and poor health in a country harms its economic perpormance, while higher life expectancy, a key indicator health status, stimulates economic growth. Therefore, it is essential to improve poor reproductive health, which remains a leading cause of death and disbility for women in Asia and to reduce unsafe sex, which is the second leading cause of death worldwide.

Maternal mortality

Todya, some 2,20,000 women in Asia die each year from complications of pregnancy and childbirth, even though we know what needs to be done to reduce maternal deaths. We known that women need access to family planning so that they can better plan and space their birth. We know that all women need prenatal care during pregnancy, and skilled attendants at birth. And we know, and this was a hard lesson, that pregnant women neen access to emergency obstetric care if complications arise. Yet today, only 48 per cent of women in Asia go through delivery with a trained attendant and the consequences are tragic.

The lifetime risk of maternal death in Asia is 18 times greater than in Europe, Fortunately, we know that progress can be achieved. Sri Lanka reduced its maternal mortality rate from more than 1,500 per 100,000 live births to 60 by making safe motherhood a priority and achieving near-universal use of skilled attendents at birth. Greater efforts are needed to reduce high maternal, infant and child mortality ratios in several countries in the region, including Afghanistan, Bhutan, Cambodia, India, the Loa People's Democratic republic, Nepal and Timor Leste. It is estimated that 22 per cent of child deaths are due to perinatal causes.

HIV/AIDS

Although HIV/AIDS came later to Asia, its spread has been swift. The most populous countries of the world particularly China and recently Indonesia, are seeing signs of rapid increases, and India has the second highest number of HIV-infected adults in the world. Unless serious measures are taken to stop the epidemic in its early stages, the consequences could be ravaging.

With no cure in sight in the near future to stop AIDS, our first line of defence remains prevention, Large-scale prevention effort have halted or reversed the spread of the epidemic in a growing number of countries, including Combodia and Thailand. We must build on these successes and expand effective interventions. Efforts must be scaled up nationwide so that information, education counselling as well as care and treatment, spread faster than the virus itself. This is the only way to stem the tide of infection.

Like all matters in reproductive health, AIDS requires a multisectoral response that reaches beyond the health system to the community. Effective strategies for behaviour change, condom programming, and targeting and involving specific sectors of society, including those living with HIV/AIDS, have been developed and need to be brought to scale to reach every citizen in the Asian and Pacific region, particularly in countries where HIV/AIDS is currently spreading.

At the United Nations Population Fund, we are focusing on three strategic interventions : ensuring that information and services reach and involve young people, especially adolescent girls; ensuring that pregnant women and their children can remain HIV-free, and ensuring that condoms are accessible, and used correctly and consistently. At the Special session on HIV/AIDS held in 2001, the General Assembly adopted the ABC approach: abstinence, be faithful, and use condoms. In line with the consensus reached, UNFPA advocates these three methods of HIV/AIDS prevention.

Changing demographics

Today, the population of Asia and the Pacific is ageing rapidly, with most of the world's elderly living in China, India and Japan. At the same time, half of the population is under the age of 25. We need to develop policy frameworks and strengthen national capacity to address the needs of adolescents and the elderly.

Adolescents comprise more than 20 per cent of the total Asian population and are the most at risk of unwanted pregnancies, sexually transmitted infections and AIDS. The reproductive health of adolescents is increasingly being recognized as a key area for UNFPA support. It is vital that they receive factual and culturally sensitive reproductive health information and services.

Asia is also home to the majority of the world's older people, the majority of whom are women, often widows living in poverty. This new emerging issue has major ramifications for the countries of the Asian and Pacific region, which still do not have systems of social protection in place.

To confront the challenges of the twenty-first century successfully, we must strive to promote, respect and protect all human rights: economic, social, civil and political. Asia has made excellent progress over the past 30 years and we must maintain the momentum. The Programme of Action of the International Conference of Population and Development and the key actions adopted at the review and appraisal of the Conference, in 1999, remain feasible, affordable and effective. We must now increase our efforts. By giving greater policy attention and generating greater resources to population and reproductive health issues, we will actually make greater progress in reducing poverty, maternal and child mortality, halting the spread of HIV/AIDS, increasing gender equality and equity and ensuring sustainable development, as world leaders agreed at the Millennium Summit.

2

Unparalleled Demographic Changes : The Asia-Pacific Experience

The past 50 years of demographic change in Asia and the Pacific is without historic parallel, altering the region's demographic landscape forever. What makes the change so striking is the rapid and unparalleled pace at which it has occurred. The change has been accompanied by significant developments in the economic, social, cultural and political fabric of the countries in the region. The process that began half a century ago continues to grip more countries and population groups of Asia and the Pacific and brings with it inevitable and significant development challenges for the future.

During the past 50 years, the Asia and Pacific region has witnessed the following developments :

- Addition of 2.2 billion persons to the 1950 population of 1.4 billion, representing 60 per cent of the total increase in world population
- Decrease of 0.6 precentage point in the population growth rate.
- Reduction in infant mortality rate by almost two

thirds, from 184 infant deaths to 68 per 1,000 live births.

- Increase in life expectancy at bith of 24 years
- Decline in the total fertility rate by more than half, from around 6 children per woman to 2.7.
- Rising female age at marriage to over 20 years.
- Deepening concentration of population within urban areas, often in one primate city.

The Populations of most countries have registered significant gains in real and disposable income, experienced massive reductions in poverty, improved their literacy and educational levels and reduced gender disparities. Druing this period, accecss to information has notably improved, and major changes have occurred in the political and planning contexts of most countries.

However, these developments have not been uniform across all countries and within countries. Consequently, at the beginning of the twenty-frist century, the Asian and Pacific region has become highly heterogeneous with regard to demographic, economic, sociocultural and political conditions. For example, although mortality and fertility have declined in many parts of Asia and the Pacific, they remain high in some others. Even as income levels have risen in many countries, about a billion people in the region are estimated to live in poverty. While more and more people are able to read and write and pursue higher education, the rate of illiteracy is still considerable.

This paper highlights the significant demographic changes that have occurred in Asia and the Pacific and discusses their underlying determinants. It also looks at the future prospects and underscores some of the challenges that lie ahead.

Dynamics of growth and age structure

The population of the Asian and Pacific region, that had stood at 1.4 billion in 1950, reached 3.5 billion by 2000, resulting in an increase in the region's share of the world population from 54 to 58 per cent. The annual rate of population growth, that had averaged around 1.8 per cent during the period 1950-1955 declined to 1.3 per cent by 1995-2000. However, this regional average masks the significant trends as well as the differences among subregions and among countries.

In the mid-twentieth century, many Asian and pacific countries had high levels of fertility, with a total fertility rate (TFR) averaging around 6.0 children per woman and relatively high levels of mortality with life expectancy at birth of around 40 years. During this time, many of the region's countries gained independence from colonial rule and initiated planned development. It was also a period when countries began to follow either the philosophy of central planning or the market economy and associated themselves politically with the major powers of the cold war era that spanned much of the second half of the twentieth century.

There is evidence that mortality, which had been declining in the region since the beginning of the twentieth century, gained momentum in the 1930s, only to be interrupted by the effects of the Second World War (Caldwell, 1999). With the end of the Second World War and the increased emphasis pleaced by Governments on controlling mortality, particularly those associated with infectious and parasitic diseases, mortality began to fall rapidly, at a pace unprecedented in human history. As a result, the annual rate of population growth began to accelerate from about 1.9 per cent in the early 1950s, peaking at about 2.3 per cent during the early 1970s (Leete and Alam, 1999).

Since the late 1960s and the early 1970s, fertility began to decline in response to government interventions and by the sustained progress in other aspects of development including imporvements in health and child survival, in incomes and in female education, as well as the rising age at marriage. Hence, the annual population growth rate dropped to about 1.3 per cent by the start of the current century. (Table 1.)

The Pattern of population growth is reflected in the different subregions (Leete and Alam, 1999). At the beginning of this century, the rate was highest (1.76) per cent) in South and South-West Asia and lowest (0.75) in East and North-East Asia, as shown in table 1. Thus, in general, the Asian and Pacific region has become highly diverse during the past 50 years, with the subregional rate for South and South-West Asia being more than twice that of East and North-East Asia. The variation in growth is even more pronounced between countries, with some approaching zero growth (Japan : 0.20 per cent) and other are depicting a very high potential for continued growth in the coming decades as a result of high fertility and population momentum combined (for example, Pakistan: 2.6 pec cent).

Table 1. Population size and growth, Asia and the Pacific : 1950-2000

Region/year, major area, Region, country or area	Population (millions		Growth rate		
	1950	2000	1950-1955	1995-2000	2000
World	2,519.5	6,056.7	1.79	1.35	1.29
Asia and Pacific	1,364.2	3,523.1	1.90	1.37	1.29
East and Northe-East Asia	672.5	1,481.1	1.75	0.84	0.75
China	534.7	1,275.1	1.87	0.90	0.80
Japan	83.6	127.1	1.42	0.14	0.20
South-East Asia	177.6	521.4	2.08	1.57	1.48
Indonesia	79.5	212.1	1.31	1.41	.131
South and South-West Asia	501.7	1,490.7	2.03	1.83	1.76
Bangladesh	41.8	137.4	1.97	2.12	2.10
India	357.5	1,008.9	1.59	2.60	2.61
Pakistan	39.7	141.3	1.96	2.66	2.60
Pacific	12.4	29.9	2.17	1.36	1.29
Australia	8.2	21.8	2.26	1.15	1.07
Papua New Guinea	1.6	4.8	1.46	2.34	2.29

Source : *United Nations (2001). World Population Prospects : The 2000 Revision, vol. 1, Comprehensive Tables (New York, United Nations).*

Note : *Countries and areas indluded in the subregions are :*

East and North-East Asia : China; the Democratic People's Republic of Korea; Hong Kong, China; Japan; Macao, China; Mongolia, Republic of Korea.

South-East Asia : Brunei Darussalam; cambodia; East Timor; Indonesia; the Lao People's Democratic Republic; Malaysia; Myanmar; philippines; Singapore; Thailand; Viet Nam.

South and South-West Asia : Afghanistan; Bangladesh; Bhutan; India; Iran; (Islamic Republic of); the Maldives; Nepal; Pakistan; Sri Lanka, Turkey.

Pacific : Australia; Fiji; French Polynesia; Guam; New Caledonia; New Zealand. Papua New Guinea; Samoa; Solomon Islands; Vanuatu.

These developments have led to a dramatic change in the population age structure. The extremes are captured in figure 1 by the age structures for Japan, on the one hand, and Pakistan, on the other. The transition from high to low fertility in Japan was completed in the 1960s. With no migration, Japan attained an age structure in which the number and proportion of people at older ages have risen dramatically over the past few decades, a trand that is projected to continue. In Pakistan, the age structure remains young, owing to significant reductions in mortality but only moderate fertility declines. As the transition to low fertility proceeds, those in the young adult and working ages will rise significantly. In Sri Lanka and Thailand, where fertility has reached the replacement level relatively recently, the age structure reflects an increase in the share of those in the young adult and working ages.

These changes have altered the relative importance of working and dependent populations over time and have had considerable consequences for savings and investment and thus on the people's employment and welfare. However, the differential development of countries were dependent on their economic and social policies, including human resource development policies, and on how such policies interacted with demographic trends. Much of the neo-Malthusian discussion (Coale and Hoover, 1961) on the impact of population change on development in the 1950s and early 1960s dealt with the emerging demographic situation in the developing world at the time and was based on this interplay of the changing age structure and savings and investment at the household and societal levels.That the changes in age structure resulting from fertility declines offer a unique window of opportunity for development, provided that it is explotied with timely human resource development policies, is a matter of contemporary discussion and dabate (Asian Develpment Bank, 1997).

Mortality and fertility transition

During the period 1950-2000, mortality declined precipitously in most countries of the region. for Asia and the Pacific, the crude death rate (CDR) decreased by nearly two thirds from around 24 per 1,000 during the early 1950s to 8 per 1,000 during the late 1990s. In all the subregions, except in the Pacific where the CDR was 12 per 1,000 the levels were close to the regional average of 24-25 per 1,000. During the period 1995-2000, the overall levels had nearly converged around 7-8 per 1,000, as recorded in table 2.

Likewise, the expectation of life at birth (e_0) in the region during the early 1950s averaged around 42 years with relatively minor differences between subregions, except for the Pacific, where it was around 64 years. By the late 1990s, life expectancy for the region as a whole had increased by 24 years, a remarkable feat by historic experience. The overall increase has been highest in East and North-East Asia (28 years), followed by South-East Asia (24 years) and South and South-West Asia (23 years). More moderate gains (10 years) in the expectation of life at birth were registered in the Pacific.

Figure 1. Age-sex pyramids of selected countries: 1950-2000

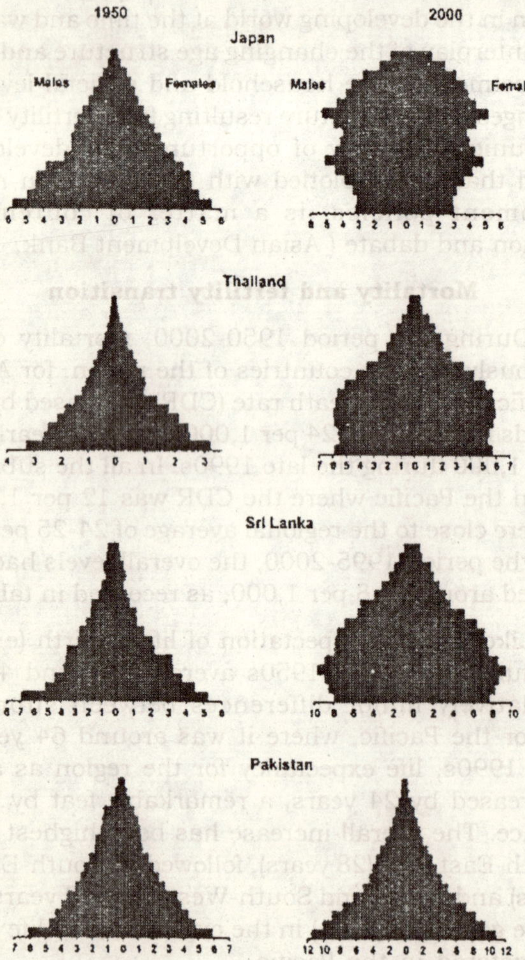

Source: Based on data provided in United Nations (2001). *World Population Prospects: The 2000 Revision*, vol. 1, *Comprehensive Tables* (New York, United Nations).

In 1950, one country in the region had a life expectancy of more than 75 years, as revealed in table 3. Only Australia; Brunei Darussalam; Hong Kong, China; Japan; New Zealand; and Singapore had expectations of life at birth that equalled or exceeded 60 years. Mortality had also started to decrease in some East and South-East Asian Countries. in the remaining subregions, life expectancy was below 45 years and in some, it was even less than 40 years. By 2000, most countries had attained life expectancies exceeding 60 years, while those that had attained more than 60 years in 1950 extended their expectations of life at birth to 75 years or more. Only a few countries in South Asia (Bangladesh, Bhutan, Nepal and Pakistan) and East Asia (Combodia, East Timor, the Lao People's Democratic Rupubilc, Myanmar) and Papua New Guinea had life expectancy less than 60 years in 2000. Afghanistan stands out as the only country in the region where it is still below 45 years (Table 3).

The gains in life expectancy at birth have been brought about by significant reductions in infant and child mortality. for example, the infant mortality rate (IMR) for the region as a whole dropped by about two-thirds of the initial level of 184 per 1,000 live births during this period, a trend that is shared by all regions. The decline was highest in East and North-East Asia (79 per cent), followed by South-East Asia (71 per cent) and South and South-West Asia (61 per cent). The Pacific, which had the lowest IMR at the beginning of the period, also recorded appreciable gains amounting to 55 per cent. Similar progress has been achieved in reducing mortality during early childhood. Compared with the regions most developed countries, such as Japan and Australia, where IMR and under-five mortality have declined to very low levels, the corresponding levels remain high in many countries of Asia and the Pacific.

During this period, the rise in life expectancy for females exceeded that of males. Even in South and South-West Asia, where life expectancy for females was lower in

1950, by 2000 it had exceeded that of males, except in Maldives, Nepal and Pakistan. The gap in expectation of life at birth between males and females has, on average, widened to two years for the region as a whole, but the difference is greater where mortality is lower. A number of factors have contributed to this unprecedented pace of mortality decline and for the differential gain in life expectancy among countries of the region. The most significant aspect of this transition is that it has taken place even with relatively modest increases in income levels. Examples include Sri Lanka and India (Kerala State), where mortality fell significantly in a very short time span. The steep decline in mortality was brought about by the prevention of deaths due to malaria, tuberculosis and cholera with the application of Western medical technology, including the use of antibiotics. The emergence of new nation-States and the emphasis given by them to providing health services, improving education and expanding knowledge of the factors affecting ill health and survival have been other important factors. Countries of the region that still lag behind (table 3) are those that have gone through periods of extreme instability, such as Afghanistan and Cambodia, or where there has been only limited progress towards education, particularly female education, as in Nepal, Pakistan and parts of India (Caldwell, 1999).

Table 2. Key indices of Mortality and fertility, Asia and the Pacific. by subregion, 1950 and 2000

Region	MortalityFertility							
	CDR	LifeExpectancy at birth			IMR	U5MRCBRTFR		
		Both sexes	Male	Female				
				1950-1955				
Asia and the Pacific	23.9	42.1	41.4	42.7	184.4	na	42.9	5.9
East and North-East Asia	23.0	42.9	41.2	44.7	181.2	na	40.7	5.7
China	25.0	40.8	39.3	42.3	195.0	na	43.8	6.2
Japan	9.4	63.9	61.6	65.5	50.6	na	23.7	2.7
South-East Asia	23.3	41.0	39.9	42.1	167.5	na	43.9	5.9
Indonesia	26.1	37.5	36.9	38.1	201.2	na	42.7	5.5
South and South-West Asia	25.5	39.2	39.9	38.5	195.9	na	45.8	6.1
Bangladesh	28.3	36.6	38.3	34.9	207.1	na	48.0	6.7

India	25.4	38.7	39.4	38.0	190.0	na	45.4	6.0
Pakistan	25.0	41.0	42.3	39.8	181.4	na	44.6	6.3
Pacific	12.3	64.0	61.7	66.4	58.6	na	27.2	3.8
Australia	9.4	69.6	66.9	72.4	23.6	na	23.0	3.2
Papua and New Guinea	29.7	34.7	33.8	38.7	157.7	na	43.1	6.2
				1995-2000				
Asia and the Pacific	8.0	66.3	64.9	67.8	68.0	92.2	22.1	2.7
East and North-East Asia	7.0	70.9	68.7	73.4	38.0	81.3	15.6	1.8
China	7.0	69.8	67.9	72.0	41.4	47.9	16.2	1.8
Japan	7.6	80.5	77.0	83.8	3.5	4.9	9.8	1.4
South-East Asia	7.4	65.3	63.2	67.5	47.2	64.4	23.8	2.8
Indonesia	7.5	65.1	63.3	67.0	48.4	62.8	22.5	2.6
South and South-Wew Asia	9.2	61.9	61.5	62.3	76.4	107.5	27.9	3.6
Bangladesh	9.8	58.1	58.1	58.2	78.8	110.8	31.4	3.8
India	9.0	62.3	61.9	62.672.5	99.0	26.2	3.3	
Pakestan	10.8	59.0	59.2	58.9	95.3	143.5	37.9	5.5
Pacific	7.6	74.1	71.7	76.6	26.2	35.6	18.1	2.4
Australia	7.1	78.7	75.9	81.5	5.4	6.7	13.4	1.8
Papua and New Guinea	10.6	55.6	54.8	56.7	69.0	95.5	34.0	4.6

Source : Based on data provied in united nations (2001) world populatin prospect : The 2000 revision, Vol. 1, Comprehensive Talble (New York, united Nations).

The 1990s have seen the emergence of HIV/AIDS in such Asian countries as Cambodia, India, Myanmar and Thailand, With no breakthrough in sight to pervent and cure this pandemic effectively, mortality levels could well rise in many countires unless countered by vigorous education campaigns and behavioural changes, particularly among men.

Table 3. Classification of countries and areas by mortality and fertility levels : 1950 and 2000 1950

e_0 /TER	e_0 <45	45<= e_0 <60	60 <= e_0 <75	e_0 <=75
TFR>=6.0	China Mongolia Combodia East Timor Lao People's Democratic Republic Myanmar Afghanistan Bangladesh India Islamic Republic of Iran Maldives Pakistan	Malaysia Philippines Thailand French Polynesia Fiji Samoa Solomon Islands	Brunei Darussalam Singapore	

	Turkey Papua New Guinea Vanuatu		
4.0<=TFR<6.0	Indonesia Viet Nam Bhutan Nepal	Macao, China Republic of Korea Sri Lanka Guam New caledonia	Hong Kong, China
2.1<=TFR<4.0		Democratic People's Republic of Korea New Zealand	Japan Australia
TFR>2.1			
		2000	
TFR>=6.0	Afghanistan		
4.0<=TFR<6.0		Cambodia East Timor Lao People's Democratic Republic Nepal Pakistan Papua New Guinea	Bhutan Guam Maldives Samoa Solomon Islands Vanuatu
2.1<=TFR<4.0		Myanmar Bangladesh	Mongolia Indonesia Malaysia Philippines Viet Nam India Islamic Republic of Iran Turkey Fiji French Polynesia New Caledonia	Brunei Darussalam
TFR>2.1		Democratic People's Republicof Korea	ChinaJapan Macao, China Hong Kong, China Republic of Korea Singapore Thailand Australia Sri Lanka New Zealand	

Source : Based on data provided in United Nations (2001). World Population Prospects : The 2000 Revision, vol. 1, Comprehensive Tables (New York, United Nations).

Declines in fertility during this period have been equally dramatic (tables 2 and 3). During the early 1950s, the TFR averaged around 5.9 children per woman in the region. In most countries it was well above 6.0. By 1995-2000, It had dropped to 2.7 for the region as a whole but with significant subregional and intercountry differences in the timing and pace of decline. For instance, while the

TFR is below the replacement level of 2.1 in East and North-East Asia (1.8), it is twice as high (3.6) in South and South-West Asia. Evidence indicates that the fertility decline began only during the late 1960s and early 1970s in the countries of North and North-East Asia, closely followed by some south-East Asian countries. While organized governmental intervention to moderate fertility began in India in the 1950s, fertility decline in South and South-West Asia did not gain momentum until the mid-1970s with not as rapid a pace of decline. In the Pacific subregion, by the early 1950s, fertility had decreased significantly in Australia and New Zealand but was very high in the other island economics. But by 2000, fertility had declined in most of these countries, with the exception of Melanesia.

Reviewing the Asian experience, Leete and Alam (1999) Have concluded that popultion Policy was the driving force, affecting both the magnitude and speed of the changes. They also concluded that the success of family planning programmes was frequently supported by positive changes in the demand for children.

In most countires, the age at marriage of females has risen markedly during the past two or three decades as a result of increasing education of girls and their participation in gainful employment (ESCAP and UNFPA, 1998; Guest, 1999). Though more recent evidence is not available, an ESCAP and UNFPA (1998) review indicated that by 1990, the singulate mean age at marriage among females had risen above 20 years in most countries and in many, it was well above 25 years. Thus, the increase in age at marriage has played an important role in fertility decline. In addition, diminishing infant and child mortality and the resulting increase in family size, rising income levels and improved access to information have created a latent demand for, and utilization of, family planning services in most countries.

In Japan, the transition to low fertility was achieved by the early 1960s. Delayed marriage and voluntary control of marital fertility, mainly throuth abortion, which was legalized in the late 1940s, were the major determinants of fertility decline. On the other hand, China achieved replacement fertility by the vigorous Government enforcement of its "one-child" policy. In Hong Kong, China; the Republic of Korea; Singapore, Sri Lanka; and Thailand preconditions for a sustained decline in fertility, in particular, lower infant and child mortality and high female education, existed by the late 1960s. However, the provision of contraceptives through government-supported progarmmes and private channels helped couples to achieve their reproductive intentions more rapidly than anticipated.

Banglades and Indonesia have reduced fertility significantly in a short time span because of consistent and high-level political support of government sponsored, externally supported family planning programmes. The decline is remarkable in the context of low income levels, low female educations, and high infant and child mortality. Recent evidence from the Demographic and Health Surveys indicates that fertility and contraceptive use have reached a plateau in these countries due in part to the high desired number of children. The Islamic Republic of Iran and Turkey are other Muslim countries in which fertility has dropped significantly even without much external donor support. In the former, the decline is due in part to its efficient health service delivery system and the more recent but strong support by the Government to provide family planning services. Among the Muslim countries, Turkey had been more progressive historically, resulting in the high educationl levels of girls and their empowerment and in the use of family planning. In multi-ethnic Malaysia, where official policy remains pronatalist, rapid fertility decline has taken place among the Chinese and Indian communities but only moderately among the Malays. In part, this is due to the higher socio-economic and human development levels achieved by the Chinese and Indian populations.

In the Philippines, support for family planning has wavered with the changes in government. Despite this and the religious opposition to family planning. fertility has decreased as a result of high female education, delayed marriage and non-marriage. In Myanmar, a Buddhist country with no religious objection to family planning, delayed marriage and non-marriage (very high compared with regional standards have played important roles in fertility reducation.

Combodia, the Lao People's Democratic Republic and Viet Nam have undergone war and/or internal strife. these countries, and Mongolia in North Asia, have followed communist/socialist ideology and their policies remained pronatalist until recently. In Viet Nam, fertility fell substantially as a result of government policies in support on family planning and abortion. With the introduction of family planning/birth spacing in Combodia and the Lao People's Democratic Republic, it is expected that fertility will soon decline, even though other preconditions for fertility decline are far from being fulfilled.

India, which was the first country in the world to adopt family planning as an official policy and programme, presents a mixed picture of progress and change. While fertility has fallen below the replacement level in Kerala, Goa and Tamil Nadu, in other states the decline has been slow. In general, there is a strong association between the level of social and human development, particularly female education, and fertility. While family planning programme efforts, though variable among the states, have played a role in reducing fertility in India, its impact has been more significant in states with higher levels of social and human development.

Fertility remains high in Afghanistan, Maldives, Nepal and Pakistan. Afghanistan has had no stable government for decades and in recent years, women's position was considerably compromised. As a result, Afghanistan ranks as the region's most backward. Support for family planning is ambivalent at best in Nepal and Pakistan. Together with lack of progress in social and human development, fertility remains at a highlevel. Likewise, in the Pacific island economies, Polynesian countries in general have moderated their fertility to lower levels in comparison with Melanesian countries, which is partly a reflection of their differences in social and human development.

Rural to urban transition

During the second half of the twentieth country, the Asian and Pacific region underwent fairly rapid urbanization and urban growth. It is the only region in the world where urbanization has consistently increased as a result of sustained improvements in urban employment opportunities (Guest, 1999).

While the world's urban population increased from three fourths of a billion in 1950 to 2.8 billion in 2000, the comparable increase for Asia and the Pacific was nearly sixfold, as depicted in table 4. Although the Asian and Pacific region is still predominantly rural, its urban population more than doubled from 17.3 to 35.9 per cent. The corresponding figures for the world as a whole were 29.7 and 47.0 per cent, respectively.

The pace of urbnization has been most rapid in south-East Asia and East and North-East Asia, followed by South and South-West Asia and the Pacific. There are variations, however, among countries within the subregions. In general, the countries of East and North-East Asia and South-East Asia, such as Malaysia, the Republic of Korea and Thailand, have followed an export-led growth policy for most of the 50-year period. Other countries, notably China, have followed the same policy more recently. Consequently, some of the region's fastest urbanization and urban growth have occurred in the afore mentioned countries. Countries in South-West Asia such as India, which followed the polity of import-substitution, have also registered moderately high rates of urban growth.

Countries where the urbanization level was high initially, such as Japan and some Pacific countries.including Australia and New Zealand, experienced modest gains in urbanization.

Concurrently, with the repid pace of urbanization, there has been an increase in the growth of large urban agglomerations in many countries. Consequently, in Malaysia, the Republic of Korea and Thailand, "primate cities" have developed. According to the United Nation (2000), the number of cities with 10 million or more population in Asia and the Pacific grew from two in 1975 to 11 in 2000. The contribution made by rural-to-urban migration to urban growth and urbanization has also been high. In general, countries that experienced rapid urban growth also had the highest share of urban growth due to rural-urban migration (United Nations, 2000 and Gubhaju and other, 2001).

Table 4. Indicators of rural to urban transition

Region/Year	1950 Urban Population (millions)	per centurban urban	Rate of Urban growth (1950-1955)	2000 per cent Population (millions)	urban urban	Rate of growth (1995-2000)
World	749.9	29.7	3.0	2,845.0	47.0	2.1
Asia and the Pacific	236.7	17.3	3.6	1,268.0	35.9	2.7
East and North-East Asia	120.8	18.0	3.9	571.7	38.5	2.0
South-East Asia	26.9	14.8	3.7	192.7	37.2	3.6
South and South-West Asia	81.2	16.2	3.1	482.3	32.1	3.1
Pacific	7.8	61.6	3.0	21.3	70.2	1.3

Source : United Nations (2000). World Urbanization Prospects, The 1999 Revision (New York, United Nations.)

Judging from the rate of growth of the urban population between 1950-1955 and 1995-2000, it appears that there has been a slight deceleration in recent years. However, the rural-urban differential in the rate of population growth remains high. Therefore, it is to be expected that with greater globalization, urbanization will continue and populations will inevitably become more urban. Reviewing the Asian and Pacific experience, Guest

(1999) concluded that the level of internal migration in the ESCAP region was growing, consisting increasingly of rural-to-urban migration. Moreover, Guest points out that internal migration involves a high proportion of temporary migrants, a significant fraction of them being females.

In countries that are at the intermediate stage of the demographic transition, such as Bangladesh, India and Indonesia, the age structure is such that it will put pressure on rural-to-urban migration as the number of new labour force entrants increases. However, countries that have completed their demographic transition, such as the Republic of Korea and Thailand, can see stabilization or even a deceleration in migration as the number of labour force entrants continues to decline in the future (Skeldon, 1991: Guest, 1999).

High and low performing countries.

From the above discussion, it is possible to classify countries into three broad categories: (a) those that have completed or are nearing completion of the demographic transition; (b) those that are the intermediate levels; and (c) those that are at early stages (table3). Countries with a TFR of less than 2.1 and a life expectancy of over 75 years can be considered high-performing countries, while those with a TFR, greater than 4 and an expectation of life at birth or under 60 years can be considered low-performing countries. In general, countries in the latter group have high infant and child mortality and low female education, while those in the former group have very low infant and child mortality and high female education.

Differences in economic development as measured by the rate of growth of gross domestic product (GDP) or the levels of per cepita income and poverty seem to be less important. For example, China the Domocratic People's Republic of Korea and Sri Lanka have completed the demographic transition while having had only modest or low levels of economic growth. Mortality has declined significantly and rapidly in most Asian and Pacific countries with relative stability and low levels of economic, social and human development. Fertility, however, has dropped rapidly in countries with high levels of political commitment in support of population policies and programmes and human capital investment. It remains high in countries with low political commitment and social and human development.

Similar patterns are also observed among the different geographic or administrative divisions and/or population subgroups with such countries as India, Indonesia and Malaysia.

The path to progress and change

Mortality decline began during the early part of the twentieth century and gathered momentum after the Second World War with the attainment of independence and self-rule in nearly all countries. Rapid gains in survival were a result of the adoption of emerging medical technologies in cambating disease and death due to infectious and parasitic diseases. Active government interventions coupled with increases in awareness among the people and rising levels of income, have contributed to this unparalleled progress made by countries in reducing mortality. Yet, high mortality still persists in many countries and population subgroups in the region. These include countries that have undergone the averages of internal conflict and war during much of the period 1950-2000 and/or countries where social and human development, particularly education, has lagged behind and poverty remains stubbonly high.

Concern with high fertility, on the other hand, was raised by non-governmental organizations, particularly in India, mainly because of its implications for the health, welfare and survival of mothers and children. Around the same time, concern was also being expressed about the adverse implications of population growth for social and economic development, a thinking that was reinforced by the seminal study by Coale and Hoover (1961); This led

India to initiate the first government-sponsored family planning an experiment in social organization and engineering which was followed by other countries,. This strategy has been used by many countries in Asia and the Pacific at varying levels of intensity. At one extreme is China, vigorously implement aed the "one child" policy by involuntary means. Likewise in parts of india during of emergency period under Prime Minister Indira Gandhi, some form of corecion was sued in controlling fertility. In many countries, however, programmes were planned and or disincentives for clients of family planning services and for service providers. As these programmes were mainly driven by the targets that were set, in most cases translated into quotas to be achieved by service providers, concerns about the rights of couples and the health of women were not, in general, matters that were considered in the equation. There are other countries, such as the Republic of Korea and Thailand, that followed a more holistic approach combined effective demand generation for family planning - which also recognized the positive impact of social and human development in this regard-and the provision of services through government outlets as well as through NGOs and the private sector.

It should be noted that where family planning services do not meet the needs of couples and individuals, it could result in increased resort to abortion. Available evidence indicates that the incidence of abortion is very high in countries such as Mongolia, Sri Lanka and Viet Nam. In countries where abortion is illegal , the high majority of these are done clandestinely and urder unhygienic conditions leading to high matermal mortality and morbidity.

The United Nations, including ESCAP and its partner agencies, in particular UNFPA, has played a vital role in creating awareness and consensus among the Asian and Pacific countries and in developing the nations technical and managerial capacity for the planning, implementing and monitoring of progarmmes. NGOs have played an important role in promoting family planning even in countries where they met with opposition for socicoultural and religious reasons. More importantly, at the 1994 International Conference on Population and Development in Cairo, NGOs played an active role in refocusing family planning programmes in the context of a broader "reproductive health" approach that addresses the needs of women, men and children during their life cycle and recognizes the rights of individuals and couples to information and quality services.

In Prospect : issues and challenges

The unprecedented progress achieved during the last half-century in most countries of Asia and the Pacific and the possible continuation of trends in the coming decades will have inevitable consequences for development. In a number of countries, particularly in Afghanistan, Cambodia, the Lao People's Democratic Republic, Maldives, Napal, Papua New Guinea, Pakistan and Solomon Islands, where the transition is still at an early stage, the challenge would continue to be to improve social and human development and to moderate their fertility and population growth. The challenge for those countries in the intermediate stage of demographic transition (Bangladesh, Fiji, the Islamic Republic of Iran and Turkey) would be to address the momentum effect of population growth as the population in the young adult ages continues to grow.

For countries that have complited or will soon be completing their demographic transition (Australia; HongKong, China; Japan; New Zealand; the Republic of Korea; Singapore; and Sri Lanka), the major issue will be to manage the effects of an ageing population for meeting both the possible shortages of labour and the health and other needs of the elderly.

The popultion of countries that are in the intermediate stage of transition will also begin to age in the not too distant future. Not only will ageing occur at a repid pace in the Asian and Pacific countries but the number of older persons in the region will also be the highest. With the number of children per women dropping to levels at or below the replacement level together with repid urbanization, internal and international migration and family nuclearization, the challenge posed by the region will be at a scale and magnitude never before experienced. The problem will be compounded by the fact that it will be taking place when the income levels of many countries will still be relatively low and the necessary social security systems will not be in place. Moreover, unless active measures are undertaken, HIV/AIDS will pose the greatest challenge for many countries, at least in the short and medium terms.

With increasing globalization, both internal and international migration will become more important issues affecting the development of many countries. Prudent migration policies, particularly those supportive of migrants, will be a subject of discussion among the receiving and sending countries in both bilateral and multilateral forums. It should also be noted that while the region as a whole was able to reduce poverty significantly during the past couple of decades, the global economic downturn that began in the late 1990s has reversed that trend in a number of countries, During the coming years Asian and Pacific countries are likely to remain vulnerable to external economic conditions, severely straining their efforts to improve social progress and human development, in particular, reducing the gender biases that continue to exist in many countries of the region.

Despite these challenges, the Asian and Pacific region as a whole is poised to move towards lower mortality and fertility levels as the level of education, of females in particular, improves and information becomes more easily accessible throughout the region. The next 50 years will witness significant shifts in population age-structure and increased migration. These changes will have an impact on development and on the well-being of the people, and hence, need to be considered as an integral part of policy of planning.

Endnote

For the purpose of this paper, the Asian and Pacific region is defined to include the countries of the following subregions: East and North-East Asia, South-East Asia, South and South-West Asia and the Pacific. The countries excluded are the countries of West Asia, and North and Central Asia.

References

Asian Development Bank (1997). Emerging Asia: Changes and Challenges (Manila, Asian Development Bank).

Caldwell, John C. (1999). "Good health for many: the ESCAP region, 1950-2000", Asia-pacific population Journal, 14 (4):21-38.

Coale, Ansley J. and Edgar M. Hoover (1961). Population Growth and Economic Development in Low Income Countries (Princeton, Princeton University Press).

ESCAP and UNFPA (1998). "Asia-population future: implications for policy". in the Asia-Pacific Population Policies and Programmes: Future Directions (New York, United Nations,) pp. 29-58.

Gubhaju, Bhakta, K.S. Seetharam and Jerrold W. Huguet (2001) Demographic dynamics in the ESCAP Region: implications for sustainable development and poverty", Asia-Pacific population Journal, 16 (1): 45-66).

Guest, Philip (1999). "Mobility transitions within a global system", Asia-Pacific Population Journal, (14(4):57-72.

Leete, Richard and Iqbal Alam (1999). "Asia's demographic miracle: 50 years of unprecedented demographic Change", Asia-Pacific Population Journal, 14(4):9-20.

Skeldon, Ronald (1991). "The relationship between magration and development in the ESCAP Region", Population Research Leads, No. 38.

United Nations (2000). World Urbanization Prospects : The 1999 Revision (New York, United Nations).

(2001). World Population Prospects :The 2000 Revision, vol. 1, Comprehensive Tables (New York, United Nations).

3

Population and Poverty : Some Perspectives on Asia and the Pacific

The International community has committed itself to an ambitious programme of social development for the opening decades of the twenty-first century. Attacking poverty directly - as a matter of human rights to accelerate development and a reduce inequality within and among countries - has become an urgent global priority. World leaders have agreed on a variety of new initiatives, including the United Nations Millennium development goals (United Nations, 2001).

Some progress in reducing the proportions of people living in extreme poverty was made in the last decade (Chen and Ravillion, 2001). However, while the absolute number of the extremely poor has decreased by over 100 million the aggregate decline has been confined to Latin America and parts of Asia. East Asia and the Pacific registered the largest absolute decline (over 185 million fewer persons lived on less than an adjusted US$1 per day in 1998 than in 1990), but China accounted for all but 38 million of that total. Despite a declining proportion in extreme income poverty (roughly 4 per cent). South Asia registered an absolute increase of 25 million. Several countries in the region have met the goal of halving poverty, while others have seen slower progress of reversals.

Since 1998, structural adjustment, the fallout of the 1997 financial crisis. socio-political conflicts and natural catastrophes have had a negative impact on several countries. Income inequality has increased in several countries, including some with rapid economic growth (ESCAP, 2002). Higher income inequality requires much higher overall growth rates to achieve progress in poverty reduction (UNDP, ECLAC and IPEA; forthcoming). The assumption that the elasticity of poverty to income gain is one that is oftern unwarranted

Further, poverty is multimidensional. Income poverty is only one aspect of the deprivation of the right to essential development assets and opportunities. Education, health (including reproductive health), nutrition, water and sanitation, employment social and political participation are additional elements of the deprivation of capability and empowerment (Sen, 1999).

The millennium development goals set targets for progress in a variety of dimensions beyond income poverty. There has been significant progress over the last decade in several dimensions, for example, educational enrolment and advancement, infant and child mortality reduction and overall longevity. However, progress in other dimensions has lagged in the aggregate and in many countries.

Population trends in the region : dimensions of diverstiy

Asia and the Pacific display one of the most diverse social, economic and demogrphich profiles. This largest of all regions contains countries at virtually all stages of demographic transition. It provides examples of the possibility of rapid change and examples of the stubborn persistence of social and demographic trends. Good overviews of recent trends are readilya vailable in the literature (Gubhaju, Seetharam and Huguet, 2001; Westley, 2001; Leete and Alam, 1999; Leete and Jones, 2002; Asian Development Bank, 2002). For current purposes, it is sufficient to note that most reviews stress the changes in fertility rates, age structures, urbanization and migration.

Linkages between population and poverty

Recent research has reviewed the long-standing skepticism by some economists of a linkage between population dynamics and macroeconomic growth and based on a more complete data record and improved techniques concluded that population has a variety of effects on development at the household and national levels (Birdsall and others, 2001). A number of mechanisms have been identified.

The demographic bonus

The change from high to low mortality and fertility can create a "demographic bonus" for countries. Mortality declines first, followed by fertility. What happens as fertility declines is that the working-age population increases relative to younger and older dependants. That creates a one-time opportunity for growth. The opportunity can be realized if countries have made the appropriate investments, not only in family planning but in health and education generally, with special attention given to the needs of girls and women, and in employment opportunities for the new and enabled workforce. Open and responsive governance makes these adjustments possible.

This phenomenon was first analysed in the "East Asian miracle" of the 1980s and 1990s (Asian Development Bank 1997). The best recent macro level research suggests that from 1960 to 1995 about a fifth of economic growth was attributable to gains in mortality and about a fifth to reductions in fertility. External financial shocks and the failure of regulatory frameworks (like those that contributed to the 1997-1998 economic catastrophe) can impede progress. But recovery since then, although held back by continuing external problems, shows the value of the earlier demographic and social changes. The collapse hit the poor hardest and they continue to bear the brunt.

The proportion of populations in the "working ages" continues to increase in many countries, particularly those at an earlier stage in the demographic transition. Many countries still have time to invest to profit from their opportunity, but investments need to be made before the opportunity is squandered.

The sheer volume effects of the demographic bonus realized through the age structure changes are supplemented by the changing opportunities for women. Female labour force participation also contributes to economic growth, particularly when it is appropriately compensated, and declining fertility is linked to increased women's employment. The rising levels of women's educations and increased demand for labour by a growing formal sector increase the opportunity cost of high fertility. Education and fertility declines can combine in a positive feedback in which the growth of the labour force increases faster than the growth of the labour age population alone.

For countries entering the post-transition period, increased old age dependency might act as a drag on further development if such a trend was not balanced by productivity gains, The evidence to date suggests that young age dependency has a stronger effect on economic growth than does old age dependency (Asian

Development Bank, 1997), but it must be recognized that the projected pace and level of population ageing are outside the range of past experience. Without accelerated accumulation of resources for old-age support and a strengthening of intergenerational linkages the net effect could be negative.

Distributional effects.

Long.-term demographic and economic data from 45 developing countries show that high fertility raises absolute levels of poverty by slowing economic growth (and reducing the poverty reduction growth can help deliver) and by skewing the distribution of consumption against the poor. Fertility reduction through greater acceptance of family planning counters both of these effects (Eastwood and Lipton, 2002). Investments in improved reproductive health help to redress gender inequities and barriers to social and economic participation.

The positive redistribution effect comes from (a) the reduction of the requirement of higher outlays for basic needs and education (with lower savings and investments in child quality) of young dependants, and (b) the increased ability of poor households to increase their labour supply and savings. Women with fewer children are more able and ofter more willing to participate in remunerative work. They are also more likely to invest their added income in the health and education of children. Societal impacts on consumption also help poor households as the increasing scarcity of labour raises wage rates - even for families whose own fertility does not decline - and lowers demand for land (reducing the costs and slowing the unsustainable fractionalization of holdings).

These consumption effects can add substantially to the gains from growth. About half the estimated decline in poverty comes from increases in economics growth and half from the consumption side.

Timing effects

At different stages in the demographic transition these effects differ. At first, when mortality declines, particularly among infants and children, increased expenditure is needed for these young dependants and growth slows. As fertility declines and aggregate growth slow, economic growth increases.

In the early stages of transition, the gap between poor and non-poor households may increase. As poorer families join in the transition (which has not yet happened in many societies in mid-transition), poverty and inequality reduction effects increase.

The poorer the country and the higher its initial level of fertility, the greater the effect of declining fertility on a decline in absolute poverty. The beneficial effects increase as the demographic transition proceeds. The faster the fertility decline, the larger the potential benefits of the demographic transition but the shorter the time period available to take advantage of them.

The magnitude of demographic effects interacts with the condition of markets, Governments and institutions. Where these institutions are weak, as in many pre-transition or early transition countries, the initial negative effects are magnified. The initial positive effects of fertility declines are likely to be reinforced where labour markets and school systems are working well and parents are prepared to invest in their children's education. Economic and social policies matter. Combined with access to reproductive health, they can accelerate poverty reducation.

The exclusion of the poor

While more people in a growing number of countries are becoming aware of the relative gains from smaller family size and larger investments in children's health and education, the poor may not be receiving the information or support that will allow them to recognize this (Merrick, 2001). As a result, they do not realize the benefits derived from smaller families. Publice economic policies may distort labour markets, leading members of poor households to expect higher returns from child labour than are realistic. They are slow to recognize changing demographics and economic conditions which are more visible to, and more quickly affect, the less marginalized. Generally they have less access to information and fewer of the assets needed to take advantage of the opportunities that societal fertility dicline produces. Where women and girls are relatively disadvantaged in decision-making and resource allocation, they bear the higher costs of high fertility but are less likely to realize the immediate gains; this undercuts their motivation to challenge the conditions that restrict their reproductive health asccess.

Gender inequality presents one of the most pervasive examples of exclusion of the disadvantaged. Reducing gender inequality can accelerate economic growth and have a powerful impact of poverty. Comparing East Asia and South Asia between 1960 and 1992, South Asia started with wider gender gaps in health and education and closed them more slowly. If gender gaps had closed at the same rate in the two subregions, South Asia Would have increased its real per capita annual growth in gross domestic product (GDP) by 0.7 to 1.0 per cent (Klasen, 2001)

Emerging population trends : selected poverty implications

Poverty and the elderly

Elderly populations are among the fastest growing segments of the age range. Increases in life expectancy and earlier population growth have increased the total number of older persons: declining fertility rates in many countries have contributed to their increasing share of total populations. Population ageing is posing a growing challenge to formal and informal support systems. Richer countries in the region have expanded the public components of systems contributing to the care of older persons (whether through pension schemes, provident funds or various subsidies and preferences in housing and other services). As in other regions, there is also evidence, however, that increased public resources can contribute to the erosion of expectations of informal familial support.

It is likely that there will be substantial increases in the numbers of elderly persons living in poverty. The legacy of earlier low coverage in public pension systems leaves many without adequate income even as informal support weakens because of increased migration, changing social attitudes and smaller family size. While such challenges can be offset by improved public support, easier transfer of resources over larger distances and increased wealth, many will be left unhelped.

The oldest old people are overwhelmingly women and they reach their later years with significant accumulated deficits from life-long discrimination and inequality in access to resources and opportunity.

HIV/AIDS and poverty

The impact of the HIV/AIDS epidemic in severely affected countries (for example in sub-Saharan Africa) is devastating. The quality of life, prospects for economic advancement, stability of family and community social systems suffer immeasurably as the pandemic progresses. In the worst-affected countries, public servants and private sector exployees are falling sick in increasing numbers; by 2020 these economies could be 20 to 40 per cent smaller than expected because of the pandemic. Damage to public services such as education and health will drive the poor further into poverty.

The prospects for the pandemic in Asia are raising increasing concern, but many countries have not yet appreciated their vulnerability. In India, more newly infected persons are being added annually than in any other country (United Nations, 2002). China is confronting the potential of a larger spread of the disease; there are acknowledged localized pockets of high prevalence, partly related to unsafe medical practices, and large-scale population movements that could readily assist the distribution of the disease. Combodia Myanmar and Thailand face a serious epidemic. Prevalence in some subgroups is also high in Indonesia, Nepal and Viet Nam.

It is hard to predict what the course of the epidemic will be in Asian countries. The potential exists (between 5 and 20 per cent of adult men visit sex workers at least once a year and many of them have wives or other partners) for expansion in several countries (Brown, 2002). Various methods of transmission may spread the disease in different countries, Intravenous drug use have been reported to have increased in several Central Asian countries. Trafficking in women and girls creates additional highly vulnerable populations.

Prevention campaigns in Thailand have demonstrated that the spread of the pandemic can be stemmed. Such programmes require the investment of political will and appropriate resources. Many countries have not mobilized themselves sufficiently, either for prevention or for programmes of treatment and care.

Adult mortality impoverishes life prospects for

children. Where HIV/AIDS is severe, it adds significantly to the number of orphans.(beyond those created by maternal mortality and other diseases). Globally, 2 million new orphans are created each year owing to the pandemic. Maternal mortality (at some 500,000) per year in South Asia) adds some 1.5 to 2 million more. Orphanhood often has serious consequences for child poverty, health (and survival prospects), education and development with subsequent negative poverty outcomes in later life

Beyond national averages[1]

Attention to progress towards achieving national poverty reduction goals should not distract attention from internal differentials. Disparities in wealth, gender nd geographical location will have to be reduced to improve the quality of life of the marginalized. These disparities are the result o complex processes of exclusion which tend to perpetuate them.

Infant mortality and poverty

Infant mortality is a traumatic societal burden. High infant mortality persists because of the prevalence of often-preventable communicable diseases. Vaccination programmes and improved nutrition have led to significant progress, but it has been uneven.

Poor infants and children are more likely to die than children in better-off families. In some countries, for example, the under-5 mortality rate of the poorest 20 per cent of the population is more than four times that of the richest 20 per cent (Adam Wagstaff, 2000). The differentials in infant mortality can be lower, but are still substantial.

Table 1. Infant mortality levels by wealth quintile, regional comparisons.

Region	Poorest	2nd	3rd	4th	Richest	National average	Poorest/ richest
East Asia and the Pacific	56.6	46.6	40.1	30.5	20.4	41.0	2.7
South Asia	97.6	105.2	99.9	83.7	56.8	90.7	1.8
Sub-Saharan Africa	107.4	107.1	99.4	91.5	66.6	96.2	1.7
Middle East/North Africa	94.7	78.2	63.5	54.6	33.5	68.0	2.9
Europe/Central Asia	67.0	58.4	56.4	47.0	36.8	54.7	2.0
Latin America and Caribbean	68.9	59.4	50.6	40.7	29.3	52.9	2.7
Asian and pacific region	72.8	72.1	67.3	56	41	63.6	
Total	90.9	87.3	79.9	70.5	50.7	78.1	
Quintile value/richest,	1.79	1.72	1.58	1.39	1.00		
total for the Asian and Pacific region	1.78	1.76	1.64	1.37	1.00		

The wealth difference in infant mortality in the Asian and Pacific region mirrors the global average (see (table 1). In some regions, progress will be more difficult. In sub-Saharan Africa and South Asia, which have the highest infant mortality rates, the gap between the richest and the poorest is smaller, and even among the richest 20 per cent infant deaths are higher than the average in other regions.

Health risks, to infants and children are worse in poor families with many children. Larger families are more common among the poor and their children in them are less likely to receive even basic preventive health care (Jensen and Ahlburg, 1999), If the children become ill, they are less likely to be treated. If the sick child is a girl, her risks can be even higher.

Table 2. Infant mortality levels by wealth quintile, ESCAP region.

Country	Poorest	2nd	3rd	4th	Richest	National average	Poorest/ richest
Viet Nam	42.8	43.2	35.2	27.2	16.9	34.8	2.5
Philippines	48.8	39.2	33.7	24.9	20.9	36.0	2.3
Indonesia	78.1	57.3	51.4	39.4	23.3	52.2	3.4

India	109.2	106.3	89.7	65.6	44.0	86.3	2.5
Bangladesh	96.3	98.7	97.0	88.7	56.6	89.6	1.7
Nepal	96.3	107.2	103.6	84.7	63.9	93.0	1.5
Pakistan	88.7	108.7	109.3	95.7	62.5	94.0	1.4
Kazakhstan	35.1	43.7	44.3	50.2	29.1	40.7	1.2
Uzbekistan	49.5	43.8	41.5	33.6	46.8	43.5	1.1
Kyrgyzstan	83.3	73.3	67.5	49.6	45.8	66.2	1.8

Overall, in countries of the ESCAP region (table 2), some of the highest wealth differentials in infant mortality are found in East Asian countries with relatively low national averages. Further progress in infant mortality reduction will require giving greater attention to equity as levels decline. The poorest 60 per cent are often the most disadvantaged.

Poverty and reproductive health access and use : differentials within countries and regions.

Some of the widest gaps within countries, and between richer and poorer countries , are in the area of reproductive health. The death of a mother in pregnancy or childbirth in hundreds of times more likely in the poorest countries. A women's lifetime risk of dying of maternal causes is as follwos: in Africa, one in 19; in Asia one in 132; in Latin America, one in 188; but in more developed countries, only one in 2,976 (Hill, AbouZahr and Wardlaw, 2001).

This reflects both higher risk and the larger number of births. Unwanted fertility is higher in poorer settings and among the poorest of the poor. There is less information on maternal morbidity[2] but the differentials are likely to be similar, since the causes - lack of information, access, community and family support, finance, transport and provider quality[3] - are broadly the same.

Fertility levels and poverty

Achieved fertility is the resultant of preferences (demand) and the availability of means to realize reproductive choice. These combine to produce significant differences in outcomes. Wealth differentials in fertility outcomes in the ESCAP region tend to be larger than the global average. (table3).

In the Asian countries reviewed (Table 4), not all the wealthy groups have reached low fertility levels. In seven, the wealthiest have reached fertility levels at or below replacement, while the porest are higher (between 3.1 in Viet Nam and 6.5 in the Philippines). Other countries are earlier in the transition. In Nepal, only the wealthiest had fewer than four children (2.9). In Pakistan, only the wealthiest had as few as four children; other groups of poorer women had between 4.9 and 5.1.

Family planning prevalence and poverty

The higher the level of women's overall contraceptive use, the lower the differental between women in the richest and poorest societal groups (see table 5). Once family planning use exceeds 40-50 per cent overall, the differences between wealth groups narrow considerably. Family planning acceptance becomes a social norm widely diffused throughout a society.

Table 3. Fertility levels (TFR) by wealth quintile, regional comparisons.

Region	Poorest	2nd	3rd	4th	Richest	National average	Poorest richest
East Asia and the Pacific	4.30	3.43	2.80	2.40	1.90	2.93	2.23
Southern Asia	4.80	4.38	4.08	3.80	2.80	4.05	1.77
Sub-Saharan Africa	6.91	6.35	6.10	5.54	4.25	5.76	1.72
Middle East/North Africa	5.55	4.50	3.80	2.95	2.50	3.80	2.27
Europe/Central Asia	3.98	3.35	3.08	2.75	1.73	2.93	2.33
Latin America and the Caribbean	6.51	4.93	3.88	2.98	2.07	3.84	3.17
Asian and pacific region	4.43	3.83	3.45	3.14	2.23	3.42	
Total	6.13	5.32	4.86	4.27	3.20	4.68	
Quinitile value/richest,	1.92	1.66	1.52	1.34	1.00		
total for the Asian and Pacific region	1.99	1.72	1.55	1.41	1.00		

In Indonesia, the Philippines and Viet Nam and some Central Asian republics, wealth differentials in contraceptive use tend to be particularly low. Differentials are largest in Pakistan, where contraceptive use is lowest (table 6).

In South Asia, the country with the lowest overall prevalence, Pakistan, at 9 per cent, 20 times as many people in the wealthiest group, use contraception as in the poorest. In Nepal, with a prevalence of 26 per cent, the difference is less than three times.

Several central Asian countries have reached overall prevalence levels close to 50 per cent, with lower differences between richer and poorer.

Recent estimates suggest that levels of unment need for family planning in Asia (excluding China and including Central Asia) and the Pacific totals around 65 million women of reproductive age, which represents more than half of the developing world total of approximately 113 million (Ross and Winfrey, 2002). The levels, however, are proportionately lower for limiting births than in other regions.

Table 4. fertility levels (TFR) by wealth quintile, ESCAP region

Country	Poorest	2nd	3rd	4th	Richest	National average	Poorest richest
Viet Nam	3.1	2.7	2.2	1.8	1.6	2.3	1.94
Kazakhstan	3.2	3.2	2.9	2.4	1.3	2.5	2.46
Indonesia	3.3	2.9	2.6	2.5	2.0	2.8	1.65
Bangladesh	3.8	3.8	3.5	3.1	2.2	3.3	1.73
Uzbekistan	4.4	3.7	3.3	3.3	2.1	3.3	2.10
India	4.1	3.6	3.2	2.8	2.1	3.4	1.95
Kyrgyzstan	4.6	3.6	3.6	3.3	2.0	3.4	2.30
Philippines	6.5	4.7	3.6	2.9	2.1	3.7	3.10
Nepal	6.2	5.0	4.7	4.4	2.9	4.6	2.14
Pakistan	5.1	5.1	4.9	4.9	4.0	4.9	1.28

Table 5. Contraceptive prevalence (percentage married women of reproductive age) by wealth quintile, regional comparisons.

Region	Poorest	2nd	3rd	4th	Richest	National average	Richest/ poorest
East Asia and the Pacific	37.6	46.3	49.7	50.0	47.2	46.2	1.26
South Asia	20.2	23.4	27.3	29.5	41.8	28.4	2.07
Sub-Saharan Africa	4.2	5.7	7.5	11.7	22.3	10.3	5.36
Middle East/North Africa	24.2	35.3	43.4	48.6	54.7	41.7	2.27
Europe/Central Asia	39.2	44.4	44.4	45.8	50.4	45.2	1.29
Latin America and the Caribbean	27.9	38.1	43.4	49.8	54.5	44.5	1.95
Asian and pacific region	32.9	38.1	40.3	41.3	46.5	39.8	
Total	16.8	21.6	24.5	28.5	36.4	24.7	
Quinitile value/poorest,	1.0	1.28	1.45	1.69	2.16		
total for the Asian and Pacific region	1.0	1.16	1.22	1.25	1.41		

Maternal care and poverty

In most regions, more than three quarters of pregnant women visit a doctor, nurse or midwife at some point in their pregnancy. Where women's mobility is more restricted, as in the South Asian countries, the figure is nearer one third. In all regions, the higher her income, the more likely a women is to seek antenatal care. The gap between wealthy and poor families is greatest when national averages are lowest. In South Asia. the gap at the extremes of the wealth distribution results from particularly high levels of care among the wealthiest.

Table 6. Contraceptive prevalence (Percentage married women of reproductive age) by wealth quintile, ESCAP region.

Country	Poorest	2nd	3rd	4th	Richest	National average	Richest/ Poorest
Pakistan	1.2	4.1	6.1	10.7	23.2	9.0	19.33
Nepal	15.7	21.2	23.2	26.6	44.9	26.0	2.86
Philippines	19.6	26.1	32.7	32.7	29.2	28.0	1.49
India	24.9	27.5	36.1	42.0	50.6	36.5	2.03

Bangladesh	38.8	40.8	43.7	38.8	48.5	42.1	1.25
Kazakhstan	44.2	48.7	40.9	47.3	48.1	46.1	1.09
Kyrgyzstan	44.4	44.9	48.4	50.9	54.4	48.9	1.23
Uzbekistan	47.2	54.7	55.1	46.4	53.5	51.3	1.13
Indonesia	46.2	55.6	56.8	58.0	56.9	54.7	1.23
Viet Nam	47.0	57.3	59.5	59.4	55.5	55.8	1.18

Table 7. Medically skilled assisted delivery levels by wealth quintile, regional comparisons

Region	Poorest	2nd	3rd	4th	Richest	National average	Richest poorest
East Asia and the Pacific	30.5	53.0	68.4	80.6	93.4	60.8	3.11
South Asia	5.3	8.1	11.7	21.9	49.3	17.7	10.49
Sub-Saharan Africa	24.6	32.9	41.2	59.2	82.1	46.2	3.46
Middle East/North Africa	12.8	21.7	37.7	58.6	82.2	38.5	6.61
Europe/Central Asia	82.7	92.3	95.1	98.6	99.7	92.8	1.21
Latin America and the Caribbean	40.2	58.4	72.9	85.6	94.3	65.8	2.38
Asian and pacific region	40.0	49.0	54.8	62.8	77.8	54.8	
Total	31.2	42.1	51.6	66.2	84.0	52.5	
Quintile value/poorest	1.0	1.35	1.66	2.13	2.70		
total for the Asian and Pacific region	1.0	1.22	1.37	1.57	1.94		

Differences by wealth level in attended deliveries are wider (table 7). The poorer segments of society are even less likely to have skilled assistance at delivery than to seek antenatal care.

In South Asian countries, women (in aggregate) are half as likely to have skilled attendance at birth as they are to have skilled antenatal care. Overall levels of pregnancy care are low; in the two poorest quintiles trained antenatal care is more than three times as common as trained delivery. In sub-Sabaran Africa, the other region with high maternal mortality, women are two thirds as likely to have skilled birth attendants as to have skilled antenatal care and the differential in the poorest strata is less marked.

Table 8. Medical-assisted delivery levels by wealth quintile, ESCAP region

Country	Poorest	2nd	3rd	4th	Richest	Na.tional average	Richest / Poorest
Bangladesh	1.8	2.5	4.1	9.0	29.7	8.1	16.5
Nepal	2.9	5.2	6.4	9.1	33.7	9.6	11.6
Pakistan	4.6	6.6	6.0	21.5	55.2	18.6	12.0
India	11.9	18.2	30.1	47.9	78.7	34.3	6.6
Indonesia	21.3	34.8	48.1	64.4	89.2	49.1	4.2
Philippines	21.2	45.9	72.8	83.9	91.9	56.4	4.3
Viet Nam	49.0	78.4	84.2	93.6	99.2	77.0	2.0
Uzbekistan	91.9	100.0	99.3	99.0	100.0	97.5	1.1
Kyrgyzstan	96.0	98.2	98.1	99.7	100.0	98.1	1.0
Kazakhstan	99.4	100.0	98.8	100.0	100.0	99.6	1.0

Increases in the use of skilled attendants relative to wealth (table 8) tand to be sharper than for other basic health-care services. Antenatal care and attended delivery are more sensitive to wealth differences than oral rehydration therapy or medical treatment for diarrhoea, medical treatment for acute respiratory infections or immunization. Attendance by a doctor is the most sensitive to income (Gwatkin and Deveshwar-Bahl, 2002).

Table 9. Adolescent (aged 15 to 19) fertility levels by wealth quintile regional comparisons.

Region	Poorest	2nd	3rd	4th	Richest	National average	Poorest/ richest
East Asia and the Pacific	85.3	64.7	38.0	29.3	12.7	46.7	6.72
South Asia	138.3	136.8	121.3	105.3	67.5	116.0	2.05
Sub-Saharan Africa	176.8	166.1	155.3	148.8	93.5	143.8	1.89
Middle East/North Africa	72.5	62.0	58.5	33.5	23.0	50.5	3.15
Europe/Central Asia	83.8	65.5	73.3	63.8	31.5	63.8	2.66
Latin America and the Caribbean	181.0	135.3	105.0	73.4	33.1	97.2	5.47
Asian and pacific region	108.8	93.7	82.8	72.1	40.2	80.4	
Total	154.7	136.4	122.0	108.3	64.4	113.6	
Quintile value/richest,	2.40	2.12	1.89	1.68	1		
total for the Asian and pacific region	2.71	2.33	2.06	1.79	1		

Childbirth at home or in a health facility is also strongly related to wealth. Nearly 80 per cent of births in the richest families are at a health facility, and most births in the two richest quintiles. At each lower wealth group, the proportion of home births increases. Nearly 80 per cent of the poorest quintile have their children at home.

Table 10. Adolescent (aged 15 to 19) fertility levels by wealth quintile, ESCAP region

Country	Poorest	2nd	3rd	4th	Richest	National average	Poorest richest
Viet Nam	51	41	27	18	11	32	4.64
Philippines	130	90	32	29	12	46	10.83
Indonesia	75	63	55	41	15	62	5.00
Pakistan	88	87	66	76	44	74	2.00
India	135	140	117	84	45	116	3.00
Nepal	143	149	132	128	90	127	1.59
Bangladesh	187	171	170	133	91	147	2.05
Uzbekistan	58	50	85	68	39	61	1.49
Kazakhstan	101	65	83	53	26	64	3.88
Kyrgyzstan	120	81	61	91	29	75	4.14

Adolescent fertility and wealth

Though adolescent fertility levels in the ESCAP region are lower than in some other major regions, the differentials between the wealth group extremes are larger: the richest attain very low levels of young fertility.

In East Asia, countries where the young are least likely to give birth have larger differences between poor and rich groups.

In Indonesia, the Philippines and Viet Nam, adolescents in the poorest segments of the population are nearly seven times as likely to have had children within the past year as their better-off counterparts. In the Philippines, poor young women are nearly 11 times as likely to have had a child. These higher levels reflect early marriage, less ability to negotiate delays in sex and reproduction and less access to family planning. In all three countries, reductions in youthful fertility are systematically related to increases in wealth. In south Asia, adolescent fertility levels are higher and only the richest quintile is regularly distinguished from less wealthy groups.

Beyond wealth

Material wealth differences are produced by disparities in physical and social infrastructure, including opportunity, resources, skills and information. They are generated and reinforced by complex social processes of exclusion. Geographical location is important; rural areas provide lower levels of services, information and opportunities than urban areas.

Some of the wealth differentials related to reproductive health services and use reflect greater poverty in more rural areas. But differences can be seen within both urban and rural areas. Fewer rural residents reach the higher income levels seen in cities, but in both settings the poorest have the worst services. In India, for example, total and adolescent fertility levels, contraceptive usage and immanization levels are highly similar across the wealth spectrum in rural and urban areas. The poorest in rural areas are more disadvantaged than their counterp arts in cities. Rural families, for example, have less access to safe dilivery services, particularly if they involve highly trained personnel or specialized facilities. In the richest groups in both settings, the differences are minor (Gwatkin and others, 2000).

Urban areas are growing repidly, and the poor of the world are increasingly urban (United Nations Population Division, 2001; Naylor and Falcon, 1996). This provides both opportunities and new challenges. Economies of scale and ease of access could increase coverage, but inequities in access within cities remain large. However, smaller cities, while better served than rural areas, compare poorly with larger cities (Hewett and Montgomery, 2001). The relative disadvantage of medium-sized cities in providing health quality and service is a growing problem as a larger proportion of urban dwellers come to live in them. Municipal and other local authorities have more responsibility under the decentralization of public health administration, without the corresponding resources or revenue-raising authority. Local governments will find it inreasingly difficult to fill the gaps in services.

Some ways forward

Most donor institutions are working to improve the positive impact of health (including reproducitve health) interventions for the poor. Health deficits for poorer populations exact a significant toll in lost productivity, human misery and missed opportunities for gender equality and accelerated development. The substantial differentials in access to information and services justify coordinated public,private and community responses on the basis of social welfare arguments and in the light of the substantial economic and social externalities. One key challenge is seeing that population and reproductive health programmes, and development programmes at large, confer their benefits on the poor, The incorporation of population considerations in emerging mechanisms for development planning (for example, in poor countries, poverty reduction strategy papers, sector-wide approaches and other elements of health sector reform) remains an important policy task. The deversity of social, demographic and economic situations in the Asian region will require the careful tailoring of policies and programmes to national realities Important principles to be incorporated include rights-based approaches, gender and cultural sensitivity, participatory mechanisms for accelerated expowerment, quality programming, efficiency, sustainability and equity. The chart suggests some important priorities for population and reqroductive health interventions with general applicability to all anti- poverty interventions.

Endnotes

1. The differentials presented here are based on the reports in the series Socio-economic Differences in Health, Nutrition and Population in [country] prepared by Davidson R. Gwatkin and others (2000) for the HNP/ Poverty Thematic Group of the World Bank. Forty-four countries with a Demographic and Health Survey were analysed . ESCAP region countries are also aggregated in this presentation. Most of the surveys date from the mid to late 1990s. work is under way to update and expand the database.

2. This is true of morbidity measures in general. The absence of effective registration systems and paucity of wealth or income measures even renders mortality comparisons within countries a difficult enterprise. (for discussion, see Adam Wagstaff, 2000).

3. Quality-of-care initiatives are an important component of most programmes of assistance to reproductive health care providers, but high or irregular workloads, poor compensation, staff turnover and underdeveloped systems of monitoring and supervision pose constant challenges to attaining and maintaining standards.

4. For comparative studies of the efficiency of service delivery systems, analyses need to be statistically correct for rural-urban proportions. Comparing access within countries looks at differentials within urban and rural places.

Reaching the Poor : towards a pro-poor agenda

Dimension of action	Key issues	Important directions
- Attend to problems that most affect the poor	-Provide basic social Services with sensitivity to people's capacity,	Provide governance and supporting environments for meeting people's needs

- Recognize the dignity of all	needs and cultures	
-Expand participation	Improve the accessibility of public and private Services. Intergated programming Qualitative approaches and active listening	Address the marginalized Women, the indigenous, the poor, those living with HIV/AIDS, people in crisis situations. Provide programmes for adolescents
Evidence based programme activities	Improve data bases on needs and situations and on effective action Ensure the availability and use of data	Expand resources for Community and individual action and choice (including microcredit) Involve local institutions including NGOs, cultural organizations and the private sector.
Improve the quality of programmes addressing basic needs, particularly of the poor.	Provide training for staff and information for potential beneficiaries Mobilize demand for quality and improve systems of accountability Make direct investments in quality improvement recruiteffective staff	Improve geographical targeting to reach those in need Respond to expressed unmet need (including thosefor reproductive Health and family Planning) Advance health sector reform in ways that attend to quality and equity.
-Improve and diversify financing and ensure Sustainability	Mobilize resources Improve monitoring and evaluation Reduce costs to the poor Involve programme staff and beneficiaries in defining and setting priorities.	Develop and improve financing systems: mobilize additional resources

Note : The general dimensions (or principles) of action that are identified in the first column are associated with the key issues presented in the second. The final column recommends particular actions that follow from this analysis.

5. See, for example, Health Systems Resource Centre, Department for international Development Health systems Resource Centre. 2001. "Health financing: designing and implementing pro-poor policies"; "Which,

healthpolicies are pro-poor?" and "Health in poverty reduction strategy papers: an introduction and early experience".

Reference

Asian Development Bank (1997). Emerging Asia (Manila, Asian Development Bank).

(2002). Key Indicators 2002 (Manila, Asian Development Bank).

Birdsall N., A.C. Kelley and S.W. Sinding (2001). Popultion Matters: Demographic Change, Economic Growth, and poverty in the Developing world (New York, Oxford University press).

Brown, Tim (2002). " The HIV/AIDS epidemic in Asia", Asia-Pacific population and policy, No 60, January 2002 (Published April 2002), Honolulu, East-West Center. Based on a chapter in the East-West Center, The Future of Population in Asia.

Chen, S.,M. Ravallion (2001). "How did the world's poorest fare in the 1990s", Policy Research Working Paper (Washington DC, world Bank.).

Eastwood, R. and M. Liption (2002). "Demogrphic transition and poverty: effectsvia economic growth, distribution and conversion", in Birdsall and others, 2001.

Economic the Social Commission of Asia and the Pacific (ESCAP) (2002). Policy issues for the ESCAP region: sustainable social development in a period of repid globalization : challenges, opportunities and policy options. Note by the secretariat, submitted to the Commission at its fifty-eight session in 2002 (E/ESCAP/1233).

Gubhaju, Bhakta, K.S. Seetharam and Jerrold W. Huguet (2001). "Demographic dynamics in the ESCAP region: implications for sustainable development and poverty", Asia-Pacific population Journal, 16(1) : 45-66

Gwatkin, Davidson R. and Garima Deveshwar-Bahl (2002). "Socio-econom ic inequalities in use of safe motherhood services in developing countries. A presentation given in London, 6 February.

Gwatkin, Davidson R., Shea Rutstein, Kiersten Johnson, Rohini P. Pande and Adam Wagstaff (2000). Socio-economic Differences in Health, Nutrition and Population in India for the Health, Nutrition and Population/Poverty Thematic Group of the Work Bank.

Hewett, P.C.and Mark R. Montgomery (2001). "Poverty and public services in developing country cities, population Council Policy Reserach Division Working Paper No 154 (New York, The Population Council).

Hill, K., C. AbouZahr and T. Wardlaw (2001). "Estimates of maternal mortality for 1995", Bulletin of the World Health Organization, 79(3):182-193.

Jensen, E.R. and D.A. Ahlburg (1999). "A multicountry analysis of the impact of unwantedness and number of children on child health and preventive and curative care", Washington DC, POLICY Project, the Futures Group International. Accessible on the web site:<www.tfgi.com>

Klasen, S. (2001). "In search of the Holy Grail : how to achieve pro-poor growth?". Paper commissioned by Deutsche Gesellschaft fur Technische Zusammenarbeit, "Growth and equity", Task Team of the Strategic Partnership with Africa (draft).

Leete, R. and I. Alam (1999). " Asia's demographic miracle: 50 years of unprecedented change", Asia-Pacific Population Journal, 14(4):9-20

Leete, R. and G. Jones (2002). "Asia's family planning programs as low fertility is attained", Studies in Family Planning, 33(1): 114-126.

Merrick, T. (2001). " Population and poverty in households: a review of reviews", in N. Birdsall, A.C. Kelley and

S.W. Sinding, eds., Population Matters: Demographic Change, Economic Growth, and Poverty in the Developing World, (New York Oxford University Press).

Ross, J.A. and W.L. Winfrey (2002). "Unmet need for contraception in the developing world and the former Soviet Union: an updated estimate", International Family Planning Perspectives, 28(3):138-143.

Sen, A. (1999). Development as Freedom (Oxford, Oxford University Press).

United Nations (2001). Road map towards the implementation of the United Nations Millennium Declaration: report of the Secretary-General, submitted to the General Assembly at its fifty sixth session (A/56/150).

(2002). World Population Monitoring: Reproductive rights and reproductive health: selected aspects, submitted to the Commission on Population and Development, 1-5 April 2002 (ESA/A/WP. 171).

United Nations Development Programme (UNDP), Economic Commission for Latin America and the Caribbean (ECLAC) and Institute for Applied Economic Research (IPEA) (forthcoming). "Meeting the millennium poverty reduction targets in Latin America", discussion draft, May 2002.

United Nation Population Division (2001). World Urbanization prospects 2001, New York, United Nations.

Wagstaff, Adam (2000). "Socioeconomic inequalities in child mortality: comparisons across nine developing countries", Bulletin of the World Health Organization, 78(1): 19-29.

Westley, Sidney B. (2001). "A 'snapshot' of populations in Asia", Asia-Pacific Population and Policy, No. 59, October 2001 (Published April 2002). Honolulu, East-West Center. Based on a chapter in the East-West Center, The Future of Population in Asia.

4

Poverty and Mortality in the Context of Economic Growth and Urbanization

Asia has always been a demographic giant, but in the second half of the twentieth century it also became an economic giant. In Those 50 years, real per capita income (expressed in purchasing power parity) in Asia multiplied by more than five, compared with a multiplication in Western countries of little more than threefold, and in Latin America and Africa by 2.3 and 1.6 times, respectively (Maddison, 2001). During this half century, the world GDP in fixed United states dollars multiplied six times but that of Asia did so by more than 12 times, taking the continent's proportion of the world economy from 18 to 36 per cent. That growth was fundamental to the mortality revolution outlined here but it was also achieved by massive urbanization, producing huge cities with savage contrasts between the living conditions of the poor and the rich. Asian urban population multiplied over eightfold from under one quarter of a billion to over two billion, and will by

2020 constitute half the population. this was partly the product of hundreds of millions of poor villagers streaming into illegal shanty towns, especially around the largest cities.

The aim of this paper is twofold. First, we will outline the macroscopic changes and than we will focus on poverty and death in the slums of one of Asia's great Cities, Dhaka, the Capital of Bangladesh, which has grown from a centre of 300,000 people in 1950 to one with around 12 million inhabitants at present. In remains a metropolis where rural-urban migration is still the major source of growth.

An outline of change

Tables 1 and 2 are constructed within a framework of real per capita income (gross national income in purchasing power parity per head) in order to overcome the distortions produced by exchange ratesin evaluating relative incomes. Excluded are those countries, mostly small Pacific ones, where the economic income calculations have not been made. the major distortion will probably arise from the omission of Afghanistan, apparently the poorest country, and certainly the one with the highest mortality (an expectation of life at birth of 43 years) in the Asian and Pacific region. The main message of the two tables is that national mortality levels are closely tied to economic development and individual economic levels, especially at the extreme ends of the income range. Indeed, among the richer populations that relationship may be becoming stronger. In group A, with per capita incomes in the US$ 15,000-25,000 range, life expectancies near 80 have now been achieved, while even the next highest income level is characterized by life expectancies not only little above 70 years but not much greater than those of countries with incomes down to about US$ 2,000.

These richer countries have achieved the additional decade of life expectancy in two ways which have become increasingly possible during the last few decades and require expensive technology. The first intervention has been the reduction of perinatal mortality by the intensive care of the newborn, especially premature and very light-weight babies. Thus, the almost incredibly low infant mortality rate of 3 per 1,000 live births has been achieved in Hong Kong, China; Japan; and Singapore, one fifththe level of the next rechest nations, and one twentieth of that not only of the poorest nations but of developed countries at the mid-twentieth century. The necessary intensive care has been achieved by the use of expensive equipment in technically advanced hospitals. The second change which has allowed the steepest declines in the whole demographic transition in the mortality of the aged populations is the product of high-technology in the form of the expensive testing and treatment of the old (United Nations, 2002; United Natinas, 2001)

This is not good news for poorer countries. The Republic of Korea, with a per capita income of over US$ 8,000 is just getting there, while Malaysia, with half the Republic of Korea's per capita income, has greatly reduced child mortality but not old-age mortality. If the lower bound for achieving really low child and infant mortality is a 1999 real per capita income of US$ 8,000, then life expectancies near 80 years will, even with 4 per cent annual growth in per capita income, not be reached by the poorest group until the late twenty-first century.

What is better news is that income is not nearly so important in determining mortality over most of the income range, certainly above US$ 2,000 per capita income. Life expectancy of 70 years is within reach by all but the very poorest countries. It can be reached, as we discuss below, by an emphasis on education and easy access to curative treatment. Much depends on the existence of an adequate public health base. This has been furthered in most Asian countries by very high rates of immunization among children, possibly higher than the Latin America and certainly higher than in africa. safar water supplies and sanitation are also important.

Where national poverty plays a decisive role is among the very poor countries, found mostly in south Asia and the old Indo-China grouping. Here, the near universal provision of safe water and sanitation has been beyond the capacity of government budgets. In 1994-1995, the proportion of the population with access to safe drinking water was 95 to 100 per cent in the group A countries except the Republic of Korea (Where it was 89 per cent), 88 per cent in Malaysia, 60 per cent in Pakistan, 48 per cent in Nepal and 39 per cent in the Lao People's Democratic Republic. An anomaly was the situation of Bangladesh, where a very high rural level of tubewells for water access has meant the almost universal drinking of bacteriologically safe water, but where it is now realized that much of this water may contain dangerous levels of arsenic. the exact danger is still undetermined (Caldwell and others, 2002). similarly, access to satisfactory sanitation in 1994-1995 fell from over 90 per cent in richer countries to 30 per cent in Pakistan, 20 per cent in Nepal and 19 per cent in the Lao People's democratic Republic.

Table 1. Parity Purchasing power per capita income (PPPPCI) and mortality, 1999-2002

Income Group (1999)	Country or area	PPPPC 1999	Life expectancy at birth (LEB) (years)	Increase in LEBs over last 25 years (years)	Under 5 mortality (per thousand births)	PPPPCI ranking	Life expectancy ranking	Relative ranking to PPPPCI ranking	Percentage urban
A. Over US$ 15,000	Japan	25170	82	7.5	5	1	1	0	79
	Australia	23850	79	7.0	7	2	3	-1	85

	Singapore	22640	78	7.6	4	3	5	-2	100
	Honk Knog, China	22570	80	7.1	4	4	2	+2	100
	New zealand	21130	78	6.5	8	5	5	0	86
	Republic of Korea	15530	76	11.7	10	6	4	+2	83
B. US$ 5,000-15,000	Malaysia	7640	73	8.9	9	7	8	-1	59
	Turkey	6440	71	11.1	50	8	13	-5	77
	Thailand	5950	73	10.1	31	9	8	-1	31
	Iran (IslamicRepublicof)	5520	70	14.1	43	10	15	-5	63
C. US$ 3,000-5,000	Kazakhstan	4790	66	-0.3	53	11	30	-19	57
	Fiji	4780	70	7.8	22	12	15	-3	51
	Maldives	4200	68	14.3	49	13	24	-11	27
	Samoa	4070	70	12.4	32	14	15	-1	22
	China	3550	71	6.6	73	15	13	+2	33
	Philippines	3390	70	10.5	36	16	15	+1	60
	Turkmenistan	3340	67	4.7	69	17	26	-9	45
	Sri Lanka	3230	73	6.5	24	18	8	+10	25
D. US$ 2,000-3,000	Vanuatu	2880	69	13.2	36	19	21	-2	21
	Indonesia	2660	67	15.9	51	20	26	-6	43
	Georgia	2540	74	3.5	22	21	7	+14	62
	Azerbaijan	2450	72	2.0	41	22	12	+10	58
	Kyrgyzstan	2420	69	3.8	47	23	21	+2	33
	Armenia	2360	73	-0.1	18	24	8	+16	71
	Papua New Guinea	2260	58	10.9	63	25	36	-11	18
	Uzbekistan	2230	70	4.1	37	26	15	+11	37
	India	2230	64	12.0	87	26	28	+2	29
	Solomon Islands	2050	70	11.8	31	28	15	+13	21
E. US$ 1,000-2,000	Pakistan	1860	61	10.0	103	29	32	-3	38
	Viet Nam	1860	69	16.9	46	30	21	+9	20
	Mongolia	1610	64	8.1	87	31	28	+3	65
	Bangladesh	1530	61	13.2	94	32	32	0	26
	Nepal	1470	60	14.0	100	33	34	-1	13
	Lao People's Democratic Republic	1430	59	12.1	107	34	35	-1	25
	Combodia	1350	57	16.2	106	35	37	-2	17
	Bhutan	1260	63	17.5	82	36	30	+6	8
	Tajikistan	1100	68	3.8	77	37	24	+13	28

Sources : United Nations (1998). world Urbanization Prospects : The 1996 Revision (New York, United Nations); United Nations (2001). World Population Prospects : The 2000 Revision, vol. 1, Comprehensive Tables (New York, United Nations); United Nations (2002). 2002 ESCAP Population Data Sheet (Bangkok, Economic and Social Commission for Asia and the Pacific).

Table 2. Average characteristics by income grouping (unweighted averages)

Group	PPPPCI (US$)	Life expectancy at birth	Under 5 mortality	Percentage urban population
A	21.815	79	6	89
B	6,390	72	33	66
C	3,920	69	45	42
D	2,410	69	48	36
E	1,500	62	89	33

Source : See table 1.

Access to curative services also falls with income.

The poorer countries usually have inferior services with low-quality staff and shortaves of drugs. Indeed, growing dissatisfaction with the lowest-level services has led to rural Chinese bypassing them and going to district hospitals and Indians increasingly turning to private practitioners. The number of private practitioners in most countries is increasing faster than the rate of economic growth and they will inevitably form an everlarger proportion of total health services. In retrospect, primary health care will be seen to have been a stopgap measure, albeit a very important one, for spreading health serives to the poor during the late twentieth and early twenty-first centuries until economic growth allowed the development of the public-private mix which has long characterized developed countries. In many countires they may be parallelled by the rise of government-organized national health insurance.

Relative success and failure in mortality improvement

There are two ways of measuring mortality advantage and disadvantage and they yield different findings, especially in the case of one anomalous group. The first way is to compare the life expectancy ranking with that of real per capita income ranking; the second way is to examine the rate of increase of life expectancey over a period such as the last 25 years, 1970-1975 to 1995-2000 (table 1).

The anomalous group is constituted by the seven Asian republics that emerged from the break-up of the Union of Soviet Socialist Republics. All had rising life expectancies up to about the 1970s and also rising incomes until around that time. Subsequently, the economic system faltered and then changed, real per capita income fell, and, rather uniquely in the modern world, life expectancy either levelled off or fell (although not to the same extent that occurred in the European segments of the former Union of soviet socialist Republics). According to the United Nations (2001) there were two patterns. In the Caucasian republics (Armenia, Azerbaijan and Georgia), mortality decline ceased or flattened out as early as the 1970s and bottomed out in the 1980s, while in the central Asian republics (Kazakhstan, Kyrgyzstan, Tajikistan, Turkmenistan and Uzbekistan), mortality declined through the 1980s only to rise or flatten out in the 1990s. What is true of all of them is that, prior to crises, the centralized system provided good educational and health systems, and subsequently high levels of education and women's independence plus a commitment to survival especially children's survival, arising from low mortality levels and an exectation of medicaltreatment. This meant that mortality levels did not fall as far as income levels. Thus, Armenia, Azerbaijan, Georgia, Tajikistan and Uzbakistan now all have life expectancy far above that predicted by incomes, Kyrgyzstan somewhat above, but Kazakhstan and Turkmenistan well below (in the latter two, the incomes figures are probably more likely to be suspect than the mortality ones). Nevertheless, the mortality crisis meant that the life expectancy gains over the last quarter of the twentieth century were all below half of the 9.5 years recorded by Asia as a whole during the period, while those of Armenia and Kazakhstan had actually fallen.

Other countries have increased their life expectancy disproportionately over the last quarter of a century : Cambodia, the Lao People's Democratic Republic and Viet Nam with peace returning to Indo-China; Bangladesh, Bhutan, India and Nepal as a second Asian economic miracle comes within reach of South Asia; Indonesia and the Islamic Republic and Iran with a greater concentration on health services; and some Pacific and Indian Ocean countries such as

Maldives, Papua New Guinea, Somoa and Vanuatu. Some of these countries and areas made gains because they started the quarter of a century from an under-performing level. In spite of their relatively repid recent progress, Indonesia, Maldives and Papua New Guinea still have lower life expectancies Than their real per capita incomes would mandate.

The important lessons come from two countries that have been singled out before as examples of the way that economies need not shackle the pursuit of good health for all: Sri Lanka and Viet Nam, ten and nine ranks respectively higher in their life expectancies than might anticipated from their real per capita incomes. Their political systems are different but the success of each depends on a relatively good situation for women, higheducation levels for females as well as males, and easy and low-cost access to an adequate health service. Both have probably been assisted by societies which are not strongly socially stratified and have largely been moulded by Buddhism (see Caldwell, 1976; Pieris, 1999). Partly as a consequence, both emphasize egaliterianism and popular involvement.

The richer countries tend to be the most urbanized, largely because they are the most industrialized. The relationship is neither simple nor linear, as is shown by a comparison of moderately prosperous Thailand, with only one third of its people in towns, with much poorer Mongolia with two thirds of the populations urbanized. The explanations lie in very different intensities of rural land use and contrasting political histories. Urbanization helps in mortality reduction for at two reasons.The first is that urban mortality in developing countires has been lower than that of rural areas since at least the mid-twentieth century because it is easier to give access for such concentrated populations or modern medical technology and specialist hospitals. Doctors prefer to live there. In contrast to the situations in early industrializing Europe where the cities were highly polluted and the killers of their inhabitants, contemporary developing country cities actually have safer water and sanitation than rural areas. The second reason for the rural disadvantage is that some of its populations are still at least partly in the subsistence sector of the economy, unused to an exchange economy or getting the most out of public facilities, with little money to spend, and often with their own explanations of disease cousation which weaken their determination to secure the most from the modern medical system. This is reinforced by lower educational levels outside the towns. Recently, it has been argued that the urban mortality advantage was disappearing (Brockerhoff and Brennan, 1998), but the case remains insecure and, in any case, was most conspicuous outside the Asian and Pacific area.

But this is not whole story, as is shown later in this paper. The new cities, especially in South Asia, are characterized by hugh socio-economic differentials in their populations, with their poor prevented from making full use of the urban health facilities.

Contemporary developing countries do have one huge advantage in achieving lower mortality over the experience of the now developed countries. Health technologies have improved and public health measures have become ever more suited to mass application. The result has been a persistent decline in the cost of achieving specific health targets. Table 3 shows that in 1990 , United States dollars purchasing power parity, Australia, the United Kingdom of Great Britain and Northern Ireland and the United States of America could not confer upon their populations a life expectancy of 60 years until their per capita incomes were arould US$

6,000. By the end of the twentieth century, Bangladesh and Viet Nam could reach this mark with only one sixth of that per capita income.

Table 3. Real per capita income in 1990 American dollars when life expectancy of 60 years was attained

Date	Country	Per capita income
1914	Australia	5 800
1919	Sweden	3 200
1931	United Kingdom of Great Britain and Northern Ireland	5 500
1933	United States of America	6 500
1935	France	4 500
1946	Italy	3 000
1948	Japan	1 700
1959	Sri Lanka	1 200
1966	Malaysia	2 000
1970	Republic of Korea	1 350
1977	Turkey	4 100
1978	Philippines	2 000
1987	Indonesia	2 350
1989	Viet Nam	1 000
1993	India	1 400
2000	Pakistan	2 100
2002	Bangladesh	900

Sources : *United Nation (2001). World Population Prospects : The 2000 Revision, Vol. 1, Comprehecsive Tables (New York, United Nations); Keyfitz, N. and W. Flieger (1968). World Population: An Analysis of vital Data (Chicago, University of Chicago Press); Maddison, A. (2001). The World Economy: A Millenial Perspective (Paris, Development Centre of the Organization for Economic Cooperation and Development).*

Emerging issues

Two further changes will have an impact on the Asian and Pacific struggle for good health for all.

The first is the continuing rise in the proportion of the aged, as is shown in table 4. This is largely a reflection of declining birth rates, with almost half the population of the ESCAP region now living in countries with below-long-term-replacement fertility. The result, unforeseen only 20 years ago, is that by 2050 East Asia will have a larger proportion of its population over 65 years of age than will North Amercia. The situation will at that date be less severe in South-East and South Asia, where the proportions of the old will the much the same as they are at present in Europe.

High proportions of the old place vary considerable burdens on government budgets, as has been demonstrated for the United States of America (Lee and Edwards, 2001). This is partly because keeping the old alive means the employment of expensive, high-technology approaches. But in the West, it has also been the product of a tradition whereby the residential family incorporates the young and meets a substantial proportion of their educational and health costs from the household budget. In contrast, the old live separately and pension, health and often residential expenses are met by the State with money raised by - often resented - taxes.

Table 4. Percentage of the population aged 65 years and over in 1950, 2000 and 2050

	1950	2000	2050
Asia	4.1	5.9	16.7
Eastern Asia	4.5	7.7	23.6
South-Central Asia	3.7	4.6	13.2
South-Eastern Asia	3.8	4.7	16.1
Europe	8.2	14.7	29.2
North America	8.2	12.3	21.4
Latin America	3.7	5.4	16.9

Source : United Nations (2001). World Population Prospects : The 2000 Revision Vol. 1, Comprehensive Tables, (New Yourk, United Nations), (Past : Estimates; Future: Medium Projection).

It has been held that Asian countries have an advantage here because of a continuing tradition of aged parents living with their married children and being at least partly supported by them. It is open to doubt whether this system can indefinitely survive rising levels of education, female employment, occupational and associated geographical mobility, and Western influences among the younger married generations. This family transition appears to be underway, albeit slowly, in Japan, If it runs its full course, the jolt in East Asia will be tremendous, for two reasons. The first is the speed with which the transformation of the age structure will have taken place. East Asia will have moved from the proportion of the population over 65 years of age being 4.5 per cent, to it being 23.6 per cent in the course of 100 years. The United Kingdom of Great Britain and Northern Ireland climbed somewhat more slowly form 4.7 per cent over 65 years in 1911 (through 6.1 per cent in 1921) and will not pass the 23.6 per cent level until almost 2030, a span of 120 years (Keyfitz and Flieger, 1968; United Nations, 2001). The second is that Europe had long since had in place various mechanisms, admittedly often deficient, for assisting the indigent old, while Asia has to invent such systems.

The second change, shown in table 5, is the rapidity of urbanization. East Asia, long thought of as one of the great agrarian regions of the world, will have half its population living in urban areas by 2014 and 60 per cent by 2030. Even more startling, a majority of the population of South-Central Asia will live in towns and cities from 2032.

Clearly, future concerns will focus more and more on urban populations, especially city ones. This is not an especially gloomy picture. Urbanizatoin is a product of economic growth and is itself an engine for achieving higher incomes and lower mortality. But, in many of the larger cities, the poor and undereducated will number millions. In the poorer parts of Asia, mostly in South Asia, intractable problems will beset the attempt to bring good health to the poverty-stricken slums often outside the planning arrangements of the Government because of the illegality of the settlements. The full range of problems is evident in Bangladesh's metropolis, Dhaka. With its population aleardy at 12 million and growing by half a million people a year.

Table 5. Percentage of the population urban in 1950, 2000 and 2030

	1950	2000	2030	Date when 50 per cent urbanized
Asia	17.4	37.6	55.2	2020
Eastern Asia	18.0	40.6	59.1	2014
South-Central Asia	16.6	30.7	48.5	2032
South-East Asia	14.8	36.9	55.0	2021
Latin America	41.4	75.4	83.2	1974
Africa	14.6	37.8	54.3	2021

Source : United Nation (1998). World urbanization Prospects: The 1996 Revision (New York, United Nations).

The Dhaka slums: good health for all

Dhaka, having been a major city as the Moghul capital of Bengal from 1608 to 1704, was then eclipsed by Calcutta and had declined to being a minor provincial centre by the begining of the twentieth century. Its modern expansion began only after it was made the colonial capital of East Bangal and Assam from 1905 to 1912 and subsequently after 1947 ,the administrative capital of East Pakistan. Intensive growth set in after in became the capital of the newly independent nation of Bangladesh in1971. From around 100,000 inhabitants in 1901, the population rose to just under 300,000 in 1951, two million in 1974 and approximately 12 million today (siddiqui and other, 1990; United Nations, 2001).

Dhaka is the main destination is Bangladesh for rural-urban migrants and in contrast to most Asian cities, this source of growth continues to outstrip its own natural increase, resulting in an annual growth rate of nearly 6 per cent (Islam, 1998:71). The growth has resulted in Dhaka being transformed from a small largely administrative town into a complex metropolis with a huge socio-economic gradient from a very wealthy elite to a vast urban poor population. This partly reflects the composition of the migrants who comprise a diverse group, some being educated individuals with skills in demand, but many being very poor families with little education, few skills, and usually little or on capital - it is the landless who have least reason to stay in the country and most to gain by migrating to the city. The poorest live in squatter settlements known as basties (bosties), with the destitute living on the streets of the main city as pavement-dwellers, both groups consisting predominantly of migrants. This enormous expansion and the growing diversity of the city have affected every aspect of the citizen's lives, including their health.

In 1999-2000, a project, Access to Health and Reproductive Health Services (AHRHS), employed survery and micro-demographic approaches to examine health among the poorer population of Dhaka. Within the framework provided by the survey information, families were identified that had experienced particular health issues, such as the death of a child, and the circumstances and outcomes explored. The survey was conducted in the last months of 1999 and the micro-demographic follow-up in the first months of 2000. Two lists were compiled covering together about one third of the city's population. One covered basties, the other poor areas. The interviewing unit was the household and the persons in it. The sample yielded interviews with 911 bestie households and 914 poor households.

The majority of migrant households reported that their health was better (72 per cent of non-bostie poor area dwellers and 64 per cent of bostie-dwellers) in Dhaka than it had been in the rural area. The main reasons they gave as affecting their health negatively was the very poor environment in which they lived (poor area 83 per cent, bosties, 92 per cent). The main positive health reasons they gave were, the presence of good doctors (poor area, 64 per cent, basties 63 per cent) and the abailability of health services (poor areas, 73 per cent, bosties, 60 per cent - respondents were allowed to give more than one reason).

Indices of health, such as infant nd child mortality, have been consistently better in urban than rural Bangladesh, but the differential appears to have diminished in recent years. For example, the under-5-year mortality rate, though declining, is only marginally better in urban Bangladesh (96.7 in 1999-2000) than in rural Bangladesh (112.6), a differential that was substantially less than earlier figures (in 1993-1994, the under-5-year mortality rate was 114.3 in urban areas and 153.2 in rural areas) (Mitra and others, 2001). For the bosties, mortality rates are in general above rural rates; AHRHS recorded a rate of 165 in the basties and 115 in non-bastie slums, thouth a truer comparison might be between the bastie-dwellers and the very deprived socio-economic strate in the rural areas from which many had migrated.

The key factors here are social composition, household and community environment, access to public services and health facilities. In terms of the composition of the population, the key factors are their poverty, the lack of eduction and the fact that many slum-dwellers, including most bostie-dwellers (poor area 50 per cent, bastie 72 per cent) and pavement-dwellers (96 per cent) are migrant households.

For the poorest households (a category excluding many bastie households), mortality rates appear to be disproportionately higher. By a household index of possessions, perry and others (1997:16) found that those with the least possessions had 88 per cent higher mortality than the. others. Caldwell and others (2001) found a 30 per cent margin. A number of factors may be involved firstly, the extremely poor may lack food security : 71 per cent of bastie-dewllers reported in the AHRHS that at some time in the past year they had no money to pay for food. Secondly, many find it difficult to afford helath care, paying not only for a doctor's examination but also for medicine and for medical tests. Many also find it difficult to afford the time required to seek treatment from a hospital. Thirdly, the very poor live in the worst, most crowded and unhygienic housing.

Bastie and pavement-dwellers, however, are not just poor. Most are also uneducated: the AHRHS found that 40 per cent of males and 53 per cent of females aged six and over in the basties had never been to school. This was also true of 22 per cent of males and 29 per cent of females in other poor areas (excluding the bosties). In comparison, the DHS found that 31 per cent of rural males and 40 per cent of rural females aged six and over had never been to school and 18 per cent urban males and 29 per cent of urban females had not (Mitra and others, 2001:13).

Caldwell and others (2001) found that eduction of the mother was a more important perdictior of child death than income or possessions. The mother's education was closely linked to whether the child had the full recommended schedule of immunizations. It was also linked to the likelihood of seeking treatment from a trained health provider for a sick child, but was less important in that respect than wealth as measured by the possessions index. Education also contributed to better hygiene. Educated mothers were more likely to wash their hands prior to preparing food. Similarly, they were much more likely to ensure that their children used sanitary toilets.

However, a household's individual characteristics constitute only one factor. The AHRHS also found that locality, and particularly living in a bastie, had an independent effect. In part, this reflects the influence of neighbours. In an AHRHS sub-study, it was found that in decisions to seek health care for yound children, young mothers were strongly influenced by the older women living in neighbouring houses. In many cases involving migrant households, these women substituted for relatives who would have made such decisions in their village homes. These women are more experienced, but as older women they are generally less educated and more traditional than the yound women they are generally less educated and more traditional than the young women they are advising. In the basties, the women can act to discourage women from seeking attention from hopitals and clinics and instead encourage them to seek attention form a *kobiraj* (practitioner of "ayurvedic" medicine, often having many aspects of a folk healer) or other traditional healer.

Locality also affects health through its environment and its access to health services. A major factor affecting health in the Dhaka slums, and particularly in the bosties and on the pavements, is, as the respondents themselves commented, the lamentable state of the environment. Overcrowding is a major problem with extremely high population density and houses squashed closely together. House quality is generally better in the urban areas, and especially Dhaka, than in rural Bangladesh. However, the bosties are exceptional in their lack of security of tenure, which means that ther is little incentive either for house-owners or tenants to improve housing conditions. Many of the houses are extremely small and poorly built. More generally, environmental conditions are unhygienic, especially in the bosties. Drainage is extremely poor, sanitation inadequate and non-existent, and rubbish, including faeces, uncollected,and indeed scattered underfoot.Basties as illegal settlements are often located in areas regarded as unsuitable for housing, for example areas subject to flooding.

More critically, because they are illegal settlements, basties receive few or no government services, such as paved roads, paved footpaths, drains, sewerage, piped water or rubbish collection. A lack of paved roads and footpaths, and a lack of drains together with poor housing mean that bostie-dwellers are in a poor position to cope with the effects of flooding.

Lack of sanitation results in a large proportion of the population using open latrines or in some cases no latrines al all. In cases where households do have access to sanitary latrines, up to 10 households or 50 individuals may share one. Young children rarely bother: their faeces are collected and thrown onto rubbish heaps, or where these are absent, simply into the open, a point that highlights the importance of municipal rubbish collection. The insecurity of tenure in the bosties means that house-owners have little incentive to improve matters by building better sanitary facilities. The lack of piped water means that most households have to share wells (themselves generally safe, but having to queue for water and carry it over a distance reduces the amount of water available for cleanliness, and storage raises the potential for contamination). The result of such poor environmental conditions is that such infections as pneumonia and diarrhoea remain major killers of children, and tuberculosis of adults.

On top of environmental conditions that are conducive to infection, Dhaka suffers from extremely high atmospheric pollution, including excessive levels of lead, nitrous oxides and suspended particulate matter owing to poorly maintained motor vehicle engines (Karim, 1999). There is strong evidence that atmospheric lead impedes the mental and physical development of children and nitrous oxides and particulate matter contribute to respiratory illnesses.

The health impact of a poor environment is compensated, to some extent, by access to health facilities and expertise, of a far higher standard, in theory than is available in rural Bangladesh. However, the health system is not fully utilized. Government health services are predominantly in the form of large specialist hospitals, with some out-service facilities, mostly found in the old part of the city, and often difficult for the poor to attend. Services that are, in theory, free usually involve payment, at least for medicine. Families usually have to queue for services, time they can ill afford away form work. On top of this, many of the poor say they are badly treated by the health workers, and are reluctant to go unless they have no choice.

Increasingly, health services are provided by the private sector. The better-off use private clinics, often staffed by government doctors after hours. somewhat cheaper services are provided by doctors who work in rooms often at the back of pharmacies. the poor who cannotafford these services use other alternatives, the most important of which is simple to ask the pharmacist for medicine. Dhaka has one pharmacy for every 1,000 people (Mookharjee and others, 1996:1). In addition, people use untrained (quack) doctors, or obtain medicine from traditional or alternative medical providers such as kobiraj fakirs or homeopaths. These providers are preferred as being cheap, convenient, polite and, in the case of traditional providers, more in keeping with the understanding of appropriate treatment of clients (Fariduddin and Khan, 1996:43; Caldwell and others, 2001).

Treatment varies according to gender. For persistent illness, Ahsan and Ahmad (1991:17) found that doctors were eventually consulted by 60 per cent of males but only 22 per cent of females. This reflects, no doubt, a male preference, a concern for the well-being of the household head, usually the main breadwinner, as well as female seclusion and modesty, which makes it difficult for women to go to male doctors, but also to female doctors in the case of reproductive tract infections (RTIs) and sexually transmitted diseases (STDs). Furthermore, men usually control the family finances and while women can in emergencies take some initiative with regard to their children, they usually do not for their own health, for to do so might be regarded as putting their own interests before that of their households. A final factor is a belief that many problems that affect women specifically are natural, and hance are not to be interfered with. This is particularly the case with childbirth, with serious implications for both mother and child.

The proportion of childbirths attended by highly trained attendants (doctors and nurse/midwives) is extremely low in rural Bangladesh (8 per cent). It is higher in urban Bangladesh but is still only about 33 per cent (Mitra and others, 2001:118) and it is clear that many dangerous cases are not being attended to in time. In answers to the AHRHS, it was clear that many women who had lost children had not sought appropriate care in time. The Women felt that childbirth was natural and were reluctant, until too late, to seek support from health-care workers, and especially male doctors. Most of the births in urban areas are attended by traditional birth attendants, a minority with limited training (9 per cent of births), but most without any (42 per cent). A substantial proportion were attended by family members (14 per cent) and a few by no one (1 per cent). Many traditional birth attendants believe that to call a doctor or nurse would be to suggest that they were not skilled enough to conduct the birth. Furthermore, in many cases, the husband was away from home working. The AHRHS interviews suggested that an important factor in not seeking medical care for newly born infants was that in many cases of serious illness, the child was believed to be suffering from conditions that could not be treated by the modern medical system but only by a traditional doctor.

In rural Bangladesh, the Government has attempted with limited success to overcome the gap between the hospital- based system and the basic health needs of the populace by creating a primary health-care system based on Union Health and Family Welfare Clinics employing a medical assistant and a female paramedic (family welfare visitor), and more recently instituting a very basic Essential Service Package. This has not been altogether successful for a number of reasons, including a lack of popular acceptors of the value of the services being offered, and lack of an effective referral system for more serious cases between the clinics and the district and subdistrict hospital system. This however, is only now being attempted in Dhaka by the Dhaka Municipal Corporation with support from the 'Asian Dovelopment Bank.

Conclusion

Poverty is inimical to good health. The very poorest countries cannot afford a minimally protective curative health service across the entire population. Only thevery richest can afford for the mass of their populations the expensive measures which keep nearly all newly born babies alive and many old sick people from prematurely succumbing to death, thus achieving life expectancy close to or beyond 80 years. In between these extremes, life expectancy can be raised to as least 70 years by comprehensive educational, public health and curative systems accessible even to the poor.

The most neglected group has been the urban poor, and this is increasingly serious because soon, and for the rest of time, most of the population in the region will be urban. In terms of health services, minimum safety nets have slowly been established in rural areas, while urban health has largely been left to the market. Such a system does not meet the needs of the very poor in the cities. In addition, the poorest, the rural-urban migrants in "squatter" areas are often positively discriminated against by being denied roads, electricity, water sewerage, and rufuse removal services on the grounds that their settlements are illegal and are subject to clearance at any time.

Dhaka provides a good example of all these problems, being a huge and rapidly growing metropolis in Asia's most health-challenged region. The settled poor are disadvantaged, but, with legal tenure, they have access to most services, although even they srffer from their constrained inability to purchase health services in a largely market situation. But themost disadvantaged are the bostie-dwellers, those in illegal shanty towns They lack most services and are often a long way from hospitals and other health provision. They can be easily missed by public health programmes. They often retain the age-old health beliefs of the rural areas. This is particularly the case among the women, a serious matter because pregnancy, birth and the survival of young children are often regarded as matters to be faced by them alone.

The way to the future is in the long-term economic growth. In the medium term, it is to move towards education for all with nearly all children progressing well into secondary education. But it is the short term that should immediately concern us, with the strongest focus being on the poorest of the poor. It is urgent that recognition be given to the reality of the continuing rural-urbanmigration of people so poor that they cannot afford to pay rent and are capable only of using free or very cheap materials to construct makeshift housing on empty government (or, less often, private) land. They must be given free or very cheap areas to settle on where there is no dispute about their right to do so or their right to services such as water, sewerage, electricity and refuse removal. There must be some kind of health service with no or low charges, not only for medical attention but also for prescribed medicines. There is a strong case for dynamic rather than passive health services. Somehow, health educators have to convey the message of the efficacy of modern medicine to the women, and the message that repoduction and infant health are the concern of husbands as well as wives. This will be helped if professional antenatal and birthing services are available for all and if families are educated to employ such services.

The urban health frontier, especially in the poverty-stricken slums, is going to present a major challenge for decades to come.

References

Ahsan; R.M. and N. Ahmad (1991). "Women nutrition and health"managing the household in slum environment in Dhaka City:, Oriental Geographer 35 (1/2):5-20

Brockerhoff, M. and E. Brennan (1998). "The poverty of cities in developing regions", Population and Development Review 24(1):75-114.

Caldwell, B.K., I Pieris and B. Khuda (2001). "Is there an urban health crisis? an investigation of the slums of Dhaka, Bangladesh", Working paper 26, Health Transition Centre, Australian National University, Canberra.

Celdwell, B.K., J.C. Caldwell, S.N. Mitra and W. Smith (2002). "Searching for an optimum solution to the Bangladesh Arsenic Crisis". to be published in Social Science and Medicine.

Caldwell, J. (1976). "Routes to low mortality in poor countries", Population and Development Review 12(2):171-220

Fariduddin, K.M. nd Amanat Ullah Khan (1996). "Health profile of the urban poor", in Nazrul Islam, ed., The Urban Poor in Bangladesh (Dhaka, Centre for Urban Studies, University of Dhaka), pp. 40-51.

Islam, Nazrul (1998). "Dhaka City: Somegeneral considerations", in Asain Cities in the Twenty first Century, Reforming Dhaka City Management, (Manila, Asain Development Bank), Vol. 3:71-82.

Karim, Md. Masud (1999). "Trafic pollution inventories and modelling in metropolitan Dhaka, Bangladesh", Transportation Research,. Part D: Transport and Environment, vol. 4:291-312.

Keyfitz, N and W. Flieger (1968). World population : An Analysis of Vital Data (Chicago, University of Chicago Press).

Lee, R. and R. Edwards (2001). "The fiscal impact of population Change" in J. Little and R. Trieste, eds., Seismic Shifts: The Economic Impact of Demographic Change.

Maddison, A. (2001). the World Economy: A Millenial Perspective (Paris, Development Centre of the Organization for Economic Cooperation and

Development).

Mitra, S.N., A. Al-Sabir, T. Saha, and S. Kumar (2001). Bangladesh Demographic and Health Survey, 1999-2000, National Institute of Population Research and Training and Mitra and Associates, Dhaka, ORC Macro Calverton, Md.

Mookherji, Sangeeta, Thomas Trudeau Kane, Shams El Arifeen and Abdullah Hel Baqui (1996). "The role of pharmacies in providing family planing and health services to residents of Dhaka, Bangladesh", Working paper 21 MCH-FP Extension Project (Urban), (Dhaka, International Centre for Diarrhoeal Disease Research).

Perry, H.B., Suraiya Begum, Jawad Bin Hussain and Abdullah H Baqui (1997). "Levels and correlates of mortality in Zone 3 of Dhaka City, 1995", Working Paper 27, MCH-FP Extension Project (Urban), (Dhaka, International Centre for Diarrhoeal Disease Research).

Pieris, I. (1999). Disease, Treatment and Health Behaviour in Sri Lanka (New Delhi. Oxford University Press).

Siddiqui, K, S.R. Qadir, S. Alamgir and S. Huq (1990). Social Formation in Dhaka City (Dhaka, University Press)

United Nations (1998). World Urbanization Prospects : The 1996 Revision (New York, United Nations).

................(2001). World Population Prospects: The 2000 Revision, Vol. 1, Comprehensive Tables (New York, United Nations)

..................(2002). 2002 ESCAP Populaton Data Sheet (Bangkok, Economic and Social Commission for Asia and the Pacific)

5

Migration and Poverty : Ambivalent Relationships

Migration can both cause and be caused by poverty. Similarly, poverty can be alleviated as well as exacerbated by population movement. Easy generalizations are impossible to make but is likely that the relative impact of migration on poverty, and of poverty on migration, varies by level of development of the area under consideration. In some parts of the world and under certain conditions, poverty may be a root cause of migration, whereas in other parts, under different conditions, the poor will be among the last to move. Equally, in some areas, migration may be an avenue out of poverty while in others it contributes to an extension of poverty.

The situation is made complex because both terms, "migration" and "poverty", are difficult semantically: both are intuitively obvious but, in practice, have proved notoriously difficult to define and to measure accurately. In this paper, all forms of human population movement will be considered under "migration", althouth "population mobility" might be a more appropriate term" that is both internal and international migrations and both short-term circular movements as well as more permanent migration will be included in the discussion. Under "poverty" a distinction between chronic, absolute poverty on the one hand and the more perceptual "relative deprivation" on the other will be drawn.

Table 1. Percentage of population below the national poverty line, 1990-2000

Country	Year	Precentage	Year	Precentage
South and South-west Asia :				
Bangladesh	1989	47.8	2000	34.0
India	1988	38.9	1999	26.1
Nepal	1985	41.4	1996	42.0
Pakistan	1991	22.1	1999	32.6
Sri Lanka	1991	33.0	1996	39.4
South-East Asia :				
Indonesia	1990	15.1	1999	18.2
Philippines	1991	45.3	2000	39.4
Thailand	1990	27.2	1999	15.9
East and North-East Asia				
China	1990	9.4	1999	3.7
Mongolia	1992	17.0	1998	35.6
North and Central Asia				
Armenia	1988	18.0	1999	55.0
Georgia	1988	16.0	1999	60.0
Kyrgyzstan	1988	37.0	1999	55.0
Tajikistan	1988	59.0	1999	83.0

Source : Extrapolated form graphs published in ESCAP/UNDP *(2002). ESCAP/UNDP Initiative for the Achievement of Millennium Development Goals in Asia and the Pacific. Millennium Development Goals : Lessons, Opportunities and Challenges (Bangkok), which were based on ESCAP, Growth with Equity : Policy Lessons from the Experiences of selected Asian Countries (ST/ESCAP/2007); ADB, Country papers prepared for the Inception Workshop on Buliding a Poverty Database; World Bank, Would Development Report 2000/2001: Attacking Poverty; IMF, and world Bank, Poverty Reduction, Growth and Debt Sustainability in Low-income CIS Countries.*

In the countries of Asia and the Pacific during the 1990s, poverty appears to have declined in Bangladesh, India, China, the Philippines and Thailand but increased in Pakistan, Sri Lanka and throughout the new republics of Central Asia (table 1). Little change in poverty levels in Indonesia and Nepal could be discerned over the some period. However, the figures for China, in particular need to be taken with a great deal of caution. It is known that the restructuring has brought about the loss of large numbers of jobs in the state sector, a trend that can only continue after that country's accession to the World Trade Organization. For example, some 26 million workers have been laid off from state enterprises since 1998 and the real rate of unemployment in 2002 may be in excess of 20 per cent in some sectors. [1]

Table 2. Offical estimates of total number of foreign workers in selected Asian economies, 1996-2001

Country or area	1996	1997	1998	1999	2000	2001
Taiwan Province of China		245 697	255 606	278 000	326 515	
Hong Kong, China [a]	164 300	171 000	180 600	193 700	216 790	
Japan [b]	610 000	630 000	660 000	670 000	710 000	
Republic of Korea [b]	210 494	245 399	157 689	217384	285 506	330 194
Singapore				530 000	612 233	
Indonesia [b]	24 868	24 359	21 307	14 863	16 836	
Malaysia [b]	745239	1 471 645	1 127 652	818 677	799 685	804 984
Philippines [c]	4 333	6 055	5 335	5 956		
Thailand [b]	1 033 863	1 125 780	1 103 546	1 089 656	1102 612	
China [c]	80 000	82 000	83 000	85 000		60 000
Viet Nam [c]					30 000	

Source : Country papers presented at the Workshop on International Migration and Labour Market in Asia, ToKyo, Japan Institute of Labor and OECD, 4-5 February 2002.

[a] Including an estimate of foreign domestic workers only ; there are no stock figures for the highly skilled.

[b] Including estimates of undocumented workers.

[c] Estimate of foreign experts only, primarily professionals, the highly skilled and teachers.

Uncertain though many of the estimates of unemployment and poverty may be, these pale in comparison with the difficulties inherent in the measurement of migration. Available data on international migration suggest that population movement is likely to have increased from all the economies under consideration (table 2). However, in several cases these figures either omit or severely underestimate the number of undocumented migrants. Any estimates of the numbers of undocumented migrants are likely to be suspect to some degree, simple by the nature of the phenomenon. These may be based on the number of apprehensions on attempted entry or on arrests in country, with assumptions make on the number of those eluding the official net, . For some countries, the number of undocumented migrants is substantial. For example, some 2.1 million illegal entrants to Malaysia were apprehended between 1992 and 2000 (Hugo, 2002:4) and estimates of the stock of undocumented migrants it that country before the 1997 financial crisis ranged up to 1.43 million (ILO, 1998). the vest majority of these migrants came from neighbouring Indonesia.

Even more difficult is the estimation of the number of internal migrants. Data for the number of movers in Thailand, where poverty levels declined markedly during the 1990s, even taking into account the impact of the 1997 financial crisis, suggest that migration might actually have slowed in the 1990s. Preliminary figures from the 2000 census indicate that the proportion of the population which had moved in the five years before the census was lower than in 1990, or 13.9 per cent in 2000 compared with 16.8 in 1990 (Thailand, 2000). To draw the conclusion that a relative reduction in mobility might be conducive to a reduction in poverty would be deceptive, if not just wrong. First, it is well recognized that the population census only captures a part of total population movement, omitting most circulation and short-term migration. Studies in Thailand, following the 1990 census, showed that a change in the reference period used to define a "migration" from the three months of the census to one month in the National Migration Survey of Thailand increased the numbers of migrants by over one fifth (Chamratrithirong and other, 1995). Second, and more critically, it is known that the number of poor in Thailand increased from 6.8 million at the beginning of 1997 to 7.9 million at the end of 1998. These figures represent an increase in the proportion of the total population classified as poor from 11.4 to 12.9 per cent (UNDP,) 1999:129). Nevertheless, it would also be deceptive to conclude that the increase in poverty as a result of the financial crisis had caused the observed decline in five-year migration. A more likely hypothesis is that the crisis stimulated an increase in precisely the types mobility that censuses and general surveys are least able to measure : that is , in short-term mobility as people moved to seek alternatives to loss of jobs in the urban sector or loss of markets in the rural Sector. Mobility could, in those years, have increased rather than decreased and been more a survival strategy than a pathway towards better opportunity.

Thus, any attempt to draw clear relationships from existing data between volume and patterns of migration on the one hand, and poverty on the other, is likely to be problematic. This paper can only seek to raise in very broad relief the likely scenarios that are the result of poverty influencing migration and vice versa. Many of the points raised below are to be considered hypotheses requiring rigorous testing rateh than statements of fact. Our empirical base and the ambivalent nature of the relationships between migration and poverty do not yet allow a more complete analysis.

Poverty as a root cause of migration

Migration is often seen simply as a flight from poverty : there are no opportunities available locally so people migrate I n order to survive. Flight from a devastating famine would appear to be the classic example of this type of relationship, well illustrated by pictures in the media of emaciated people who have walked great distances of reach feeding stations run by international agencies and charities. Unequivocally, such cases exist but these are generally restricted to the poorest parts of the world, and primarily to parts of sub-Saharan Africa. In Asia, such cases, although still found in pockets across that vast area, have become less common given the rapid economic development over the last half to the twentieth century. Examples within living memory include the "Great Hunger" in China, 1959-1960, when millions moved in edesperate attempts to find food, although millions more were prevented from moving by the authorities. The real impact of this last great famine in China on population migration has yet to be reported, although general discussions are included in Becker (1996) and Banister (1987). Other, more limited but more recent examples can be found in South Asia such as Orissa in India in 2001.

The survival migration of the poorest is likely to be mainly local, or regional at most, and primarily within country. In apparent contradiction to the logic of survival migration, the general finding of most studies of migration in non-disaster situations is that it is not the poorest who move but those with access to some resources, no matter how meagre these might appear. Migration always involves some costs of transportation and the abandonment of many of the few possessions the poor might have. The poorest of the poor cannot afford either risk or movement and the majority starves in situ.

Even in the "Great Famine in Ireland 1845-1950:, it was rarely the poorest who emigrated to North America. The more able-bodied among them could perhaps reach the United Kingdom but many of the rest perished. Emigration rates from the hard est-hit counties were often significantly less than from those counties not so affected (see Miller, 1985).

In a different continent in a different era, the majority of those who fled from China to Hong Kong, China after the victory of the communist forces in 1949 might have had a "well-founded fear of being persecuted" (the definition of a refugee) but over half claimed that they had moved for "economic reasons" (Hambro, 1955). They were not among the poorest in China at the time. This discussion is not to deny that poverty is an important cause of migration but to suggest that there are other factors at work. Except in particular areas and at particular times, it is not absolute poverty as such that is significant in accounting for migration but whether people feel that they are poor.

Migration as the result of poverty

Poverty as the root cause of migration and migration as the result of poverty might suggest the same thing but there are significant differences. Migration as the r esult of poverty shifts the focus to the issue of feeling poor: relative rather than absolute deprivation. Migration, either of outsiders into a community, or of natives going outside their community, establishes linkages between origins and d estinations. These linkages spread knowledge about conditions in a wider world that can transform communities from conditions of "subsistence affluence" (Sahlins, 1974) to those of relative deprivation without any significant real changes in the quantity of subsistence in the community.

What changes is the less tangible quality of life when the number of potential migrants increases as a consequence of community members beginning to judge their own conditions relative to those of people living elsewhere. Thus, migration creates the conditions that lead to people feeling themselves to be poor, which in turn leads to further migration as they move in order to satisfy new-found aspirations. This process is perhaps at the root of most migration, giving the impression that poverty is the driving force but in reality is the product of the desire to better oneself against new standards rather than the result of absolute deprivation. Migration is thus both the creator and the product of poverty.

Most of those who can respond to the information coming into any community are the more innovative, the better-off and the better educated even if these qualities themselves are relative. In an isolated rural community, for example, the better educated might be those with just the most basic primary education among the many with no formal education at all. Migrants need not always, or even generally, respond to information coming into a community: they may be selected by labour recruiters or other representatives of an expansionary urban-based group. Again, recruiters are unlikely to select the weakest or poorest members of any group. Migrants are either a selected or self-selected group within any population. Thus the general conclusion is that migrants from any community, and particularly the initial migrants, are among the most innovative and dynamic members of that community (see Skeldon, 1990). Whether their loss can contribute to poverty creation will be considered in a later section.

Migration as a cause of poverty

Nevertheless, there are ways in which migration can lead directly to an increase in the number of absolute poor. The clearest way is through forced relocation without adequate planning and support. In many cases, the forced relocation is essentially the product of development, mainly through the creation of lakes and reservoirs that are the result of the construction of dams, although displacement for roads and urban expansion is also important. For example worldwide, it is estimated that between 90 and 100 million people were involuntarily displaced by infrastructural development projects during the last decade of the twentieth century (Cernea and McDowell, 2000:2). In India alone, some 20 million people are estimated to have been displaced over about 40 years, the majority of whom became impoverished (Cernea, 2000:12) while in China over a similar period, well over 30 million were displaced (Meikle and Zhu, 2000:128). The Three Gorges Project, currently under construction on the Yangtse is estimated to displace will over a million people.

Perhaps the key difference separating forced population displacement due to development policy from other types of migration is that the numbers moving and the timing of the movement are known. Thus, if poverty is indeed the result of the forced migration it is the fault of inadequate planning rather than of the movement itself. There is no necessary reason that the migration must lead to an extension of poverty although this often appears to be the result. There can be little excuse for a lack of adequate reconstruction and this particular relationship between migration and povety appears to be one that is ideally suited to effective policy intervention.

A more difficult dimension of migration leading to an extension of poverty relates to the loss of innovative and educated community members: in essence, a "brain drain" whether at national or village levels. It has proven singularly difficult to demonstrate empirically a fall in macro-level economic indicators in the face of a marked exodus of the educated at the national level.Equally, the evidence for a decline in either agricultural production or productivity upon rural-to-urban migration at the village level is elusive. Much of the difficulty is derived from the fact that the much of the migration may be circular in nature. Both the educated at the national level, and workers moving from village to town, either return at a later stage, or move to extend the resource base of their families by incorporating new resources elsewhere.

The so-called "brain drain" argument is difficult to sustain at the macrolevel in East Asia. Tens of thousands of students left Japan; the Republic of Korea; Taiwan Province of China; and Hong Kong, China for study overseas from the 1960s at precisely the time that these economies began to grow rapidly (Skeldon, 1997a: 108-115). It is difficult to see that these economies could have grown even faster than they did if the students had stayed home. Over time, increasing numbers returned and there clearly was a "brain gain" rather than a brain drain in these economies. This scenario, however, need not necessarily apply more generally. The loss of relatively small numbers of the educated from marginal economies such as many in sub-Saharan Africa may indeed contribute to slower or even declining growth. Ghana, for example, has lost 60per cent of the doctors trained in the 1980s and a total of about 60, 000 highly skilled workers are reputed to have fled African economies during the last half of 1980s (Harris, 2002). The loss of large number of Russian technicians may also be a significant factor in the rising poverty observed in the Central Asian republics. While the assessment of the impact of the loss of the highly educated and skilled needs to be carried out on a region-by-region basis, a critical factor will always be whether there is something for the educated to return to in their economies of origin. Where there is little to return to, a brain drain is more likely to occur, but where origin economies are more dynamic, a brain gain may be result.

At the local level, assessments of the impact of outmigration of production of equally problematic although few studies support the idea that there is a negative impact on farm production (Simmons, 1984). An assessment in China has shown that the loss of labour due to outmigration can have a negative impact on income from cropping but has no impact on crop yields (de Brauw and others, 2001). Where the impacts become intense in marginal areas and migration develops to such an extent that the reproductive capacity of a village is eroded, leading to ageing and declining populations, then pockets of deprivation may emerge even in the most developed societies. For example, the severely depopulating area (kaso) in Japan present a challenge to policy makers to supply adequate services to ageing populations. Agricultural income in these area was 70 per cent of the national average in the mid-1990s and they covered almost half of the total land area of the country but represented only 6.3 per cent of the total population (Skeldon, 2001). In poorer economies, those left behind may be those most likely to experience "chronic poverty" (Kothari, 2002) with poverty thus a residual of migration.

Finally, in this section, the question is whether migration concentrates the poor in destination area, and primarily in the largest metropolitan centres of the developing world. Even if it is not the poorest who migrate from the villages, relative to city people in destination areas they are often poor and their concentration may be a drag on development. Here again, the evidence to support the apparent logic of this statement is far from conclusive. There is little evidence to suggest that migrants are overrepresented among the urban poor, with migrants tending to have higher labour force participation rates than native-born in cities in the developing world. This statement should certainly not imply that the living conditions of all migrants in towns are satisfactory or that they do not appear among the ranks of the urban poor. Many of the occupations filled by migrants, and particularly those undertaken by poorly educated migrant women, are badly paid, insecure and often require work under appalling conditions, However, given that migration is generally not the principal component of urban growth in the developing world (natural increase is usually more important), and that migrants have higher rates of employment than the local urban-born, the principal causes of urban poverty are to be found in the metropolitan regions themselves rather than in migration to them.

Poverty alleviated by migration

Implicit in much of the discussion thus far has been an underlying assumption that the relationship between migration and poverty should in some way be negative: either that migration was the result of deprivation or that migration leads to the impoverishment of certain areas. While these statements cannot be discounted in very case, there is a lack of empirical data to support them as general conclusions. The weight of the evidence provides support for a very different conclusion: that the movement of population can be a significant factor for the alleviation of poverty. The principal reason lies in the nature of the migration process itself. Migrants rarely move simply from A to B but their movement is a complex system of circulation between two, or among several, destinations. Also, migrants are rarely individuals operating in a social vacuum but are meshed into family, household and community networks. Migrants, rather than individual income maximizers can be conceptualized as existing with in a communal risk- minimizing strategy. Such an interpretation falls within the so-called "new home economics" approach to theories of migration (Massey and others, 1993; Stark, 1991).

Migration can therefore be seen as a system linking origins and destinations in which flow not just people, but also money and goods. The incorporation of new destinations broadens the resource base of a household, perhaps allowing a more optimal deployment of labour as those underemployed during the slack part of the agricultural cycle can find work on a plantation or in town. Gender differences can become important. In areas where males undertake most of the agricultural work, as in Latin America, for example, women can be released from rural households to access off-farm activities in town, and vice versa in areas where women dominate labour input into agriculture as in much of Africa. The diversification of resource base, labour input and gender role can all act to alleviate poverty where household are dependent upon a single resource at one location. In such diversification, however, there is always the possibility of the exploitation of migrants at destinations and the social disruption that can ensue upon separation of family members. These negative consequences need to be balanced against possible improvement in status of migrants who may acquire skills or pursue education at destinations. Here, in particular, there appear significant gender issues as women, by absenting themselves even temporarily from patriarchal structures, can improve their status (Hondagneu-Sotelo, 1994). Temporary absences of men, by thrusting the women left behind into positions of responsibility to run the households, can also elevate their status and, indirectly or directly, reduce the incidence of deprivation.

Where the migration is essentially circular in nature, it is likely to be a support for the communities of origin but when migrants begin to spend longer away from home, over the long term, the outmigration may eventually act to undermine the demographic and economic viability of the community. The resultant transformation need not necessarily imply an extension of poverty as more capital-intensive forms of economy may emerge. Even when migrants spend longer at destinations, they rarely cut off relations with their areas of origin: they go back at regular intervals and they send goods and money to relatives in their home country, village or town which introduces the critical issue of remittances.

Like so many components of migration and poverty, remittances are notoriously difficult to measure accurately. Unless specialized surveys are undertaken, estimates of the amounts of money and goods remitted by internal migrants within a country are impossible to make. While there are estimates of the volume of flows remitted by international migrants, it is recognized that these capture only those that flow through official channels: much is transmitted through informal channels through relatives or when the migrants return. What is indisputable is that the volume and importance of these flows are vast. In 1990, it was estimated that the observable volume of global remittances was $US 71.1 billion per annum, making it second only to oil in terms of value in international trade (Russell, 1992). Considering the global flows from developed to less developed countries only, the volume probably doubled from about $US30 billion in the late 1980s to more than $US60 billion a decade later (Martin and Widgren,

2002).

In Asia, the Philippines is the country of emigration par excellence with some 7 million Filipinos from a resident population of 78.7 million in mid-1992 living or working overseas. In 2000 alone, more than 800,000 workers were deployed overseas with more than $US6 billion in foreign exchange remitted back to the Philippines (Go, 2002). Remittances from overseas workers are also important for many other labour exporters such as Bangladesh, India, Pakistan and Sri Lanka. For the Pakistan of the mid-1980s, they represented about 9 per cent of GDP and were "an important factor in allowing Pakistan to sustain the highest growth on the South Asian subcontinent through most of the 1970s and 1980s" (Addleton, 1992). In the state of Kerala in the 1990s, remittances accounted for 21 per cent of state income (Kannan and Hari, 2002). Even Viet Nam, a relatively recent entrant into regional and global labour markets, had around 300,000 workers overseas in 2000, who were remitting some $US 1.25 billion annually (Nguyen, 2002).

Although the important dimension of foreign exchange earnings is missing in remittances from internal migrants, these, too, are significant for communities of origin. The data from the National Migration Survey of Thailand showed that over one quarter of outrmigrants had sent money or goods back to their households of origin during the 12 months prior to the survey (Osaki, 2002). The data also showed that the proportion remitting tended to increase with time spent away from home and that one third of those who had been away for more than 10 years were still sending money back home. Given that the number of internal migrants in any country vastly exceeds any numbers going overseas, the volume of money sent back to the rural sector from cities in the developing world is likely to be significant, even if amounts sent by overseas migrants are likely to be greater on a per capita basis simply because, on average, they earn more. In China, studies suggest that households that send out internal migrants are able to increase the per capita income of those left behind by between 14 and 30 per cent (de Brauw and others, 2001).

More important than the actual amounts, however, are the uses to which the monies are put and the impact that the remittances are likely to have on the areas of origin of migration. Perhaps *the* critical issue in the migration and poverty equation is whether remittances can help to alleviate poverty. One perspective is that remittances tend to be used for conspicuous consumption rather than investment: for house construction or the sponsoring of weddings, and the like, rather than improvements that are likely to lead to increasing agricultural productivity. A common use of remittances, nevertheless, is also to pay for the education of the next generation and that does appear to be a clear investment strategy.

However, a clear distinction between investment and consumption may be difficult to maintain in the context of the use of remittances. Expenditure on house construction, for example, can stimulate local building enterprise, thus generating employment and trade in materials. Even something as apparent an example of conspicuous consumption as wedding feasts generates demand for local foods, supports local musicians, and so on. Thus, there are important indirect effects of remittance money in the villages. The general conclusion from studies of the use of remittances is that migrants tend to use their wealth wisely and the benefits appear to more than counterbalance costs (Gunatilleke,1986).

More difficult to assess is the impact of remittances on inequality. Given that those who move tend to be from the wealthier families in any community, the remittances logically flow back to those families, exacerbating or at least reinforcing existing inequalities. Poverty can be measured by the proportion of wealth controlled by the various quintiles in any population and if the upper 20 per cent are increasing their "share" as a result of migration, and the lowest fifth decreasing their share, it could be argued that migration was indeed contributing to the intensification of poverty in a society. Yet again, the evidence is contradictory. In Pakistan, although inequalities increased between migrant and non-migrant households, the distribution of remittances appears to have spread benefits to a greater range of groups and areas that could effectively "undermine the centre" of traditional power (Addleton, 1992). Migration flows do tend to be generated out of specific "niches" or areas of origin.

Hence, certain micro-regions may benefit relative to those areas that send relatively few migrants, increasing regional as well as social inequalities (Seddon and others, 2002). Nevertheless, data from Thailand show that though the per capita amount of remittances to poor households may be much less than to wealthier families, they have a much greater relative impact and help to alleviate poverty (Osaki, 2002). Thus, migration may help to reduce absolute poverty among some while simultaneously acting to increase feelings of relative deprivation among others. Overall, people may be better fed as a result of migration but the feelings of deprivation may generate resentment. Migration has been shown to be a significant component in the development of particular social and revolutionary movements, a theme that remains under-researched

(Skeldon, 1987). The results of those movements have led in the past to destruction that has extended poverty on a massive scale.

The final issue related to migration as a factor in the alleviation of poverty, and one that returns the debate to the macrolevel, emerges from the nature of the migrants arriving at destinations, both domestic and international. It has been emphasized that migrants tend to be among the more innovative and better-educated members of any population. A small number of migrants are traders and entrepreneurs who are the brokers of economic exchange generating not only wealth for themselves but employment for locals at origins and destinations that can help to generate prosperity. Entrepreneurship, often associated with particular ethnic groups, the Chinese or the Jews, for example, is perhaps more a function of situations and linkages that are the result of migration than of particular ethnic charactristics. Entrepreneurs are the minority among the migrants, the "essential outsiders" (Chirot and Reid, 1997) who generate capital accumulation. Migration, both internal and international, is thus an integral part of the whole process of economic development which must underlie any attempt to alleviate poverty.

Conclusion: policy dilemmas

This discussion should have revealed the complexity of the relationship between migration and poverty. In most areas migration appears, on balance, to bring an improved probability of survival and often an alleviation of poverty. At the same time, exploitation and disruption can be an integral part of the transformations associated with the population movement. Amid the uncertainty of outcome, several policy-relevant propositions can be advanced. First, constant attention needs to be directed towards the protection of migrants, both male and female. Second, migration is not a new phenomenon even if there are certain novel aspects about the current situation: it has characterized all societies at all times. Thus, migration is not suddenly going to stop and cease being a characteristic. Governments need to learn to plan for it and attempts to control population movements within countries have invariably met with a distinct lack of success over anything but the immediate short term. Attempts to control movements across international borders have met with greater success but at huge cost both financially and often socially and politically. The issues of border control remain beyond the limits of this paper but policy makers need to address whether the restriction of movement is in the best interests of their own population as well as the populations of origin areas.

The weight of the evidence is that mobility enhances economic growth and improves the lot of most, but not all, of the population. Generally, spatially static populations are likely to be economically stagnant populations. A paper presented by the Organisation for Economic Cooperation and Development (OECD) to the Earth Summit 2002 argued that if the European Union, Canada, Japan and the United States allowed migrants to make up just 4 per cent of their labour force, the returns to origin areas could be in the region of $US 160-200 billion a year, a sum far greater than any potential debt relief (cited in *The Guardian,* 26 August 2002). Migration may not. be able to eradicate all types of poverty, and may even exacerbate some, but the alternative of attempting to limit or restrict migration is likely to be much less productive. The words of John Kenneth Galbraith appear to capture the essence of the whole relationship:

Migration is the oldest action against poverty. It selects those who most want help. It is good for the country to which they go; it helps to break the equilibrium of poverty in the country from which they come. What is the perversity in the human soul that causes people to resist so obvious a good? (cited in Harris, 2002:119)

However, it is important to recognize that migration can involve costs, economic and social, as well as benefits. The challenge to policy makers is to facilitate the types of movement that are most likely to lead to an alleviation of poverty while protecting migrants from abuse and exploitation. This paper has attempted to draw attention to the range of possible outcomes. It is likely that the relationship between migration and poverty will be different in the dynamic economies of East Asia, for example, than in the more stagnant economies of sub-Saharan Africa. Within regions and within countries, there will also be variations. There can be no universal policy recommendation just as there is no single and simple interrelationship between migration and poverty. While accepting a variety of outcomes, this writer stands by a generalization made earlier in the pages of this journal that "policies that accept the wider mobility of the population are likely to accord with policies that will enhance the well-being of greater numbers of people" (Skeldon, 1997b). More recent work of others appears to advocate similar approaches (de Haan, 2002 and Kothari, 2002), yet the immediate challenge remains the need to incorporate an appreciation of the potentially positive role of migration in poverty reduction programmes.

References

Addleton, J.S. (1992). *Undermining the Centre: the Gulf Migration and Pakistan* (Karachi, Oxford University Press).

Banister, J. (1987). *China's Changing Population* (Stanford, Stanford University Press).

Becker, J. (1996). *Hungry Ghosts: China's Secret Famine* (London, John Murray).

Cemea, M.M. (2000). "Risks, safeguards, and reconstruction: a model for population displacement and resettlement", in M.M. Cernea and C. McDowell, eds., *Risks and Reconstruction: Experiences of Resettlers and Refugees* (Washington, The World Bank), pp. 11-55.

------------and C. McDowell (2000). "Reconstructing resettlers' and refugees' livelihoods", in M.M. Cernea and C. McDowell, eds., *Risks and Reconstruction: Experiences of Resettlers and Refugees* (Washington, The World Bank), pp. 1-8.

Chamratrithirong, A, K. Archavanitkui, K. Richter, P. Guest, V. Thongthai, W. Boonchalaksi, N. Piriyathamwong and P. Vong-Ek (1995), *National Migration Survey of Thailand,* Publication No. 188 (Salaya, Institute for Population and Social Research, Mahidol University).

Chirot, D. and A. Reid (1997). *Essential Outsiders: Chinese and Jews in the Modern Transformation of Southeast Asia and Central Europe* (Seattle, University of Washington Press).

de Brauw, A., J.E. Taylor and S. Rozelle (2001). "Migration and incomes in source communities: a new economics of migration perspective from China", a paper produced in the Department of

Agriculture and Resource Economics, University of California, Davis.

de Haan, A. (2002). "Migrants, livelihoods, and rights: the relevance of migration in development policies", London, Department for International Development, Social Development Department, Social Development Working Paper No.4.

Go, S.P. (2002). "Recent trends in migration movements and policies: the movement of Filipino professionals and managers", paper presented at the Workshop on International Migration and Labour Market in Asia, Tokyo, Japan Institute of Labor and OECD, 4-5 February.

Gunatilleke, G. (1986). *Migration of Asian Workers to the Arab World* (Tokyo, United Nations University).

Hambro, E. (1955). *The Problem of Chinese Refugees in Hong Kong* (Leiden, A. W. Sijthoff).

Harris, N. (2002). *Thinking the Unthinkable: the Immigration Myth Exposed* (London, I. B. Tauris).

Hodagneu-Sotelo, P. (1994). *Gendered Transitions: Mexican Experiences of Immigration* (Berkeley, University of California Press).

Hugo, G. (2002). "Introduction", in *Migration and the Labour Market in Asia: Recent Trends and Policies* (Paris, OECD), pp. 7-16.

ILO (1998). *The Social Impact of the Asian Financial Crisis* (Bangkok, Regional Office for Asia and the Pacific of the International Labour Organization).

Kannan, K.P. and K.S. Hari (2002). "Kerala's Gulf connection: remittances and their macroeconomic impact", in K.C. Zachariah, K.P. Kannan and S. lrudaya Rajan, eds., *Kerala's Gulf Connection: CDS Studies on International Migration from Kerala State in India* (Thiruvananthapuram, Centre for Development Studies), pp. 199-230.

Kothari, *U.* (2002). "Migration and chronic poverty", Chronic Poverty Research Centre, Institute for Development Policy and Management, University of Manchester Working Paper No. 16.

Martin, P.L. and *J.* Widgren (2002). "International migration: facing the challenge", *Population Bulletin,* 57(1).

Massey, D.S., *J.* Arango, G. Hugo, A. Kouaouci, A. Pellegrino, *J.* Edward Taylor (1993). "Theories of international migration: a review and appraisal", *Population and Development* Review, 19(3):pp 431-466.

Meikle, S. and Zhu Youxuan (2000). "Employment for displaces in the socialist market economy of China", in M.M. Cernea and C. McDowell, eds., *Risks and Reconstruction: Experiences of Resettlers and Refugees* (Washington, The World Bank), pp. 127-143.

Miller, K.A. (1985). *Emigrants and Exiles: Ireland and the Irish Exodus to North America* (New York, Oxford University Press).

Nguyen, N.X. (2002). "International migration of highly skilled workers in Vietnam", paper presented at the Workshop on International Migration and Labour Market in Asia, Tokyo, Japan Institute of Labor and OECD, 4-5 February.

Osaki, K. (2002). "Internal migration and remittances in Thailand: economic necessity or social institution?", paper presented at the IUSSP Regional Population Conference, Bangkok, Thailand, 11-12 June.

Russell, S. (1992). "Migrant remittances and development", *International Migration,* 30(3/4):267-287.

Sahlins, M. (1974). *Stone Age Economics* (London, Tavistock).

Seddon, D., J. Adhikari and G. Gurung (2002). "Foreign labor migration and the remittance economy", *Critical Asian Studies,* 34(1):19-40.

Simmons, A.B. (1984). "Migration and rural development: conceptual approaches, research findings and policy issues", in *Population Distribution, Migration and Development,* ST/ESA/SERA/89 (New York, United Nations, Department of International Economic and Social Affairs), pp. 156-192.

Skeldon, R (1987). "Protest, peasants and the proletariat", in R. Ghose, ed., *Protest Movements in South and South-East Asia* (Centre for Asian Studies, University of Hong Kong), pp. 3-18.

(1990). *Population Mobility in Developing Countries: A Reinterpretation* (London, Belhaven).

(1997a), *Migration and Development: A Global Perspective* (London, Longman). (1997b). "Rural-to-urban migration and its implications for poverty alleviation", *Asia-Pacific Population Journal,* 12(1):3-16.

(2001). "Ageing of rural populations in South-East and East Asia", in The *World Ageing Situation: Exploring a Society for All Ages,* ST/ESA/271 (New York, United Nations, Department of Economic and Social Affairs), pp. 38-54.

Stark, O. (1991). The *Migration of Labor* (Oxford, Blackwell).

Thailand (2002). Advance results from the *Population and Housing Census 2000* at <www .nso. go. th/ pop2000/report/adv _e. htm>

UNDP (1999). *Human Development Report of Thailand 1999* (Bangkok, United Nations Development Programme).

6

Education and Health in South Asia:

During the last decade, at least three international conferences (the World Conference on Human Rights in Vienna in 1993, the International Conference on Population and Development in Cairo in 1994 and the Fourth World Conference on Women in Beijing in 1995) sought to reshape a vision of women's lives by placing gender equity, women's rights, empowerment, health (including reproductive health), quality of life, equality and freedom at the centre of population and sustainable development policies and programmes. In the period since these international events, almost all States, as signatories of the action agenda of the conferences, have attempted to move closer to fulfilling many of the commitments. In this endeavour, they have also sought the help of both national and international non-governmental organizations, institutions and corporate sectors. However, certain challenges remain for many of the countries in terms of access to services for some of the marginalized groups. Perhaps more innovative approaches rather than the standard poverty alleviation approaches are needed to bring all within the fold of development.

In the last three decades, almost all countries in the ESCAP region have made noteworthy progress in improving women's overall status and more specifically their health and education indicators, two areas where female disadvantages have traditionally been conspicuous. In the first section, this paper outlines the achievements or improvements made in access to the basic health and education status of women in four countries in the Indian subcontinent (Bangladesh, India, Nepal and Pakistan; however, Sri Lanka and the other small or island countries are omitted). The factors that constrain progress in achieving the goals set by the international conferences such as the International Conference on Population and Development as well as by the countries themselves, are also discussed. The measures needed to reach the goals to improve the health and education status of women in these countries are outlined in the subsequent section. Unequal access to development associated with poverty is a cross-cutting theme throughout the paper.

All four countries have articulated women's concerns and made provision in their plans and programmes to address those concerns and their development. However, despite the rhetoric and some measures that have been initiated, women's participation in almost all sectors remains very limited. This is a consequence of both their low educational achievements and the biases favouring males in all walks of life. The persisting gender disparities in regard to various benefits and opportunities are brought out by the data and analyses presented below.

The data quality, breadth of issues covered and the time duration for which information on various indicators is available vary a great deal between the countries under consideration. An effort is made, however, to cull out those data which are more or less comparable in terms of both estimations and the time period to which they refer. They do provide the flavour of the prevailing situations in each of the countries and also point to the country-specific issues. Except for Nepal, the countries are large in terms of population and show wide interregional variations within them. However, in the broad canvas that is presented here, it is not possible to address this important issue. Wherever appropriate, reference will be made to the differences within the countries.

Access to education

Illiteracy contributes to women's marginalization within the family, workplace and public arena. The large gender gap prevailing in most countries in the South Asian region in levels of education results in women's powerlessness or non-involvement in decision-making at home. Illiterate women are also caught in a vicious cycle of poverty, repeated childbearing and ill-health. At the workplace, women without education are engaged in low-paid irregular wage employment, work long hours and also face the threat of unemployment. In the public arena, they face indifference or receive scant attention from providers of health-care or other services. Education is essential to enable them to break out of this predicament. The advantages in providing education to women have been well established throughout the world. It elevates women's status in all spheres of life and decisively determines their access to paid employment, earning capacity, overall health, control over fertility, family size, spacing of births and decision-making. Educated ,women are able to ensure that their children, both boys and girls, attend school, receive good-quality education and have access to health care.

However, until recently South Asia countries have had practically no tradition of providing education to women. When they adopted universal primary education as a fundamental goal, barely 3 to 7 per cent of women were counted as literate in India or Nepal. The situation in Bangladesh and Pakistan was equally dismal. Since then, there has been a considerable increase in the enrolment of girls at the primary level of education. While the gender gap in literacy has somewhat narrowed because of the rapid increase in the literacy level of women, there is still a long way to go in universalizing education among girls. To provide education to all in the South Asian countries would require not only strong political will, serious bureaucratic commitment, mammoth investment in the development of infrastructure, such as school buildings and teacher training, but also social engineering in order to mobilize the parents to send their daughters along with their sons to schools.

Table 1. Changes in the educational profile of women andmen in South Asian countries, various years

	Male	Female	Male	Female	Male	Female
Bangladesh	1974		1981		1991	
Percentage Literate in 10 and over population	37.2	13.2	39.7	18.8	45.5	24.2
Percentage literate in 10-14 age group	37.9	28.1	-	-	-	-
Percentage literate in 20-24 age group	14.2	1.1	12.2	2.3	-	-
India	1971		1981		1991	
Percentage literate in 10 and over population	49.9	22.6	57.0	29.0	64.3	38.1
Percentage literate in 10-14 age group	59.8	38.1	66.8	44.8	77.0	59.7
Percentage literate in 20-24 age group	60.7	28.7	66.6	37.1	71.5	43.8
Nepal	1971		1981		1991	
Percentage literate in 10 and over population	24.7	3.7	34.0	12.0	54.5	25.0
Percentage literate in 10-14 age group	-	-	50.8	21.2	76.0	49.3
Percentage literate in 20-24 age group	-	-	41.7	12.6	64.3	26.3
Pakistan	1972		1981		1991	
Percentage literate in 10 and over population	30.2	11.6	35.0	16.0	-	

Percentage literate in 10-14 age group	31.4	16.4	31.3	19.6	-	-
Percentage literate in 20-24 age group	40.3	15.7	46.0	22.8	-	-

* For India, the category "literate" also includes those who report themselves as literate without any formal schooling.

Sources: United Nations, 1995, 1996, 1997; Visaria and Ramachandran, 2002.

As shown in table 1, all four countries have indeed made considerable progress in providing education to women and men in the past three decades. It may, however, be noted that the increase in education is a recent phenomenon in all the countries. The spurt occurred in India a decade or two earlier than in the other countries and, although recent data for Pakistan are not available, its education revolution has just begun.' All the same, the backlog of illiterate population will remain with all the countries for the next four or five decades. Around 1990, only 24 per cent (Bangladesh) to 38 per cent (India) of females 10 years of age and over and 45-64 per cent of adult men in this region were reported to be literate. Since then, in the past 10-year period, these countries have reportedly made significant progress in improving the literacy status of its young population; however, detailed data from the latest round of censuses are yet to become available.

Further, the literacy level is considerably higher in the urban areas compared with rural areas in all the countries (not shown in the table). In Bangladesh, for example, according to the 1991 data, the urban female literacy rate of 52.5 per cent was more than twice the corresponding rural rate of 20 per cent. For the same year in India, 31 per cent of rural women were reported to be literate as against 64 per cent of urban women (the 2001 census data are not yet published). During the past three decades, Nepal has also made considerable progress in developing its national education system. Despite a significant improvement in the proportion of literates in the population since 1971, only a quarter of the adult females were reported to be literate in 1991, the majority of whom live in urban areas. Although data for the 1990 decade are not available, the situation in Pakistan is likely to be much more dismal, partly because until recently there was no tradition of providing education to women in many parts of the country. Concerns of safety of girls, limited supply of female teachers etc. have hampered providing literacy to girls.

The fact that the spread of education is a recent phenomenon is evident in the data in table 1. Nearly 76 per cent of boys and 50 per cent of girls aged 10 to 14 were literate in Nepal in 1991 (as against 42 and 24 per cent of men and women aged 10 years and over, respectively). India is the other country for which similar data are available; it shows a similar pattern, with a much higher percentage of children than adults (77 per cent of boys and 60 per cent of girls aged 10-14 years were reported to be literate) as literate. The 1991 figures for Bangladesh and Pakistan by age are not available but the situation is unlikely to be different. Among the 20-24-year-old young adults in 1991 who would have enrolled in school in the mid-1980s, the percentage literate among men ranged between 65 and 71 per cent, but among women, between 26 and 44 per cent, with Nepal at the lower end and India at the higher end of the scale. This suggests a gender lag in the provision of education; boys began to receive education in large numbers earlier than girls, who began to enter schools in large numbers a decade or more later.

The overall literacy rates do not give an indication of the level of education that the women and men attain. One summary measure available is the mean number of years of schooling estimated for the adults 25 years and over, for years around 1980 and 1990.

Estimates given in table 2 clearly indicate that in 1990 males and females had received on an average three and one year of schooling, respectively. The situation had marginally improved in.one decade but is not very different in the four countries under consideration. The implications of such a low level of education for the well-being of the population in general and women in particular are discussed in a later section.

Table 2. Mean years of schooling (25 and over) in South Asian Countries, 1980 and 1990

Country	1980			1990		
	All	Male	Female	All	Male	female
Bangladesh	2.0	3.1	0.9	2.0	3.1	0.9
India	2.2	3.3	1.1	2.4	3.5	1.2
Nepal	1.8	2.7	0.9	2.1	3.2	1.0
Pakistan	1.7	2.7	0.7	1.9	3.0	0.7

Sources: *United Nations, 1995, 1996, 1997; Visaria and Ramachandran, 2002.*

Some further data on education presented for the four countries in table 3 suggest that school participation by girls relative to boys is much less and girls drop out of the school system earlier than boys do. Despite the fact that equal access to education opportunities for both sexes is guaranteed by Bangladesh's constitution, and girls comprised almost 45 per cent of the primary school-age population, the participation of girls in the education system was significantly lower than that of boys. At the secondary level, only 15 per cent of all girls were enrolled in school as against 32 per cent of boys, and girls comprised 34 per cent of all children. At the higher level of education, the share of girls would be even smaller. Further, while in recent years a large percentage of children in the primary school age group may be enrolled in schools, the percentage of those attending classes regularly is likely to be much smaller, and more so in the case of girls. As evident in the average number of years of schooling, the completion rate of even the primary cycle is very low. The drop out of the system at various stages of the primary cycle occurs even before attaining the minimum educational standards or literacy skills. Poverty, non-conducive social norms and values and insecurity are important factors contributing to the high dropout rates in Bangladesh.

The Nepalese Government had subscribed to the goal of achieving universal primary education by the year 2000 and has made the five-year primary education programme starting at 6 years of age officially compulsory and free of charge in government schools. Considerable efforts have been made to expand primary school education and increase the participation of girls in schooling, by establishing schools in remote areas, providing free tuition and books and giving special incentives to encourage teachers to work in these areas. Despite these efforts, and a dramatic increase in enrolment at the primary, lower secondary and upper secondary levels of general education, available data indicate that girls lag behind boys in school enrolment, and in literacy and educational attainment. In 1991, girls constituted only 37.2 per cent at lower secondary and 28.7 per cent at upper primary levels. Further, about half of the males and three fourths of all females in the appropriate age groups were not participating in secondary education. The low level of literacy among females in Nepal is due to social prejudices against female education, restrictions on their mobility and their overall low social status. The system of early marriage further leads to lower participation by women in formal education.

In recent years, the Government of Pakistan has also accorded priority to education; however, allocations to the education sector have until recently been around 2 per cent of gross national product, one of the lowest levels in the world. Consequently, all levels of Pakistan's education system have been underdeveloped and underfinanced, in both absolute and relative terms. Pakistan continues to have very high illiteracy, low rates of participation and very limited educational opportunities for many children, particularly for girls in the rural areas, despite a dramatic increase in student enrolments at the primary, middle and secondary levels in the late 1980s and early 1990s. However, despite the increases, girls constituted only about 31 per cent of all students enrolled at the primary and middle levels of education in 1993-1994. Although reliable and up-to-date information is not available, it is generally accepted that nearly 50 per cent of girls who enter the primary level at grade 1 drop out before completing grade 5 and the highest dropout rate occurs between grade 1 and 2. The low enrolment and high dropout rates, particularly for rural girls, are due to a number of reasons such as poor physical facilities in schools, long distance to school and shortage of teachers, especially of female teachers. Further, schooling in Pakistan involves substantial cost to parents, which influences their decision about sending girls to school given the economic and socio-cultural constraints.

Given the inadequate investments in education by the Government, resulting in inadequate school facilities in terms of separate schools for girls (only about a third of primary schools are for girls), and an unsafe school environment, religious schools have become an alternative avenue for the education of girls in rural areas where there are no facilities for primary education or where the primary schools are located at a considerable distance from the village. In the mosque schools, the Imams teach children Islamic studies and in the Mohallah schools literate women in the local area teach girls the Islamic studies and skills of home management. The very low female enrolment in formal schools implies that a very limited pool of educated women from which teachers are recruited is available in Pakistan, which in turn further limits the educational opportunities for girls, particularly in the rural areas.

Table 3 : Education profile of countries in South Asia, decade of the 1990s

Item	Bangladesh	India	Nepal	Pakistan
Female teaches as percentage of total				
Primary	-	-	-	-
Secondary	10	36	10	15
Female pupils as percentage of total				
Primary	48	45	42	32
Secondary	51	38	38	31
Adult illiteracy rate (aged 15 and over)				
Male	48	32	42	43
Female	71	56	77	73
Youth illiteracy rate (aged 15-24)				
Male	40	21	24	30
Female	61	36	59	59
Combined primary/secondary gross enrolment ratio				
Male	49	81	94	53
Female	38	62	53	26
Children out of school (percentage of age group				
Primary – Male	20	17	7	-
Primary – Female	30	29	38	-
Secondary – male	73	29	32	-
Secondary - Female	84	52	60	-

Sources: United Nations, 1995, 1996, 1997; Visaria and Ramachandran, 2002.

India, on the other hand, appears to be in a somewhat more fortunate position with regard to enhancing enrolment of boys as well as girls at the primary level compared with its neighbours. The Government's efforts to provide schools throughout the country seem to have contributed to the achievement. Despite the criticism that a significant proportion of rural schools are single-teacher schools, the statistics suggest that enrolment at the primary level has become universal for boys and that girls are not lagging far behind throughout India. However, household data collected by the National Sample Survey do not fully corroborate the official service statistics. For example, as opposed to officially 82 per cent of all girls enrolled at the primary level of education in 1996, the Survey reported 68 per cent of girls being enrolled and 63 per cent attending school. According to the 1991 census, 45 per cent of all girls and 39 per cent of rural girls aged 6 to 10 years were reported to be attending school.

Table 4. Health Profile of South Asian Countries, various years in the decade of 1990s

Item	Bangladesh	India	Nepal	Pakistan
Life expectancy at birth				
Male	60	62	58	61
Female	60	63	57	63
Life Expectancy at age 60				
Male	15	16	15	17
Female	16	17	16	18
Infant mortality rate				
Male	78	67	81	75
Female	79	78	84	73
Child mortality rate (1-4 years)				
Male	14	29	NA	9
Female	16	42	NA	10
Maternal mortality rate	600	440	830	200
Prevalence of anemia (Percentage of pregnant women)	53	88	65	37
Percentage of women receiving pre-natal care	23	62	15	27
Percentage of all births attended by skilled health staff	12	42	11	18
Percentage women among adults with HIV/AIDS	15	24	40	19

Sources: United Nations, 1991,2000.

However, evidently the decade of the 1990s has witnessed a major achievement in school attendance in India. The overall achievements, however, mask the important fact that the spread of education has been quite uneven. Not only do women continue to be at a disadvantage compared with men, but this also applies to rural areas as compared with urban areas. Within rural areas, certain segments of the society, such as those belonging to scheduled tribes and other economically and socially backward groups, have lagged behind. The stated reasons for non-attendance at school for girls have ranged from high cost of education, lack of interest in studies, and the perception of parents that education is unnecessary for girls. Lack of proper school facilities and marriage, were also important reasons for girls not going to school or dropping out of schools. These reasons have to be understood in a wider context in order to evolve appropriate policy prescriptions.

Health care: existing situation and access

South Asia is the only region of the world where men outnumber women in the total population. This deficit of women relative to men stems from various forms of lifelong discrimination against girls and women, particularly from the inferior nutrition and health care that girls receive early in life and during their childbearing years. Even though women are the main providers and carers of family members, their own health needs are inadequately addressed almost everywhere. In all the four countries of the Indian subcontinent under review, boys are more valued than girls, who have less access to health care. Discrimination is reflected in the female infant and child mortality rates, which are higher for girls than for boys.

Although data on food distribution within the household are difficult to collect, there is enough microlevel evidence to show that it is not always equally distributed among all family members. In all South Asian countries, there is a practice of men and boys eating first, and whatever is left is then distributed among the girls and women. Invariably, the adult women end up eating less food that is of inferior quality and nutritive value. As a result, girls and women in these countries are much more likely to be malnourished or anaemic compared with boys. These practices are further aggravated when family incomes shrink; women are the major sufferers of deprivation.

Table 4 presents a comparative picture on several health indicators derived from recent data available from the countries. The life expectancy at birth and at age 60, shown in the table, indicates that, except for Nepal, women in the countries concerned live slightly longer than men (about one year). However, until very recently, this was not the case. Men outlived women in this entire region for several decades. With the spread of immunization services and the control of many of the communicable diseases, the natural biological advantage of women has finally taken precedence. The female advantage in life expectancy at birth is expected to increase in the coming decades in all the countries.

The life expectancy of women at older ages (at age 60 and above) is also about a year higher than that of men. A somewhat higher life expectancy of women compared with men at older ages implies that women will have to spend a part of their old age without partners because, besides living a little longer, women tend to marry older men and do not generally remarry when widowed. Given their minimal literacy attainment, the elderly women are more likely than elderly men to live in poverty. Further, widowed and other women are also restricted in their employment opportunities, property rights and social behaviour and movement in public space.

On the other hand, the infant mortality rate for girls in the early 1990s was slightly higher than that of boys in Bangladesh and Nepal, and significantly higher in India. Pakistan was the only exception, with a female infant mortality rate lower than the male rate by two points. At the same time, female child mortality (mortality at ages 1 to 4 years) is significantly higher than male child mortality in all the countries. Not only that: there has been no improvement in the relative death rates of females at childhood ages; if anything, the situation seems to have worsened. Preference for sons is widespread throughout this region. Studies conducted in these countries have shown that behavioural factors, including care-seeking practices, operate against young female children. Girls are less likely to receive medical attention than boys, and if they do receive treatment it tends to be at a later stage of illness and provided by less qualified personnel (Waldron, 1987). Many of the discriminatory practices involved are subtle and lie deep within intimate family behaviour.

In the entire South Asian region, it is difficult to obtain reliable estimates of maternal mortality. In Nepal, the indirect estimates of maternal mortality rate have ranged from 510 per 100,000 live births for the country as a whole, to 850 based on three rural districts (United Nations, 1996, p. 21). The levels observed in the neighbouring countries of Pakistan and Bangladesh and in certain States of India are also similar. The high maternal mortality in this region is attributed to several causes, such as complications during pregnancy and delivery, indirect obstetric causes such as aggravation of pre-existing conditions, and deaths arising from a condition not related to pregnancy but occurring within 42 days. In Pakistan, an estimated 20,000-30,000 women die every year from complications of pregnancy, childbirth or unsafe abortion. Again, the majority of maternal deaths that occur during or soon after birth are caused by haemorrhage, sepsis, toxaemia, labour and primitive abortion methods.

Except for Pakistan, the prevalence of anaemia among pregnant women in the countries concerned exceeds 50 per cent; in other words, more than half of all pregnant women are anaemic. This adversely affects not only the health of the mothers but also of the infants born to them. A sizeable proportion of infants are born with low birth-weight.

In Nepal, less than 10 per cent of deliveries take place in a health facility and, given the mountainous terrain and poor road and transport network, access to emergency obstetric care is virtually impossible for most of the rural women. In Pakistan also, a very substantial percentage of birth deliveries take place at home with the help of *dais* or traditional birth attendants. According to the 1990-1991 Pakistan Demographic and Health Survey, 52 per cent of all births were attended by *dais*, while relatives attended another 12.5 per cent.

Although the majority of current HIV infections are still among men not only in the world but also in South Asia, AIDS is increasingly spreading among women. The recent estimates suggest that almost 40 per cent of HIV/AIDS cases in Nepal are women. While the proportion in the other three countries is small, there is no reason to be complacent. Largely monogamous women are increasingly exposed to the infection owing to the behaviour of their husbands.

The other major health problems faced by women stem from poor environmental sanitation, high prevalence of communicable diseases, nutritional deficiencies and parasitic infections. Despite the progress made in all the South Asian countries in expanding health facilities and services, the morbidity and mortality situation of women remains unsatisfactory. Malnutrition, caused by a combination of low income, inadequate or poorly balanced diets and poor food hygiene, has been one of the key determinants of ill health among the poor, and women are at a much greater risk than men. The problem is aggravated by cultural barriers, which prevent women's mobility to access health care when it is not available within the village where they live. It is also aggravated by the fact that many rural health institutions, such as primary health centres, have problems in attracting staff at all levels. This problem is even more acute with respect to female paramedical personnel owing to the severely restricted supply of qualified girls and problems of their safety in remote locations.

Challenges ahead

In the developing countries, including those of South Asia, health sector reforms are being implemented and issues related to financing, resource allocation and management have become very important. We need in-depth and dispassionate research on what impact these reforms have on the poorer sections of the societies and particularly women. Women comprise a large segment of the vulnerable population group in these countries and since access and the utilization of heath services are influenced by cultural and social factors, we need to highlight the gender issues in health sector reforms. Especially in this context, issues such as the introduction of user fees and what impact it would have on the access of women to health care must be fully understood. Questions such as whether vulnerable groups will be appropriately served by the private sector must be addressed and debated (Filmer and others,1998).

Another challenge is involving women themselves in some way in the design, implementation and evaluation of both health and education policies and programmes. Their voice must receive more than token representation. Along with that, the policy makers and concerned personnel of both health and education departments will have to be educated to "listen" to women.

We also need to understand why the poor are less educated and suffer greater mortality and morbidity. Many of the determinants of illiteracy and poor health would require taking a broader view and going beyond the health or education sectors. Issues of sanitation, clean water, employment etc. are all closely interlinked and a holistic approach would be needed if we aim at the well-being of all, including women.

Also, innovative approaches such as providing support for girls' secondary education in Bangladesh (where girls have been exempted from paying tuition fees and are given cash incentives) need to be carefully reviewed for possible upscaling. Similarly, the education guarantee scheme of Madhya Pradesh in India, which has reportedly increased school participation among girls from backward communities, also need to be carefully evaluated for possible lessons and replication in other parts of the country.

Endnotes

1. Overall, India has fared better than its neighbours and declared to provide free and compulsory education to all children by 1960. The goal of universal education even today remains elusive but certain pockets, such as the southern State of Kerala, have managed to nearly universalize literacy but the proportion of literate girls has been very small in the tradition- and caste-ridden north Indian States of Uttar Pradesh and Bihar.

2. According to the National Family Health Survey, two conducted in India in 1998-1999, 72 per cent of urban women and 44 per cent of rural women were reported as literate. The corresponding figures for men were 87 and 69 (IIPS, 2000).

3. Gross enrolment ratios include under-age and over-age students as well as repeaters, and thus tend to exaggerate the enrolment situation.

4. According to the latest Education Survey available for 1993, 83 per cent of habitations and 94 per cent of the population in India have a primary school within a distance of one kilometre. It is in the very small villages and hamlets located in remote areas that schools have not been set up. However, alternative schools have been set up in many such areas in the last 8-10 years, which has resulted in a tremendous increase in enrolment at the primary level (Visaria and Ramachandran, 2002).

5. In the case of Nepal and, to a smaller extent, Bangladesh, the excess of females in the total population is explained in terms of net emigration of men to countries like India in search of work. However, males have outnumbered women in the young age group 0-14 in both these countries - a fact that can be explained largely in terms of higher female infant and child mortality compared with male mortality.

6. Several United Nations reports have estimated the maternal mortality rate for Pakistan at 600 per 100,000 live births in 1988, while the Government's Eighth Five-year Plan estimates the rate at 300 for 1993.

References

Filmer, Deon, Elizabeth M. King and Lant Pritchett (1998). *Gender Disparity in South Asia: Comparisons Between and Within Countries* (Washington, DC, World Bank, Development Research Group on Poverty and Human Resources).

International Institute for Population Sciences (IIPS) (2000). *India, National Family Health Survey (NFHS-2), 1998-99,* Mumbai.

United Nations, Economic and Social Commission for Asia and the Pacific (ESCAP) (1996). *Women of Nepal: A Country Profile,* Statistical Profiles, No.4 (New York, United Nations).

(1997). *Women of Pakistan: A Country Profile,* Statistical Profiles, No.8 (New York, United Nations).

(1995). *Women of Bangladesh: A Country Profile,* Statistical Profiles, No.2 (New York, United Nations).United Nations (1991). *Women: Challenges to the Year 2000* (New York, United Nations).

(2000). *The World's Women: Trends and Statistics* (New York, United Nations). Visaria, Leela and Vimala Ramachandran (2002). "What DPEP and other data sources reveal", in: Ramachandran, V.

Gender and Social Equity in Primary Education (New Delhi, The European Commission).

Waldron, I (1987). "Patterns and causes of excess female mortality among children in developing countries", *World Health Statistics Quarterly,* vol. 40.

7

Transforming Rural-Urban Interactions and Social Networks Through Globalization

Recent globalization processes have changed significantly the conditions and features of female rural-to-urban labour migration in Thialand, particularly in terms of social networks and rural-urban interactions. The Thai case is specifically interesting because the Thai societal model is often said to support female migration better than other cultures. Thai female migrants encounter globalization, especially when they search for employment in the industries of Bangkok and its vicinity, the site of condensing economic globalization. The "feminization of urban employment" and the "feminization of labour migration" actually represent two sides of the same coin.

Development in a globalized world comprises apparently contradictory trends, an encompassing networking at all levels on one side,and more rapid and unpredictable socio-economic changes, disconnections and disjunctures on the other. Likewise, the female migrant workers experiences are somewhat caught between (a) their roles as cheap, flexible labour force; (b) a new environment of urban modernity, consumerism and social grouping; and (C) the traditional norms conveyed through relationships with their rural home. While moving between village and city, each migrant must negotiate shifts, not only in space but also in terms of personal identities and social relations: literally, the "good daughter" meets the "modern woman".

The resulting social networks and overall rural-urban interactions represent powerful vehicles and expressions of contemporary social-spatial dynamics. Women's mobility towards employment in Bangkok is asserted to be one example for continuity and change, as well as convergence and conflict of the people and the environment in present future Thailand. Against this wide-ranging background, the key questions of the paper are outlined as:

1. What dynamic interrelationships exist between and determine the development of gendered rural-urban migration, industrial labour and globalization in Thailand?

2. What impacts do the migrants social relationships with rural areas have on the geography of rural-urban circulation? Is female labour migration situated within a Bangkok-periphery divide or continum?

Hence, the paper's key objective is to identify, analyse and explain how socio-economic processes at the global and national levels are reflected in the practical experiences of Thai female labour migrants and their relationships with their rural families and communities left behind. The study investigates specifically rural-urban migration streams towards Bangkok and its vicinity and the target group of female migrant factory workers.

Migration is understood as a social, rather than a demographic process. Therefore, it is necessary to begin with understand the move from the periphery to the city as a passage from a relatively traditional to a modern context (United Nations, 1993a). In this paper,the macro-level background of the national political economy and the Thai societal system are related to the micro-and meso-level network structures of migrants and the resulting processes in their rural-urban interactions.

Methodology

This article summarizes the findings of a larger paper which reported on a research carried out over a three-month period in Bangkok (from November 2000 to January 2001). A mixed research approach was chosen including (a) 14 problem-centred and focused expert interviews; (b) visits to six industrial areas/trade union centres where eight female migrant manufacturing workers in three groups were interviewed; plus (c) the analysis of related statistics and existing research results. To evaluate the qualitative interviews, all information was thematically structured in categories, compared and analysed for sets of female labour migrants' typical patterns of social behaviours. The quantitative analysis mainly relates to the first key question, whereas the qualitative research concerns the second key question.

The variety of data sources creates difficulties for comparisons, especially regarding migration data, because sources employ varying definitions. However, the statistics are mainly used to illustrate overall trends and patterns. The available data sufficiently meet these expectations. Another problem is that most statistical sources use either regional or provincial classifications for analysis. Data in spatial categories that would fit the perspective of the paper, i.e. Bangkok Metropolis plus its vicinity against the four remaining regions of Thailand (the Southern, Northern, Central and North-Eastern Regions). are not available. The vicinity stands for the five provinces of Samut prakan, pathum Thani, Nonthaburi, Nakhon Pathom and Samut Sakhom which surround Bangkok Metropolis and belong administratively to the Central Region. Because they are assumed to be mostly urban, the municipal areas of the Central Region are used as spatial category instead. In cases where the urban character is only relevant in sociocultural terms, i.e. the statistical differentiation is not important, "bangkok" refers to the Metropolis and vicinity.

The expert interview partners were selected by their institutional and personal backgrounds. They comprise (a) academic institutions (Mahidol University and Chulaongkorn University, Thailand Development Research Institute (TDRI); (b) United Nations agencies (United Nations Population Fund, United Nations Development Fund for Women, United Nations Economic and Social Commission for Asia and the Pacific; and (c) five non-governmental organizations.

The interviews with the female migrant workers took place during field visits to industrial production areas and trade union centres. Culture and language barriers tied the author to other institutions for contacts with the female migrants. This dependency on NGOs and governmental bodies opened up doors for supposedly more selective insights, especially as two cooperating NGOs approach the workers through trade unions only.

Migration and globalization

Migration and globalization are tied together across many dimensions. Globalization jeopardizes and reworks the traditional ideas of geography and social actions within space. Generally speaking, globalization stands for ever-increasing worldwide networking that takes place simultaneously at various levels and dimensions (Beck, 1999; Cohen and Kennedy, 2000). Its major underlying component is a new, all-encompassing compression of time and space. Economies, cultures and societies are squeezed together towards increased mutual interaction. Consequently, peoples' biographies change. Particularly, mobile people encounter new ways of life. They have to face a new, disjunctive relation between space, place and cultural identity. Rural-urban interactions, as constructed by migrants and their families left behind, are both part and result of these network structures over space and time. The wider social, political, economic and spatial contexts become interconnected with the practical experiences of migrants and their families.

Local cultures remain vivid but widen their reference points by adopting and adjusting "global" symbols and products. Individual lives, cultures and identities are caught in between different places, networks, the global, and the local. As a result, they redefine themselves - a process that is expected to bring about personal, familial and societal tensions and conflicts (Appadurai, 1996; Werlen, 2000).

The consequences of migration are closely interlinked with its initiation and perpetuation processes. particularly significant for this study is the "new econimics if migration" or "household survival" approach. It comes close to a "meso-theory" that is appropriate for the chosen integrative research approach. The concept presumes that the decision to migrate is taken as a combined household strategy. Motivations are primarily the minimization of risks associated with unforeseeable market failures, resource diversification and in the second place, income maximization (Chant, 1998; Massey and others, 1993; Stark, 1991).

Economic globalization and female labour migration

Economic globalization in Thailand, as elsewhere, occurs in the form of political-economic interactions between global and national forces leading to an integration of labour, trade and capital markets. The outcomes are profound structural socio-economic changes, particularly in terms of altering employment patterns, regional disparities, migration and a policy shift towards family and community cohension in place of macroeconomic goals.

Thailand entered the global economy as it is understood today after 1985, when the Government applied the industrializing strategy of labour-intensive export orientation which set off intensified local private and particularly foreign direct investment (FDI). Subsequently, the country experienced an economic boom. Gross domestic product (GDP) grew massively and relatively unexpectedly in 1987-1988 by 13.3 per cent, continuing at an average 9 per cent until 1995. The percentage of the population living below the poverty line fell from 32.6 to 11.4 per cent during the period from 1988 to 1996 National Economic and Social Development Board; Skeldon, 1999). Thailand was quickly termed a "newly industrialized country" with economic globalization appointed to be the impetus and upholder of the boom. An expansion of FDI, particularly by Hong Kong, China; Japan; and Taiwan Province of China into Thailand has followed the appreciation of the yen since 1986. These processes caused exceptional growth in the merchandise exports of industrial goods, from 55.35 per cent in 1986 to 84.27 per cent in 1999 (TDRI, 2000b). The country entered the world trade market and joined the international division of labour. Many transnational corporations (TNCs) relocated their manufactures to Thailand because it offered the favourable factor conditions, specifically a large pool of unskilled, cheap female labour (Krass, 1996a, 1996b; Sussangkorn, 1997; Ogena and others, 1997).

However, in 1997-1998, globalization exposed its risks and in particular Thailand's dependency on foreign capital, in the form of a severe economic crisis. The GDP growth decreased to -10.8 per cent in 1997-1998, and the percentage of Thais living beneath the poverty line rose again to 12.9 per cent. The demand for goods fell, factories closed, employees were laid off, working hours and wages were cut (Gray, 1999; TDRI, 2000a). In 2000, GDP growth slowly recovered at 4.5 per cent but the socio-economic effects of the crisis are still visible.

Representing one factor condition in Thailand's global integration, Thai women became increasingly engaged as cheap, flexible and unprotected workers. This feminization of employment is most apparent in the five major export-oriented, labour-intensive industries, which are electrical machinery, electronics and computer parts; textiles and ready-made garments; chilled, frozen and canned food; precious stones and jewellery; and footwear. In 1999, the proportions of female workers varied from 55.44 per cent (precious stones and jewellery) to 75.94 per cent (textiles and ready-made garment) (GDRI, 2000).

The Thai women's labour participation rate has always been and is still high at 60-70 per cent (16-17 per cent lower than the male rate in 1999-2000) (NSO, 1999-2000). Yet, their traditional tasks were closely tied to unpaid family work. Nowadays, if a family expects the daughter to support it more successfully than the son, she is the one to work outside the household, even at the expense of migration. The proportion of economically active women who work as employees increased from 17 to 25.6 per cent between 1980 and 1990 (Phananiramai, 1996).

Thai female industrial workers experience higher socio-economic independence and "empowerment", which paradixically take place in a gender segregated and biased labour market. The majority of Thai female workers face vulnerability and marginalization in terms of low wages, bad working conditions, health risks and insecure jobs. Generally, the higher the wages and education, the wider the gap between male and female workers (GDRI, 1999).

Growing disparities between Bangkok and the periphery

As a second major outcome, economic globalization especially the power of TNCs does not balance, but on the contrary widens local and regional disparities. The outcomes are , on the winning side, new "marketplaces" of globalization - here, Bangkok and its vicinity - and, on the losing side, most of the remaining marginalized peripheral regions that have lost the contest: since the 1980s, 75 per cent of all investment has been concentrated in Bangkok and its vicinity. The city's population totals about 16 per cent of the whole Thai population and 60 per cent of the urban population. Fifty per cent of the GDP was generated in Bangkok and its vicinity in 1998. Likewise, in 1999, 45.6 per cent of all establishments and 48 per cent of all manufacturing establishments were located in Bangkok, 7.2 and 13.5 per cent in the vicinity. With regard to employment structure in 1999, 41.5 per cent of all Thai employees (28.5 per cent of factory labourers) worked in Bangkok, 20.13 per cent (33 per cent) in the vicinity and 17.15 per cent (22.7 per cent) in the remaining Central Region[2] (TDRI, 2000b; Ministry of Labour and Social Welfare,1989, 1999; Kittiprapas, 1999).

Thailand has one of the most concentrated patterns of industrial development worldwide. Bangkok faces the problematic situation of being jammed between national requirements and reverse-oriented international forces. Necessary national balancing policies collide with - and have so far failed against - the interests of the global economy. Recent policy shifts towards stronger regionalization and decentralization have not yet shown profound results (Wongsuphasawat, 1997; Krass, 2000).

Summarizing, economic globalization operates as occupationally-selective in manufacturing, spatially-selective in Bangkok and its vicinity, and gender-selective for the female sex. These regional, sectoral and sexual disparities in Bangkok-periphery relations are reflected in human migration behaviour, to be discussed in the following.

Mobility patterns, migrants' socio-economic profile and links to factory workers

Rural-to-urban migration in Thailand is being feminized, accelerated and reinforced. In August 2000, 14 per cent of the Thai population aged 13 and over had changed their residence from one village or municipal area to another in the previous five years, 1.4 per cent more than in 1985 (aged 11 and over) (NSO, 1985, 2000). Male and female shares among migrants in Bangkok and the Central Region are consistently fairly equal. With regard to migration flows, however, female migrants usually dominate urban-ward and male migrants rural-rural migration (Pejaranonda and others, 1995). Interestingly, the 2000 Labour Force Survey data do not reflect the female dominance, with the exception of migrants in the Central Region. Percentages are also generally lower. Whether this is the beginning of a new trend or an exceptional situation cannot be said at this stage (NSO, 2000).

There are no official data on the proportion of migrants among factory workers. But according to the interview conducted, such workers comprised about 80 per cent of the workforce in the industrial areas visited. Census data in 1990 and Thonguthai and Pattaravanich's labour market survey (1993) revealed that factory workers typically comprised the largest proportion of young Thais (age 15 to 30), followed by rural-to-urban migrants and all migrants. Female rates usually exceeded male rates in this age group, except from female "all migrants", who surpassed men only at ages 10-14 and 15-19. In 1997, migrants , as well as the surveyed manufacturing workers, were more likely to be single than non-migrants, especially in Bangkok with 58 to 59 per cent singles (36 to 38 per cent of non-migrants). As a matter of fact, in industry, singles are often favoured over married workers because they offer the required "factor condition) of flexibility. Moreover, the majority of migrants had, in contrast to non-migrants, finished at least elementary schooling. Fewer women than men attended secondary school. Factory workers in Bangkok were generally better educated than the whole group of migrants, those employed in services and commerce, as well as non-migrants (NSO, 1997). Also, in 1992, the better educated the migrants the more likely they were to move towards Bangkok (Chamratrithirong and others, 1995). Matching this pattern, a disproportionately high number of migrants in Bangkok and the Central Region (40 to 60 per cent) worked in the industrial sector in 1997 (20 to 25 per cent non-migrants) (NSO, 1997). Accordingly, the female migrants' spatial concentrations followed the relocations of industries from the "full" Bangkok Metropolis (12.7 per cent migrants, August 2000) to the municipal Central Region (24.5 per cent migrants compared with 15.2 per cent in non-municipal areas) (NSO, 1999-2000).

Seasonal mobility in rural and urban areas is a common phenomenon in Thailand. However, it is more common among male than female migrants. Factory workers are typically permanent movers and forced to stay in Bangkok owing to their contract obligations (Chamratrithirong and others, 1995)

In terms of regional streams, the mobility processes establish a kind of regional economic migration system between Bangkok/ the urban Central Region and the North Eastern Region/ the rural Northern Region. The latter two regions, being largely neglected by industrialization, direct investment and tourism, provide the economic heartland of Bangkok and the municipal Central Region with relatively cheap labour (Parnwell and Rigg, 1996). Hence, the globalized Thai labour market determines the volume, direction, nature and type of female rural-to-urban migration in Thailand.

Analysing the impact of migration

The following two sections summarize the findings of the qualitative research on migrants' network structures and processes of rural-urban interactions (key question two), supplemented by other investigations. Specific interview references are only given after direct quotes, and additionally utilozed literature is explicitly quoted.

Communicating material and immaterial goods

In analysis, (a) flows of material and social remittances and (b) sustained migration through networks are regarded as the distinguishing aspects for the dynamics of migrants' exchange networks. The interviews indicate that the major contact points of migrants and their rural origin are material remittances. Concisely, remittances consist of money and "special items" like seafood, clothes, television sets, refrigerators, rice cookers, radios and dried fruit. Gender-specifically, a higher percentage of women remit higher percentages of their salaries, often more than what they keep for themselves (at least at initial stages of migration).

Thai migrant women also transfer so-called social remittances, here ideas, patterns of behaviour, identities, attitudes, skills and practices to their family and/or community (Levitt, 1998). Firstly, the migrants were said to take back with them new habits and attitudes of urban "modern" lifestyle, possessions, consumerism and materialism. For explanation, the interview partners referred to the Thai Buddhist image of people possessing what they deserve - in spite of sincere buddhism actually rejecting all kinds of possessions. Eng (1997) and Mills (1997) infer that for young Thais, wealth determines social status: the purchase of "than samay", the modern lifestyle, has replaced religion at the centre of their social life. Secondly, migrants, particularly, females, adopt new education targets. They learn in Bangkok that "opportunities are dictated by education". As a consequence they "send money back for the education of the children so that they, when they start to go to the job market, would have a better chance in life". (expert interviews 3,8). Thirdly, some experts noted (while others denied) that return migrants transfer new political ideas and take on initiatives for local political empowerment. The fourth kind of social remittances is the communication of expertise. Mentioned examples include the utilization of newly acquired sewing, computing, accounting or mechanic skills, and knowledge of how to open up businesses.

Importantly, migrants' exchange networks always stand for a two-way relationship in material and immaterial dimensions. The interviewed women stressed the emotional support the migrants receive from their parents while living in Bangkok (Curran, 1998 and Mills

1999a). Material support flows from the rural areas exist, too, although to a smaller extent than remittance streams.

Focusing on the family basis, interview partners often reason the existence of networks with Buddhist tradition: migrants pay back gratitude to their parents through material remittances.

"They are not economic ties. Although they do still provide support to their parents and their siblings who need it. If they need it they give them support. It's an ethnic, it's a cultural trait to give money to your parents. You know you are supposed to return what you got from them" (expert interview 8).

Thus, children feel a sense of continuous obligation to their parents in reciprocity for their parents' care - in Thai called "bun khun". Gender-specifically, the traditional Thai societal model conditions that daughters are more committed to provide remittances than sons: "Daughters are usually the ones to take care of the parents [...] the sons could go to the monkhood to pay debt of gratitude to their parents. But the girls cannot be a monk" (expert interview 1, see Pramualratana, 1992; Osaki, 1999). Both experts and interviewed workers emphasized that female migrants commonly support their parents plus their (male) siblings' education and/or livelihood, even if they are migrants themselves. In this respect, Thai internal migration functions as a household survival strategy as posited by the "new economics of migration" theory.

Sustaining the migration chain: the human dimension of networks

The remittance flows create yet another from of linkage between migrants and their rural origin: migration chains which perpetuate mobility. Their mechanism was depicted thus:

"A women who is working in a factory or any employment in Bangkok goes home. She has got some money, she has got new clothes, she has seen the world, she knows Bangkok. And she tells her friends: if you come with me you can stay with me and I know that my factory is employing" (expert interview 9). So "when these women come back to the village they want to show that they are better off. [...]. So they become role models for the other women who want to migrate. Because they think this women is successful" (expert interview 6).

Consequently, the urban migrants mobilize the remaining people in the rural areas and channel their movement to Bangkok. For example, seven interviewed workers came to the city following a relative, usually their sister, and two of them have asked younger sisters to join them.

The migrants' outer appearance and behaviour transmit an idea of the "than samay" lifestyle, associated with modernity and autonomy offered by the Bangkok surrounding. The rural women feel relatively deprived and follow their more experienced role models in search of the same "imagined identity". Importantly, the migrants' appearance and their real "than samay" experiences must not necessarily correspond. Any failure of migrants in the city is hidden because "all of the parents would like to see progress of their children", which is equated with money, clothes and make-up (expert interview 5).

Thus, women's decisions to migrate reflect filial responsibilities and their independent ambitions for unique types of personality and material goals. Hence, "there is a great deal of both family and individual decision involved in migration. It's not so simple, it is a family decision". To the speaking expert, this applies specifically to Thais who, according to their (Buddhist) societal model, are very individual within their families I think more than in other Asian cultures" (expert interview 9).

Moreover, the social networks facilitate adjustments and socialization of newcomers to Bangkok. Migration chains are tools to make the migration experience less risky and difficult. Almost all but especially female, movers have some personal contact net. Thonguthai and Pattaravanich (1993) discovered that 81 per cent of their surveyed female factory workers (compared with 69 per cent of male) relied on networks for information about job availability. Interestingly, factory owners were said to prefer the recruitment of friends and family of their trusted workers over recruiting agencies because it is cheaper and more effective.

Changes as the migration experience proceeds

The described exchange relations change as the migration experience proceeds. During the interviews, a wider understanding of changing behaviour was pronounced. The interviewed experts' assessment of changes varied. The two recurring themes were that (a) material remittance streams usually decline with time, and that (b) the migration chain may stablize or may gradually be replaced by "ethnic" communities in Bangkok.

Remittances are "... much higher for recent migrants and taper off over time. So if you get migrants who have been in Bangkok for 5 or 10 years, then their remittances as a percentage of their salaries have gone down quite a lot. They don't remit as frequently" (expert interview 9). The interviewed migrants and Mills (1997) confirmed these observations. The numbers of households receiving support in 1992 declined from 10.3 per cent for recent migrants to 5.5 per cent for old-time migrants (moved more than two years ago) (Osaki, 1999).

With regard to migration chains "as you move along the way that's when you bring in members of the family to help you and also it changes the entire relationships in the sense that the more productive members at the place of origin are coming to the city and you are creating your own [...] networks [in Bangkok]" (expert interview 6). Through stabilizing migration chains and with time, the migrants create their own "ethnic" communities in Bangkok, based on social capital in the form of solidarity through identical ethnic and regional backgrounds. Indicators are shared accommodation places, "ethnic" meetings at certain sites like Lumpini Park in Bangkok, and the organization of regional cultural festivels in Bangkok. "Ethnic" communities create many small "ethnic" clusters in the city which are hardly recognizable to an outsider.

Hence, traditional networks are reworked in the new Bangkok environment or, as one expert puts it "So in a sense it's a kind of a village home transplanted" (expert interview 9). The "ethnic communities" are equally part of urban life and a vivid connection to the rural areas. Like migration chains, "ethnic" communities serve as shields against vulnerability, offer hold and reduce homesickness: "With a dozen of your friends from the village around it's not like you are totally anonymous [...] you are really in a group" (expert interview 9).

On the whole, the findings suggest that networks of kinship obligation and of shared understanding are crucial for migration preparation, its realization and urban adjustments. The "ethnic" communities in the city play an essential role at a latter stage of life establishments.

New relationships at destination Bangkok

A third alternative of social support, besides

retaining links with the rural areas and the creation of "ethnic" migrant communities, was defined. Some migrants are said to lead an "urbanized" way of life, including the construction of new, ethnically independent social networks. The research revealed, however, that female factory workers do not necessarily create exclusive, long-lasting networks. As industrial workers, they obviously experience sectoral, spatial and sexual concentrations. Nonetheless, many migrants frequently shift their workplace and their social environments in search of ideal occupational conditions, more consumer culture and better social collectivity. Therefore female migrant factory workers' urban networks are distinct in some respect, but also share many characteristics with other occupational migrant groups. These include personal background and motivation to migrate, age, children, upward social mobility and job hierarchy, gender, generation, education, role within the household, experiences in Bangkok and the duration of the sojourn. The women's stage of life cycle, i.e. whether they are married or single, was ascribed particular importance.

In contrast to the exchange, urban workers' networks comprise both informal and formal structures. Informal friendship networks are almost omnipresent and especially important for singles in matters of education, health, politics, entertainment, sports, religion, money or personal issues. At the factory, personal life and work are closely connected: "The workers here work together, always. So we are friends. So our friend is like the workers here" (group interview 2). Their social closeness is facilitated by spatial closeness. For example, at one visited industrial site in Samut Prakan, most single female workers lived together in small dormitores or rented apartments. Other locations to socialize were the factory canteen and a food and shopping centre, which exist in most industrial areas.

Meanwhile, the social and spatial focal points of married women differ. Together with their husbands they tend to move away from the industrial production area (e.g. into downtown Bangkok). Their social networks shift. Contacts with their new neighbourhood and immediate community are often more intense than with their colleagues in the industrial area. Married workers also tend to discuss family matters in their own circles.

With regard to formal organizations, trade unions, if they exist, take over many central functions in the workers' everyday life. In total, only about 2 per cent of the Thai private labour force is unionized and membership is risky. Therefore, the following discourse may not be transferred to the situation in the entire Thai manufacturing sector. Formally organized groups are generally rare in Thailand. Thais often show a political passiveness and avoidance of conflicts which are rooted in a strict hierachical patron-client system determining all social intercourse, behaviour and communication.

"I think they are not political. They would not be concerned. They don't relate to the macro-level, only their own economic, needs and that of their family [...] everything is micro for them" (expert interview 6) (Yoddumnern-Attig, 1992).

The two visited trade unions are, with 80 per cent worker' participation, exceptionally active organizations in the Thai context. They represent gathering sites of the labour movement and the locations for multiple activities, including education and training, saving groups, cultural activities, entertainment and sports, and shopping. The unions established tourist trips for the workers, a music band, and a shop offering special deals to the workers. In addition, the unions provided assistance in legal and health matters. They literally functioned as the workers' mediator to the world "outside" the industrial areas. And importantly, field observations suggested that the formal Thai trade unions bear significant informal functions. For instance, the visited workers informally gathered hours before an official union meeting. Their sense of familiarity and level of confidence seemed to be strongly developed, and they showed intense, frank and very private communication behaviour.

The above discussions may lead to the conjecture that urban workers' relations in Bangkok are based on social capital in the form of enforceable trust (in more utilitarian networks) and solidarity (in emotionally closer networks). Evidently, the workers' networks are part of the life establishment in the city, hence a later stage of the migration cycle.

Rural-urban interactions in transition

Thai women's localized identities and their expression in rural-urban interactions

This section explores how migrants' network formations shape rural-urban interactions. Thai female migrant factory workers' daily lives were identified to be positioned in between three different kinds of social networks which are representative of distinct spheres and locations (here: the factory environment in Bangkok, the urban "ethnic" community and the rural place of origin). How does each migrant woman deal with the different spheres: does she produce a continuum or a divide between her rural and urban existence?

There is no straightforward answer. Obviously, exchange and urban "ethnic" networks stand closer to each other, and somewhat in opposition to the urban workers' relations, since both are connected with the rural. In general, however, the decision of any migrant to take on or not to take on her "bridging function" between Bangkok and the periphery is decisive for the resulting form of social networks, which again shape rural-urban interactions. Thus, rural-urban interactions are here understood as forms of socially constructed spaces in a globalized context. Characteristics pointing to the migrant's position between divide and continuum are (a) the nature and transformation of her social exchange networks, and (b) her personal localized identity, here her own perception of belonging and affiliation and where, in Bangkok or the periphery, these are located (Massey and Keynes, 1998). The qualitative research came up with three "typical" experiences of Thai migrants. These are by no means exclusive and may overlap.

Pattern one: the "modern women" takes over

In this case, urban and exchange networks prove to be competing social spheres to the migrant. The women's traditional roles no longer fit their modern images. "Urbanized" identities of mobility, independence, sexuality, consumerism and self-assertion confront established rural ideals of thrift, modesty, social harmony and familial responsibilities.

Following pattern one, the women find their identity, here their home, in the city. They "forget about it (the rural way of life) and lead an entirely different lifestyle" (expert interview 6). Friends and family who share their urban lives, participation in consumer culture and concentration on their own aspirations are focal points of their "than samay" life. Consequently, the migrants do not envisage or long for return migration and tend to change their official household registration to the city. As a result of these processes, one expert claimed, migration "... has already changed the culture of the people. So they have no rural culture any more, they belong to the urban culture. So they fit to the [...] luxurious thing in Bangkok" (expert interview 11). Long-term movers, i.e. most factory workers, are more likely to undergo such diverging dynamics. Educational targets and marriage can also be influential factors (Ogena and Dejong, 1999).

Pattern two: filial obligation or the adventure of life

In pattern two, the migrants continuously regard their rural village as their home despite their city sojourn. They encounter the three social spheres in Bangkok in a harmonious way or show a clear preference for the rural-urban exchange and related "ethnic" networks. for example, two interviewed migrant workers uttered a relatively negative attitude towards their Bangkok existance:

"During time of working they are thinking of it like a jail [...] they don't like [Bangkok] but [...] they have no opportunity, no choice because they try to work in order to send back money to their parents" (group interview 1).

Their filial obligation overweighs their personal interests. Bangkok life is viewed as an unfortunate necessity. Overall, their localized identity lies unmistakably with their rural origin. In the city...

"...it's kind of weird, I don't think that they feel they have another home. Only that they have another friends, another surroundings, another new things here, but it's not home. It's something else but not home" (expert interview 14).

Migrants either develop some compromise between their urban and rural ways of life, or explicity voice their unease through e.g. trade union membership (as in the case at hand). Their urban networks (formal and informal) are generally less dense for they aim at the migrants' practical survival and ultimate return (usually they do not change their household registration). Contradictory interview statements revealed, however, that they, despite their disapproving attitudes on the surface, adopt and take some "urban" concepts to the rural areas (see social remittances above).

Migrants may choose pattern two in the alternative context of the "adventure of life". Here the sojourn in the strange urban world is an individually motivated, temporary exciting encounter without familial pressure. One expert reported from her own research that such "adventurous" stay(s) had been the favourite way of life of most elderly rural people before they married and settled in the provinces. Their Bangkok experience had upgraded their personal, familial and community-wide status.

On the whole, the migrants who choose the second path establish continuous rural-urban interactions. Firstly, they live a continuum themselves, consciously or subconsciously, by mixing rural and urban attitudes within their personal identity. Secondly, they take on their bridging function by maintaining intensive linkages until their own return. Thirdly, migration in the "adventure of life" context always implies an individual choice factor. Its harmonizing effect favours the construction of a rural-urban continuum.

Pattern three: Ambivalent feelings amidst reality and commitment

Pattern three is multi-faceted, more ambiguous and was most popular with the interview partners and in the literature. The women of pattern three manage an emotional and economic compromise between their traditional and new economic roles. They consider that their rural and urban lives serve different purposes. Concisely,

"They miss home and they would like to be home, I think. But the difficulty is most people will say in the same breath virtually: but, there is no money at home

[...] and so there is probably an internal conflict. You can't have both" (expert interview 9).

In other words, the migrants' attachment and commitment are still in the rural areas, but their real life takes place in Bangkok because "there is no future in the village" (expert interview 10). Especially long-term migrants feel uneasy about the city's alien and alienating aspects; they still turn towards their rural home for advice.

"When we stay here we are quite lonely but we have the friends. So this is like compensation. We can consult many topics with the friends but not exactly like we consult with the parent".

Positively, Bangkok offers the jobs, and "in our province life is backwards, no so modernized. But here we have everything. Modern. Everything is convenient here". Moreover, the work "makes us to have responsibility [...] for ourselves" and provides educational upgrading. Negatively, life in Bangkok also implies that "we need to fight for survival" whereas "when we go back to our hometown, it is quiet, smooth, peaceful" (group interview 2). As the quotes illustrate, migrants' life in Bangkok functionally represents the place for work, "than samay" lifestyle, and personal status accumulation whereas the rural origin is the emotional home and place of rest. The latter is related to the parents, the former stands for friendships.

When asked which place the female migrants identify themselves with, they stated: "All of us think our home is still home, so but, because of the fact we have to work here and we work already a long time, so this is like second home" (group interview 2). The migrants' rural and urban existances are functional complements in one overall "system of life", hence they construct a rural-urban continuum. Migrants also take on their "bridging role", participate in exchange relations and create a connected space of exchanges. To one expert, these processes suggest that "... maybe the cultural divide is not that great. ... it could be valid that the people don't feel it" (expert interview 9).

Thai answers to the cultural divide and continuum: pragmatism and flexibility

Some specific features of the Thai people facilitate the migrants' lives across space and time and influence the migrant workers' overall perception of their "problematic" situations. Essentially, Thai female migrants are likely to deal with conflicts differently from Western people. Even if they are aware of conflicts, they usually do not spend much time contemplating or discussing them. Believing in the Buddhist thought of "karma", Thais are generally less anxious and more accepting (Kraas, 1997). Pragmatism and flexibility are crucial Thai coping strategies that are particularly relevant to migrants, or put differently:

"Thais are open [...] society here is very progressive, open. Because they just say, well there are the breaks and you have to take the good and the bad, and the bad and the good [...] So tolerant. And it is not our business. Very like this: Take the advantage of everything!" (expert interview 8).

How does such an attitude influence their assessment of problems? The interviewed female workers seemed aware of problems at the workplace but stressed only those issues which are commonly discussed at their trade union (the "typical Western" ideas of problems of equality, exploitation, and the lack of legal protection). Matters connected with gender roles or their migration experiences, e.g. disconnections were not tackled. Generally, the Thai labour movement is disproportionately exposed to "Western" attitudes because it is financially supported by NGOs. Through these channels a "Western" image of the problems of female industrial workers finds access into the Thai orbit and into the present study: experts with an international background and those practising a gender-specific approach commonly supported the same "Western" argumentation.

Importantly, the women's own problem-awareness might be essentially different: "It is so easy to say that these people are disadvantaged and marginalized and so forth. But you see this is relative. It is how the woman compares herself in this setting and in another setting and which is better. And my theory is women make choices as they move alone. They weigh you know the benefits and cost of each choice". Hence, a problem in Western thinking is not necessarily a problem from a Thai point of view.

Hence, labour migration can be defined as a way for Thai people to make the most of their opportunities. It contains advantages and disadvantages - "That is simply the way life is" (expert interview 9). The westernized approaches to problems of equality, exploitation and human rights issues are surely meaningful, yet they should consider that typical Thai attitudes, and thus the viewpoint of the people concerned, may be disparate.

The rural and the urban areas as safety nets? Social cohesion during the 1997 economic crisis

The circulation of goods, money, ideas and people has considerable potential to create a dynamic, wealthier economy and society in the interconnected rural and urban sectors. Rural-urban household and community links function as an informal, non-institutionalized social safety net. Migration then becomes crucial for poverty alleviation, especially since a formal "western-style" social safety system does not exist in Thailand (Skeldon, 1997).

Changes in social safety nets and migrants' social capital during and after the economic crisis are controversially debated. On the one side, Thai group dynamics were eroded as the provinces lacked the capacity to absorb the return flows of migrants, and adverse trends in educational enrolment, child care, suicides, divorces, crime and drug use as well as declines, although not a stop, in remittances declined were apparent (TDRI, 2000a; World Bank Thailand Office, 2000). On the other side, compared with the violent outbreaks that accompanied the crisis in many other Asian countries, the situation in Thailand remained relatively calm, thanks to the traditional, conflict-rejecting societal model, as well as the at least partially functioning social back-up systems (UNDP, 1999). Social capital also increased with people consulting and sharing with each other more and more. With respect to the Bangkok industrial production environment, the labour movement uprisings were viewed as a positive sign for an emerging new collective identity and political empowerment. Many female migrants have redefined their individual-centred images and now collectively challenge the customary avoidance of "macrolevel" affairs (Mills, 1999a). However, a female migrant worker who is actively engaged in urban-based movements may eventually abandon those in the rural areas. In this case, her family's dependence and reliance on her as a personal safety net are indeed destabilizing and risky (United Nations, 1993b).

In summary, the crisis has highlighted the risk inherent in diverging interactions in terms of fading social security between people from the periphery and from Bangkok. Therefore, as mentioned, the Government nowadays acknowledges and supports the social importance of traditional rural-urban interactions. Further, the crisis has introduced new forms of social cohesion and political participation. These alliances concentrate either in Bangkok or in the rural areas; rural-urban interactions are not importnat. Hence the crisis has intensified the existing rural-urban divide(s), and equally pushed counteractive trends (Kraas, 2000; Suwanraks, 2000).

Conclusion

Revisiting the role of globalization in socio-spatial transformations in Thailand

Economic globalization and industrialization produce the structural setting of sectoral, sexual and spatial disparities which trigger off and determine female labour migration from the rural provinces to Bangkok. The female workers simultaneously experience socio-economic empowerment and exploitation.

In this structural area, female labour migrants' life in industrial Bangkok takes place in between three different socio-spatial environments which reflect their culturally determined, sex-specific family roles and personal, more utilitarian choices: firstly, networks of material, non-material and human exchanges with the rural origin; secondly, migrants' "ethnic" community networks in Bangkok; and thirdly, urban factory workers' networks. Depending on their relation in terms of collision, harmonious combination or coexistence, each woman produces a distinct pattern of Bangkok-periphery interactions. In what way are these dynamics interrelated with globalization?

Rural people encounter the "imagined worlds" of Bangkok, either through old-time migrants or media information flows. the globalized technology and communication systems reach every region of Thailand with the same intensity in contrast to economic globalization. They spread the popular "than samay" images concerning the display of commodities and the meaning of progress - a possible explanation for their crucial role in exchange and urban networks (Mills, 1997; UNDP, 1999). As the migration proceeds, the advanced communication and transport systems facilitate rural-urban connections.

At least at initial stages of life establishment, many women are physically present in Bangkok but still participate in the socio-economic life of their rural homes. They can be said to lead a translocal life (Olwig, 1997). Thai female labour migrants define their cultural selves across a geographically fragmented space which they link through social actions. They are not socially disconnected but belong to two places. Bangkok and the periphery become part of several socioeconomic translocal migration systems based on family and friendship.

In the face of the increasing concentration of economic choices in the "global marketplace" of Bangkok, many Thai migrant women decide to carry on their translocal life as their migration experience proceeds. They create a vivid rural-urban continuum. Each location fulfils specific functions, and together they shape a "system of life": the rural origin offers religion, emotional support and personal roots, whereas Bangkok provides opportunities for personal and familial socio-economic upgrading and future perspectives (pattern three).

In the long run, the "functional system of life" is possibly gradually replaced by the new, globalized orbit at the destination. In the Thai case, these processes happen in an ambivalent setting, as demonstrated by the example of the economic crisis: on the one hand, the recession intensified the familial safety net functions across space: on the other , the broadening of individual;

choices through globalization supported the individualized, as well as collective search for new, exclusively urban gender identities and collective urban safety nets. Circumstances like marriage or generation differences can also cause the "modern woman" to take over. Consequently, the image and way of life of a "good daughter" are rejected, rural-urban interactions are cut, and a rural-urban divide is produced (pattern one).

One needs to consider that many of the debated socio-spatial transformations began in Thailand alongside industrialization in the 1960s and 1970s. Globalization has undoubtedly deepened and reinforced the processes and their resulting structures, yet the Thai societal model, the family and the individual play an equally important role. For instance, some migrants reject the modern Bangkok life and regard their urban sojourn as an unfortunate family responsibility, or as a temporary adventure (pattern two).

To sum up, globalization in its various dimensions initiates spatial mobility and social networking across space and time in Thailand. It is also partially responsible for the intensification and acceleration of spatial mobility and increases circular migration. Specifically, it creates bridges of imagination for the migrants who themselves automatically work as driving mechanisms of globalization through the rural-urban connections they establish. National and global political economies in Thailand form the structural context of internal gendered labour migration. Meanwhile, the spatial and sociocultural dimensions of globalization are the major forces behind migrants' changing biographies and are at the same time reworked in a self-reinforcing process. These changes are particularly apparent in the transition of rural-urban interactions, but in fact reflect the modification of the entire Thai societal structure. Consequently, both rural-urban divides as well as continuums are produced. “In-between” categories increasingly replace stereotypical categories of “the”rural and “the” urban.

The impacts of globalization are always incorporated in local behaviours and norms. For instance, Thais’ social traits of acceptability and pragmatism reduce potential instabilities that arise with globalization. Thus, migrants’ actions across space and time are expressions of their lives in the local area and simultaneously in the global sphere.

Policy implications

The research on which this paper is based was not meant to extent to issues of government policy, nor was the paper intended to provide policy guidelines or recommendations. Nonetheless, the interviews with migrant workers and with United Nations and other experts on the subject led to a few policy implications.

In the majority of factories in which migrants work, labour union membership is far from universal. Even where membership is high, the union functions more as an employees’ social club than as their representative in collective bargaining with management. The social function is extremely important at the factory level because most employees are migrants who are relatively new to Bangkok and whose stay is expected to be temporary. The labour union would benefit workers more, however, if it had a greater voice in determining working conditions and was involved in other worker protection systems, such as health insurance and pension schemes.

A number of workers who were interviewed explained that they had imgrated because of the lack of opportunities at home in the rural areas. This situation points to the need for more effective refional and rural development. Roughly 70 per cent of the population of Thailand still resides in rural areas and about half of the labour force is employed in agriculture. In this situation, rural and agricultural development remains essential to national economic and social development. The Government should continue to encourage rural-urban linkages. One way to do so is by promoting industrial decentralization, which requires the appropriate tax and investment frameworks but also good infrastructure in the rural areas. The Board of Investement provides tax incentives for manufacturing plants to locate outside of Bangkok. The non-governmental sector can also play a role. The Thailand Business Initiative for Rural Development (T-BIRD) encourages firms to locate plants in rural areas as a sound business decision. By doing so, the company can often attract more dedicated workers at lower wage levels.

The study has highlighted the importance of social infrastructure to economic growth. Rural-urban links stimulate economic innovations in the rural through the transfer of skills and capital. The networks could be used more efficiently if organized institutionally.

Endnotes

1. It should be forgotten, however, that the majority of Thais still works in agriculture. Moreover, the informal sector plays a significant role for migrants, but is excluded here.

2. In Buddhism, life is mainly an individual responsibility. Therefore merit-making ("tham bun") which aims at the collection of positive "karma", is an essential part in Thais' daily routine. As a consequence, living conditions, status and power justify themselves and are widely accepted as a manifestation of earlier

actions (Richter and Yoddumnern-Attig, 1992; Weggel, 1997; Mulder, 1996).

3. The "Thai people" comprise many ethnically distinct groups. Some have sustained their own ethnic identity despite being "Thai", some have not.

References

Appadurai, A. (1996. Modernity at large (London, Minneapolis, Cultural dimensions of globalization).

Beck, U. (1999). Was ist Globalisierung? (Frankfurt am Main).

Chamratrithirong, A., K. Archavanitkul, K. Richter, P. Guest, V. Thongthai, W. Boonchalaksi, N. Piriyathamwong and P. Vong-Ek (1995). National Migration Survey of Thailand, Publication No. 188, (Salaya, Institute for Population and Social Research, Mahidol University).

Chant, S. (1998). "Households, gender and rural-urban migration: reflections on linkages and considerations for policy", Environment and Urbanization, 10(1):5-21.

Cohen, R. and P. Kennedy (2000). Global Sociology (London).

Curran, S. (1998). "Migration and cultural change: a role for gender and social networks?", The Center for Migration and Development Working Paper Series No. 6 (Princeton, Princeton university Eng, P. (1997). "Thai democracy: the people speak", The Washington Quarterly, 2(4):169-189.

Gender and Development Research Institute (GDRI) (1999,2000). Data on the socio-economic situation of Thai women in 1998/1999, not yet published at the time of research (Bangkok).

Gray, R. (1999). "The effects of globalization on labour force and migration in Thailand", Population and Development Working Paper Series No. 8 (Bangkok, United Nations Economic and Social Commission for Asia and the Pacific).

Kittiprapas, S. (1999). "Role of Bangkok and its periphery in the Asia-Pacific region: towards globalization economy and sustainable development", Quarterly Review, 14(3):18-24, (Bangkok, Thailand Development Research Institute (TDRI).

Krass, F. (1996a). "Ungeplante Megastadtentwicklung durch Wirtschaftsboom and soziokulturelle persistenzen", in Geographische Rundschau, 2:89-96 (Bangkok).

(1996 b). "Thailand - a newly industrialized country? Die industrielle entwicklung seit ende der Achtziger jahre", in Zeitschrift fur Wirtschaftsgeographie, 40(2):241-257.

(1997). "Megastadte; urbanisierung der erde and pronleme der regierbakeit von metropolen in entwicklungslandern" in Holtz, U. Probleme der Entwicklungspolitik Bonn (=Cicero Schriftenreihe 2):139-178.

(2000). "Ursachen and folgen der thailandischen Wahrungs, Finanz - and Wirtschaftskrise", in I. Sander and G. Reinecke, eds., Thailand: Aktuelle Wandlungsprozesse in Politik, Wirtschaft, Umwelt and Gesellschaft, 328:107:141 (Hamburg, Mitteilungen des Institute fur Asienkunde Hamburg).

Levitt, P. (1998). "Social remittances: migration driven local-level forms of cultural diffusion", International Migration Review, 32(4):926-948.

Massy, D.S., J. Arango, G. Hugo, A. Kouaouci, A. Pellegrino, j. Edward Taylor (1993). "Theories of international migration: a review and appraisal", Population and Development Review, 19(3):431-466.

Massy, D. and Keynes, M. (1998). "'Identity' : some parallels between feminist debate and the identity of place", in Berichte zur deutschen Landeskunde, 72(1):53-59.

Mills, M.B. (1997). "Contesting the margins of modernity: women, migration, and consumption in Thailand", American Ethnologist, 24(1):37-61.

(1999a). "Thai women in the global labor force", Consuming Desires, Contested selves New Brunswick, New Jersey and London.

(1999b). "Migrant labor takes a holiday: reworking modernity and marginality in contemporary Thailand", Critique of Anthropology, 19(1):31-51.

Ministry of Labour and Social Welfare 1989, 1999). Yearbook of Labour Statistics (Bangkok).

Mulder, N. (1996). Inside Thai society. Interpretations of Everyday Life The Hague).

National Statistical Office (NSO (1985). Report of the Labour Force Survey, Whole Kingdom, Round 3, August (Bangkok.

(1997). Report of the Migration Survey (Bangkok).

(1999). Report of the Labour Force Survey, Whole Kingdom, Round 3, August(Bangkok).

(2000). Report of the Labour Force Survey, Whole Kingdom, Round 3, August (Bangkok) (unpublished at the time of research).

Ogena, N.K. Soonthorndhada, K. Rojnkureesatien, and J. Bumronglarp (1997). Globalization with Equity: Policies for Growth in Thailand", publication No. 214 (Bangkok, Institute for Population and Social Research, Mahidol University.

Ogena, N. and G. Dejong (1999). "Internal migration and occupational mobility in Thailand", Asian and pacific migration Journal, 8(4):419-446.

Olwig, K.F. (1997). "Cultural sites: sustaining a home in a deterritorialized world", in K.F. Olwig and K. Hastrup, eds., Siting Culture, The Shifting Anthropological Object (London), pp. 17-38.

Osaki, K. (1999). "Economic interactions of migrants and people of Isan, Thailand: missing out of the economic boom?", in D. Dwyer and D. Drakakis-Smith, eds., Ethnicity and Development, Geographical Perspectives (Sussex), pp. 215-248.

Pejaranonda, C., S. Santipaporn, P Guest, (1995). "Rural-urban migration in Thailand", in ESCAP, Trends, Patterns and Implications of Rural-urban Migration in India, Nepal and Thailand, Asian Population Studies Series No. 138 (New York, United Nations), pp. 171-243.

Phananiramai, M. (1996). "Changes in women's economic role in Thailand", in S. Horton, ed., Women and Industrialization in Asia (London, New York), pp. 274-306.

Pramualratana, A. (1992). "The impact of societal change and the role of the old in a rural community in Thailand", in B. Yoddumnern-Attig, K. Richter, A. Soonthorndhada, C. Sethaput and A. Pramualratana, eds., Changing Roles and Statuses of Women in Thailand: A Documentary

Assessment, Publication No. 161 (Salaya, Institute for Population and Social Research, Mahidol University),pp. 44-54.

Richter, K. and B. Yoddumnem-Attig (1992). "Framing a study of Thai women's changing roles and statuses" in B. Yoddumnem-Attig, K. Richter, A. Soonthorndhada, C. Sethaput and A. Pramualratana, eds., Changing Roles and Statuses of Women in Thailand: A Documentary Assessment, Publication No. 161 (Salaya, Institute for Population and Social Research, Mahidol University),pp. 1-7.

Skeldon, R. (1997. "Rural-to-urban migration and its implications for poverty alleviation", Asia-Pacific Population Journal, 12(1):3-16.

(1999). "Migration in Asia after the economic crisis: patterns and issues", Asia-Pacific Population Journal, 14(3):3-24.

Stark, O. (1991). The Migration of Labor (Cambridge, United Kingdom).

Sussangkorn, C. (1997). "Thailand: looking ahead to 2020 in light of global and regional changes", Quarterly Review, 12(2):3-13 (Bangkok, Thailand Development Research Institute (TDRI).

Suwanraks, R. (2000). "Sufficiency economy", summary of discussion: the 1999 TDRI Year-end Conference, Thailand Development Research Institute, TDRI Quarterly Review, 15(1):6-17.

Thailand Development Research Institute (TDRI) (2000a). Social impact assessment: synthesis report (Bangkok).

(2000b). Labour Market in Thailand and the Southeast Asian Transitional Economies:

Growth, Poverty Reduction and Adjustment to Crisis, unpublished when received in December 2000 (Bangkok).

Thonguthai, P. and U. Pattaravanich (1993). "Employment and mobility in the Bangkok labour market with special reference to women in the manufacturing sector", in Promoting Diversified Skill Development for Women in Industry, volume II (New York, Economic and Social Commission for Asia and the Pacific (ESCAP), United Nations Development Program (UNDP), International Labour Organization (ILO),pp. 91-150.

United Nations (1993a). "Types of female migration", in Internal Migration of Women in Developing Countries, Proceedings of the United Nations Expert Meeting on the Feminization of Internal Migration, Aguascalientes, Mexico, 22-25 October 1991, United Nations Department for Economic and Social Information and Policy Analysis, (New York),pp. 94-115.

(1993b). "Report of the meeting and recommendations to improve the status of female migrants", in Internal Migration of Women in Developing Countries, Proceeding of the united Nations Expert Meeting on the Feminization of Internal Migration, Aguascalientes, Mexico, 22-25 October 1991, United Nations Department for Economic and Social Information and Policy Analysis, (New York),pp. 21-38.

United Nations Development Programme (UNDP) (1999). Human Development Report Thailand 1999 (Bangkok).

Weggel, O. (1997). Die Asiaten, Gesellschaftsordnungen, Wirtschaftssysteme, Denkformen, Glaubensweisen, Alltagsleben, Verhaltensstile, Munchen.

Werlen, B. (2000). "Die Geographie der Globalisierung, Perspektiven der Sozialgeographie", geographische revue, 1:5-20.

Wongsuphasawat, L. (1997). "The extended Bangkok Metropolitan Region and uneven industrial development in Thailand", in C. Dixon, D.W. Smith, Uneven Development in Southeast Asia (Singapore, Sydney)pp. 196-219.

World Bank (2000). Thailand Social Monitor, Social Capital and the Crisis (Bangkok).

Yoddumnern-Attig, B. (1992). "Thai family structure and organization: changing roles and duties in historical perspective", in B. Yoddumnern-Attig, K. Richter, A. Soonthorndhada, C. Sethaput and A. Pramualratana, eds., Changing Roles and Statuses of Women in Thailand: a Documentary Assessment, Publication No. 161 (Salaya, Institute for Population and Social Research, Mahidol University) pp. 8-24.

8

Viet Nam's Older Population : The View from the Census

Viet Nam, as many other countries in East and South-East Asia has been successful in its policy to lower fertility in the interest of national development. According to United Nations estimates, the total fertility rate fell from over six, just three decades ago, to close to the replacement level by the turn of the twenty-first century. Life expectancy at birth increased during the same time by almost 20 years to close to 70 (United Nations, 2001a). Past high fertility, combined with mortality decline, is resulting in substantial growth in the numbers of the older persons and, in conjunction with the subsequent fertility decline, to an increasing share of the overall population who are at older ages. Recent United Nations projections indicate that the population aged 60 and over will increase by 80 per cent in size in the first two decades of this new century and grow fivefold by mid-century (United Nations, 2001b). By 2050, persons aged 60 and over will constitute almost a quarter of the total Vietnamese population.

Most of what we know about Viet Nam's older population derives from a few small-scale studies and two regional surveys of older persons (Bui The Cuong and others, 2000). Although important characteristics of the older population can be derived from the recent national censuses, published reports contain very little information for older age groups. Tabulations typically group persons 50 and over into a single age group. Thus, although recent censuses are generally of high quality, so far they have not been exploited to yield detailed information on the older population.

The purpose of the present study is to redress this situation by providing a descriptive analysis of Viet Nam's older population based primarily on special tabulations from the 3 per cent public use sample of the 1999 census. Results are weighted to be nationally representative. We draw on a public use CD-ROM that allows original tabulations from the 100 per cent count to provide a detailed examination of the age structure. Finally, we use the 5 per cent public use sample of the 1989 census to examine changes in living arrangements. We define the older population as those ago 60 and older. Although this definition is somewhat arbitrary, it reflects the mandatory age of retirement in the public sector for men in Viet Nam and is the most commonly used age cut-off to demarcate the older population in Asian countries.

Although by its very nature the census is quite restricted in the amount of information it can collect for any individual, it nevertheless covers some crucial characteristics that bear on the well-being of older persons and the context in which they live. In this study, we examine the age distribution of older persons, marital status, education and literacy, work status, religious affiliation, housing quality and media possession, and living arrangements. We typically, focus on differences between men and women, between rural and urban residents, and among age groups within the older age span since these basic background characteristics can be strongly related to some of the characteristics we examine. In the case of living arrangements, we examine regional variation and incorporate information on the gender and marital status of co-resident children. We also appraise evidence of change in living arrangement patterns between 1989 and 1999.

Table 1. Age and sex distribution of older population by sex and residence, Viet Nam 1999

	Total	Sex		Residence	
		Men	Women	Urban	Rural
Population aged 60 and over as percentage of total population	8.0	6.7	9.3	7.5	8.2
Percentage distribution of 60+ population :					
60-64	28.5	30.1	27.3	30.1	28.0
65-69	26.8	28.8	25.5	27.0	26.8
70-74	19.7	19.8	19.7	19.3	19.9
75-79	13.4	12.2	14.2	12.5	13.6
80+	11.6	9.1	13.3	11.1	11.7
Total	100	100	100	100	100
Sex ratio (men per 100 women) by age :					
60-64	77	-	-	78	76
65-69	79	-	-	81	78
70-74	70	-	-	74	69
75-79	60	-	-	60	60
80+	48	-	-	46	49
Total	70	-	-	72	69

Source : 1999 census (100 per cent count).

Note : A hyphen (-) indicates that the item is not applicable.

The age distribution of older persons

Table 1 summarizes the age and sex distribution of the older population of Viet Nam based on the full 100 per cent count of the 1999 census. Approximately, 8 per cent of the total population was aged 60 or over of whom a fourth are aged 75 and over. The extent of population ageing, however, differs by gender. Both the share of older persons relative to the total population and the share of the older population that is in age groups 75 and over are greater among women. This reflects lower female than male mortality throughout the lifespan, a factor that is likely to have been somewhat exacerbated through excess male military casualties during the prol on g ed periods of war dating from before mid-twentieth century through 1975 (Hirschman, Preston and Vu Manh Loi, 1995). In addition, as indicated by the sex ratios, older women outnumber older men with the imbalance increasing with each successively older age group. This pattern reflects the continuation of higher male than female mortality into the elderly age span. Among persons 80 and older, women outnumber men by more than 2 to 1. Despite higher fertility in rural areas, and thus higher proportions of children, the proportions in older ages are also modestly higher in rural than urban areas, which probably reflects rural-to-urban migration among younger adults.

Table 2. Martial status distribution of older population by age and sex, Viet Nam 1999

	Total	Men	Women
Percentage Currently married :			
60-64	75.5	92.8	61.9
65-69	69.3	88.9	53.5
70-74	58.6	83.6	40.6
75.79	45.7	75.0	28.1
80+	27.8	60.2	12.1
Total	61.1	84.8	44.2
Percentage Widowed :			
60-64	21.9	5.9	34.4
65-69	28.7	9.9	43.8
70-74	39.8	15.2	57.4
75-79	52.6	23.7	70.1
80+	70.9	38.5	86.6
Total	37.0	14.0	53.3

Percentage single, separated, divorced			
60-64	2.6	1.3	3.6
65-69	2.0	1.3	2.6
70-74	1.6	1.2	1.9
75-79	1.6	1.2	1.9
80+	1.3	1.3	1.3
Total	2.0	1.3	2.5

Source : 1999 census (3 per cent sample)

The 1999 census indicates that population ageing has progressed further than anticipated by the United Nations in its 2000 assessment, which presumably was made before the census results were available. According to United Nations estimates, only 7.5 per cent of the population was anticipated to be aged 60 and over by 2000, compared to the censuses result of 8.o per cent in 1999 (United Nations, 2001b). This could reflect a faster fertility decline than anticipated by the United Nations. Additionally, the sex ratio of the older population according to the census is considerably lower than that estimated by the United Nations (70 versus 88 men per 100 women.)

Marital status

Over the recent past, marriage has been close to universal in Viet Nam. Thus, few of today's older persons have never been married. Likewise, divorce and permanent separation are relatively uncommon, so that 98 per cent of older Vietnamese as enumerated by the census are either currently married or widowed. As table 2 shows, the balance between these two statuses shifts rapidly with increasing age and differs markedly by gender. Currently married persons form the majority of the older population in age groups under 75, but the widowed population dominates in older age groups. The majority of older-aged men, however, remain married in all age groups, including even those aged 80 and over. In contrast, more than half of women aged 60 and over are widowed and only among those under age 70 are most currently married.

The fact that older men are almost twice as likely as older women to be currently married is attributable to several factors. As higher male than female mortality persists through the older ages, older women are at increasingly higher risk of widowhood than are men and hence gender differences in marital status increase. In addition, older men who experience the loss of a spouse are more likely to remarry than are older women.

Education

As table 3 shows, there are pronounced cohort differences in education among Viet Nam's older population reflecting a steady improvement in literacy and formal schooling during the period that today's older population passed through their school ages. Thus, over three fifths of those aged 80 and over are illiterate compared to less than a fifth of persons aged 60 to 64. Gender differences, however, are particularly pronounced and, although not as striking, the urban and rural populations also differ substantially.

The census reveals that older women are clearly disadvantaged compared to older men in educational backgrounds. They are much more likely to be unable to read or write and to lack any formal schooling than are men of the equivalent age group and are much less likely to have any secondary education. The gender gap in both literacy and the lack of any schooling increase with age. Overall, almost half of older Vietnamese women are illiterate and fully three fourths of women age 80 and older cannot read or write. In contrast, less than 15 per cent of men 60 and older and less than a third who are 80 and older are illiterate. The fact that the percentage of both men and women who are illiterate exceeds the percentage who had no schooling indicates that some have lost this ability to read and write over time.

At all ages the urban population of older persons is characterized by higher levels of education than their rural age peers. Urban-rural differences are particularly striking with respect to achievement of secondary education. For almost every age group, the percentage with secondary education is at least twice that for urban elders than for those residing in rural areas.

Table 3. Literacy and educational attainment of older population by age, sex and residence, Viet Nam 1999

	Total	Sex		Residence	
		Mele	Female	Urban	Rural
Percentage illiterate:					
60-64	19.4	7.3	28.9	12.5	21.4
65-69	26.3	10.5	39.0	18.3	28.5
70-74	38.0	15.8	53.9	27.7	40.8
75-79	48.6	22.7	64.3	37.2	51.7
80+	62.5	34.6	75.9	49.3	66.0
Total	33.7	14.2	47.6	24.3	36.4
Percentage with complete Primary (at least grade 5) :					
60-64	45.7	66.4	29.5	61.8	41.1
65-69	37.2	57.1	21.1	41.4	33.2
70-74	27.4	47.5	13.1	40.9	23.8
75-79	21.1	39.0	10.2	33.1	17.9
80+	13.1	28.3	5.8	22.4	10.6
Total	32.8	53.2	18.3	46.9	28.9
Percentage with some secondary or higher education (grade 6+) :					
60-64	29.2	48.4	14.2	46.0	24.3
65-69	22.3	38.6	9.1	36.0	18.5
70-74	14.9	28.7	5.1	26.9	11.7
75-79	10.3	21.3	3.6	19.9	7.8
80+	5.7	13.7	1.9	12.4	3.9
Total	19.3	35.3	8.0	32!5	15.6

Source : 1999 census (3 per cent sample).

Economic activity and household work

The continuation of work into older age may reflect a variety of influences and circumstances, ranging from economic necessity to a desire to keep active to provide personal fulfilment and a sense of purpose.Likewise, the cessation of work may reflect the loss of physical stamina, mandatory retirement rules, or a desire for relaxaton and leisure. As already noted, in Viet Nam, under most circumstances in the state sector, retirement is mandatory at ages 60 for men and 55 for women. The majority of the population, however, does not work in the formal states sector and those who do may switeh employment to the non-state sector once they pass the mandatory retirement age (Friedman and others, 2001).

The 1999 Vietnamese census asked what type of work, if any, each individual in the household spent most time on during the prior 12 months. Household work is recorded as a separate category in the census form and not considered as part of economic activity. Such a definition is common in many countries and reflects the centrality of the market as symbolic of the economy with a focus on commodity production and on production for exchange rather than production for use. Nevertheless, the exclusion of household work from the definition of economic activity is coming under increasing criticism, particularly because it tends to understate the contribution of women to the economy (Editor, Gender Dialogue, 2001; Clark and Anker, 1993). In the present analysis, we examine both economic activity (as more narrowly defined) and household work.

Table 4. Economic and Housework activity by age, sex and residence, Viet Nam 1999

	Total	Sex		Residence	
		Male	Female	Urban	Rural
Percentage economically active in the last 12 months prior to the survey (excluding household work					
60-64	44.1	54.2	36.3	27.1	49.1
65-69	30.2	38.9	23.1	18.0	33.5
70-74	15.9	22.7	11.0	9.3	17.6
75-79	8.5	13.3	5.6	4.8	9.5

80+	2.4	4.5	1.4	1.4	2.7
Total	25.3	34.1	19.0	15.5	28.0
Of those economically active, percentage in agriculture :					
60-64	84.7	83.3	86.3	38.0	92.3
65-69	85.2	85.8	84.4	40.0	90.0
70-74	85.4	87.1	82.9	42.8	91.5
75-79	84.9	87.6	81.2	34.0	91.7
80+	81.9	80.3	84.4	30.4	89.4
Total	84.9	84.8	85.1	38.9	92.0
Percentage who primarily did household work :					
60-64	16.9	4.0	26.9	22.1	15.3
65-69	14.3	3.6	22.9	15.3	14.0
70-74	10.8	3.4	16.0	9.3	11.2
75-79	7.8	3.1	10.6	6.4	8.1
80+	3.1	1.4	4.0	2.0	
Total	12.2	3.4	18.4	13.6	11.8

Source : 1999 census (3 per cent sample).

As table 4 shows, only a fourth of the population age 60 and older were economically active during the 12 months prior to the census. Even among persons aged 60 to 64, the majority said they had not worked. Women are far less likely to be economically active for all age groups. The largest absolute gender difference in terms of percentage points is among those in their 60s. It is unlikely that the differences in the mandatory retirement ages for men and women account for much of this difference since the declines in the percentage economically active between 50-54 and 55-59 do not differ greatly between men and women (results not shown in table). Economic activity decreases steadily with age among both older men and women but the gender gap in participation persists at all ages.

Economic activity rates among older persons also differ substantially between rural and urban areas. Older-aged persons in rural areas are almost twice as likely as their urban counterparts to be active. Moreover, a rural urban contrast is evident for all age groups. This is clearly related to the higher percentage working among persons for whom agriculture has been their major livelihood (Friedman and others, 2001). Thus among those older persons who are economically active, a very high proportion are engaged in agriculture, accounting for well over four fifths of both economically active older men and women. Even among older-aged urban residents, almost two fifths reported agriculture as their main work.

A substantial share of persons who did not report themselves as economically active reported that they were doing household work. Although only 12 per cent of all persons aged 60 and older reported household work as their major activity during the prior 12 months, this was far higher for women than for men. Household work is also somewhat more common among urban than rural elderlyalthough the differenceis not very p r on oun ced.As with economic activity, performing household work diclines with each successive age group within the older-age span.

When household work is considered together with economic activity, gender diffference in terms of work disappear. As figure 1 indicates, the percentage who are eithereconomically active or do household work is almost identical for men and women age 60 and over (37.5 vs. 37.4 per cent). Moreover, this combined percentage is slightly higher for women than men in their 60s, although in both c ases at least half are active in one or the other sense.

Religious adherence

In many societies, older persons play important roles as religious leaders and old age is associated with increasing preoccupation with religious matters (Cowgill, 1986). In Viet Nam, however, as table 5 indicates, only a minority of the older people profess a religion, likely reflecting a de-emphasis of religion as part of the long-standing socialist orientation of the

Government. Overall, just modestly more than a fourth (28 per cent) of the older population profess a religion according to the 1999 census. There is only a very slight tendency for the proportion doing so to increase with age within the elderly age span. More pronounced is a gender difference with older women likely than men to profess a religion. In addition, religious adherence is higher among urban than rural elderly.

Figure 1. Economic activity and household work by gender and age, Viet Nam 1999.

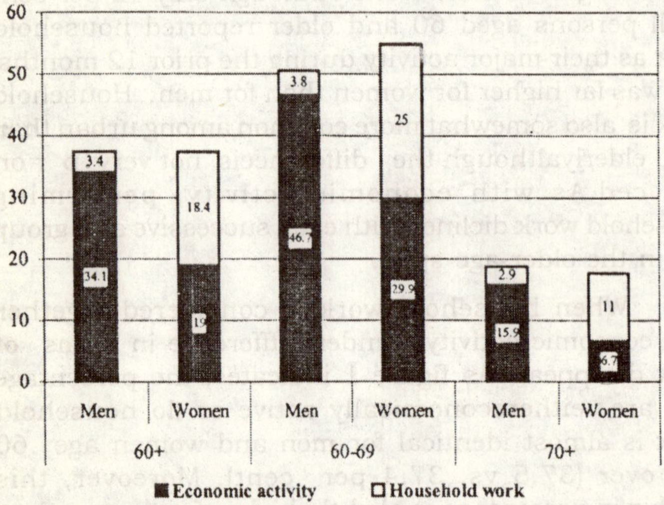

Clear regional differences, not shown in the table, exist with half (50 per cent) of the older residents of the South-East region and over two fifths (43 per cent) of those in the Mekong Delta indicating a religious affiliation. Among older persons who profess a religion, almost two thirds (64 per cent) are Buddhists and over one fifth (22 per cent) are Catholics. The remainder are accounted for mainly by two indigenous regional religious sects, Cao Dai and Hoa Hoa. Adherents of the former are largely concentrated in the South-East and

Mekong Delta regions and the latter are almost exclusively restricted to the Mekong Delta.

Housing quality

The census provides information on housing characteristics, including permanency of dwelling unit, the type of toilet, access to electricity, and the type of water supply. In addition, the census records whether or not the household had a television or radio. These items can be used to judge the quality of the dwelling unit and reflect the material wealth of the household. Table 6 presents each of these items individually as well as a summary index of housing quality that is based on a weighted combination of all. While the possession of television or radio is not literally an aspect of housing quality, it is also included in the table since it can serve as an additional indicator of the material wealth of the household. Moreover, having a teleivision or radio is important in its own right given that access to the media can serve not only as an important source of entertainment but as a crucial channel through which older persons become informed about ongoing changes in the Vietnamese society and economy.

Table 5. Religious adherence by age, sex and residence, Viet Nam 1999

	Total	Sex		Residence	
		Male	Female	Urban	Rural
Percentage who profess a religion :					
60-64	26.9	21.7	31.0	33.9	24.9
65-69	27.8	23.1	31.5	34.2	26.0
70-74	29.3	23.8	33.3	34.3	28.0
75-79	28.6	23.2	31.9	32.8	27.5
80+	30.1	27.5	31.4	34.6	28.9
Total	28.2	23.2	31.7	34.0	26.6
Percentage distribution by religion among those who profess a religion :					
Buddhist	63.8	56.5	67.6	68.6	62.1
Catholic	22.4	26.1	20.5	24.0	21.9

Cao Dai	6.0	7.0	5.4	3.9	6.7
Hoa Hao	6.2	8.4	5.1	2.7	7.5
Othera	1.6	1.9	1.4	0.8	1.8
Total	100.0	100.0	100.0	100.0	100.0

Source : 1999 census (3 per cent sample).

[a] Category "Other" excludes those whose religion is not classifiable.

The census distinguishes between four different tpyes of housing structures in terms of their degree of permanency. Only a little over a tenth of older Vietnamese live in what are considered to be the most permanent structure, while almost a fifth reside in structures that are considered least permanent. The large majority of Vietnamese elderly have access to electricity but only a small minority have piped water. Although the vast majority have a toilet, only a smallminority have a modern (flush) toilet in the house. There is very little difference between older men and women in their quality of housing as indicated by the overall house quality index. However, older persons in urban areas live in substantially better housing than those in rural areas. Over half of older persons in Viet Nam live in a household with a television. At the same time, 30 per cent have neither a TV nor radio in their house. Women are moderately less likely to live in a household with a TV and slightly more likely to live in one that lacks both a TV and a radio. Older persons in rural areas are far less likely to have a TV and much more likely to have neither a TV nor a radio.

Table 6. Housing quality and possession of T.V. and radio by gender and marital status, Viet NAM1999

	Total	Sex		Residence	
		Men	Women	Urban	Rural
Housing Quality :					
Percentage living in a permanent house	11.6	11.8	11.5	27.0	7.4
Percentage in temporary housing	17.1	16.4	17.6	8.5	19.5

Percentage with access to electricity	81.5	81.5	81.6	96.6	77.4
Precentage with piped water	12.4	12.7	12.2	50.7	1.8
Precentage with modern toilet	16.0	16.4	15.7	58.5	4.2
Precentage with no toilet	13.7	13.0	14.2	6.8	15.6
Overall house quality index	4.5	4.6	4.5	6.5	4.0
Television/radio possession:					
Precentage with a TV	55.3	58.1	53.4	80.7	48.3
Precentage with neither a TV or radio	30.4	26.6	33.2	14.3	34.9

Source : 1999 census (3 per sample).

Living arrangements

In Viet Nam, as in many other Asian countries, living arrangements are closely interwined with the support provided to older persons by their families. Co-residence with a spouse and a married child is the social norm for older persons whose children are adults and constitutes an important part of the context in which inter-generational exchanges of support occur (Truong Si Anh and others, 1997). Elderly persons who live alone, or with only their spouse, could be among the most vulnerable within the older-aged population. Some who live alone or only with a spouse, however, may do so out of a preference for privacy, especially if they have adult children living nearby. In these cases, their ability to do so may reflect a greater physical and financial ability to live independently.

Table 7. Living arrangements of the older population by sex, age residence and region, Viet Nam 1999

	Percentage living with any child	percentage living with any married child	percentag living alone	percantage living only with spouse
Total	77.6	53.8	5.8	11.5
Age :				
60-64	83.4	46.2	3.4	9.4
65-69	77.8	51.3	4.6	12.6
70-74	74.0	56.7	6.8	13.8
75-79	71.8	60.6	8.6	12.9
80+	74.8	66.7	9.2	8.5

Sex :				
Men	78.0	47.4	2.7	14.7
Women	77.2	58.4	7.9	9.2
Residence :				
Urban	82.7	59.3	3.9	7.3
Rural	76.2	52.3	6.3	12.7
Region :				
Northern Uplands	82.7	63.7	8.5	18.2
Red River Delta	68.6	46.1	3.4	9.7
Central North	73.5	48.8	6.3	16.3
Central Coast	75.9	46.5	8.2	10.3
Central Highlands	85.2	56.2	2.5	8.0
South-East	83.9	58.6	4.4	5.9
Mekong Delta	83.9	60.0	3.9	5.3

Source : 1999 census (3 per cent sample).

Several measures of living arrangements can be directly calculated or estimated based on the census. These include co-residence with adult children (based on information on relationship to head of all household members) living alone, and living with a spouse only. Table 7 indicates that most Vietnamese elderly persons in 1999 co-resided with their children. Over three fourths lived with at least one child and just over half lived with a married child.

Co-residence with any child is higher for younger than elderly persons undoubtedly reflecting a life cycle process for the family in which children move out of the parental house as they get older and as their parents age (Knodel and others, 1996). In contrast, co-residence with a married child is highest for the older elders again reflecting a life cycle process in which, as parents age, their adult children get married. There is little difference between men and women with respect to the percentage who co-reside with any child, although elderly women are more likely than men to live with a married child. This difference largely reflects the fact that women typically marry men who are older than themselves and thus, compared to men of the same age, have been married longer and have older children on average, who in turn are more likely to be married. Hence, more children of women 60 and over are married than of men at the same age.

Co-residence levels vary considerably by region and moderately by rural-urban residence. Co-residence is least common in the northern regions of Viet Nam, especially the Red River Delta, while southern regions in general exhibit the highest levels. Co-residence is higher in urban than rural areas, a common pattern found in a number of developing countries, perhaps in part reflecting differential costs of housing (Hashimoto and others, 1992).

Only a small minority of older persons in Viet Nam live alone and only a moderately higher percentage live only with a spouse. The proportion living alone increases with age although even among persons 80 and older less than a tenth live in solitary households. Living alone is more common for women, while living only with a spouse is more common for men, reflecting gender differences in mortality and remarriage. In addition, as noted above, the children of women over age 60 are older on average those of their male age peers and thus are more likely to have left the home.

Co-residence levels by gender and marital status of child are shown in table 8. Summary ratios of co-residence with sons to daughters indicates the dominance of children of one sex over the other within each martial status category in the living arrangements of older Vietnamese. The summary ratios of elderly persons living with single sons as opposed to single daughters exhibit little gender preference on the part of the elderly parent. In contrast , Vietnamese elderly persons are almost four times as likely to live with a married son as opposed to a married daughter, suggesting a clear son preference with respect to co-residence with a married child. This varies little with the age or gender of the parent. Regional variation in this respect, however, is substantial. The preference for married son co-residence is much greater in the northern than the southern regions. Rural-urban differences in the predominance of co-residence with married sons rather than married daughters are pronounced. This regional variation in married son co-residency is consistent with other evidence, indicating a greater prevalence of patriarchal and patrilocal practices in the north of Viet Nam than in the more southern regions (Knodel and others, 2000).

Equivalent measures of living arrangements can be calculated from the 5 per cent sample of the 1989 census and compared to those from the 1999 census, thereby providing evidence to judge the extent of change between the two censuses.Such a comparison is of

Table 8. Co-residence patterns of the older population by sex of co-resident child, age, sex, residence and region, Viet Nam 1999

Percentage	percentage Living with a single son	percentage living with a single daughtger	Ratio of co-residing with a single son to single daughter	percentage living with a married son	percentag living with a married doughter	Ratio of co-residing with a married son to a married daughter
Total	23.9	22.4	1.1	44.5	11.9	3.7
Age :						
60-64	41.0	33.9	1.2	38.2	11.3	34
65-69	27.7	24.8	1.1	43.1	11.4	38
70-74	15.5	16.9	0.9	47.7	11.6	4.1
75-79	7.9	12.0	0.7	49.9	12.2	4.1
80+	3.3	8.5	0.4	52.8	14.8	3.6
Sex :						
Men	31.8	28.7	1.1	39.8	10.5	3.8
Women	18.2	17.8	1.0	48.0	12.9	3.7
Residence :						
urban	29.7	26.8	1.1	43.8	22.1	2.0
Rural	22.4	21.2	1.1	44.7	9.1	4.9
Region :						
Northern Uplands	19.0	15.1	1.3	57.6	7.0	8.2
Red River Dalta	17.5	16.9	1.0	40.1	6.8	5.9
Central North	20.7	19.7	1.1	43.6	5.9	7.4
Central Coast	30.3	27.9	1.1	35.9	13.2	2.7

Central highlands	31.7	21.3	1.5	42.7	15.9	2.7
South-East	32.7	31.2	1.0	42.2	24.0	1.8
Mekong Delta	28.6	28.9	1.0	46.9	17.6	2.7

Source : 1999 census (3 per cent sample).

particular interest given that the intervening decade was marked by very substantial transformations in the Vietnamese economy, including the extension a series of free market reforms, commonly known as Doi Moi (literally "New Change"). As figure 2 shows, living arrangements have remained remarkably stable. Co-residence with any child or with a married child remained barely changed between 1989 and 1999, despite the dynamic social and economic environment that characterized the decade in between. While solitary living declined slightly between 1989 and 1999, living only with a spouse increased slightly so the combined percentage in these categories remained virtually unchanged.

Figure 2. Living arrangements of the older population, Viet Nam 1989 and 1999]

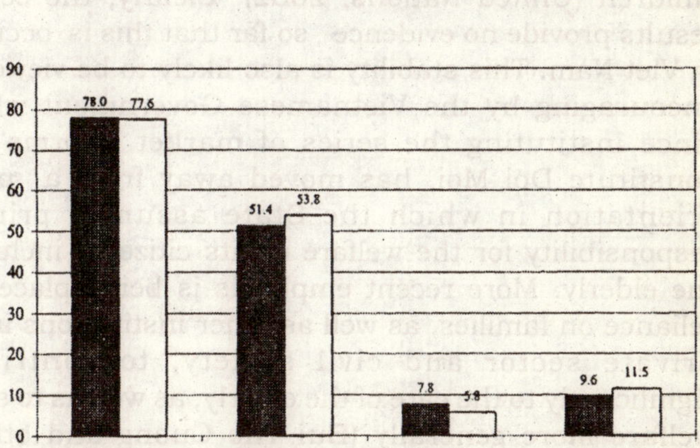

Conclusions

The Vietnamese census is a valuable source of information on the older-aged population. The availability of microsamples permits exploration of numerous characteristics of the elderly that are either not tabulated in sufficient detail or not available at all in published reports and thus provides an important basis for informing policies and programmes related to population ageing and the welfare of older persons in Viet Nam.

Perhaps the most remarkable finding of our examination of census data related to the Vietnamese elderly is the remarkable stability in their living arrangements with respect to co-residence with children. A common fear, embodied for example in the International Plan of Action adopted by the United. Nations-sponsored Second world Assembly on Ageing, is that development will be associated with desertion of elderly parents by socially or residentially mobile adult children (United Nations, 2002). Clearly, the census results provide no evidence so far that this is occuring in Viet Nam. This stability is also likely to be viewed as encouraging by the Vietnamese Government which, since instituting the series of market reforms that constitute Doi Moi, has moved away from a policy orientation in which the State assumed primary responsibility for the welfare of its citizens, including the elderly. More recent emphasis is being placed on reliance on families, as well as other institutions in the private sector and civil society, to contribute significantly to the care of the elderly, as well as to social welfare more generally (Bui The Cuong and others, 2000).

The census results also reveal substantial rural-urban contrasts among Viet Nam's older population.

Rural elderly are clearly disadvantaged in terms of educational attainment, housing quality, and access to the mass media. Also, much higher percentages of rural elderly remain economically active, quite possibly out of necessity. Policies directed to the social the economic welfare of the older population in Viet Nam clearly need to target disproportionately the elderly living in rural areas.

The findings in relation to gender are of considerable interest. Non-governmental agencies and international organizations, including the United Nations, frequently argue that older women are disadvantaged compared to men on virtually every dimension related to social, economic and physical well-being (United Nations, 2002; World NGO Forum on Ageing, 2002). The census evidence, however, provides only limited confirmation of a disadvantaged situation for older Vietnamese women compared to men. Blanket recommendations (such as contained in both the United Nations and NGO plans of action emerging from the recent World Assembly on Ageing) that ageing policies include a heavy emphasis on women thus may be not be fully appropriate for Viet Nam.

Women clearly compare unfavourably to men with respect to formal educational attainment and literacy. In addition, older women are far more likely to be widowed than are men of the same age. Given that marital status is likely to have an important bearing on material and emotional well-being, the higher incidence of widowhood among women can clearly be considered a disadvantage (although it is in part due to the women's advantage in mortality risks).In contrast, gender differences in terms of housing quality are almost non-existent and women are only modestly disadvantaged with respect to access to modern mass m edia (television and radio). Perhaps most significantly in terms of its implications for well-being, there is no gender difference in the likelihood of co-residing with any child and older women areactually more likily to live with a married child than are men.

While olderwomen are less likely to be economically active than men, they are more likely to be activ e in housekeeping and related work. Overall, when these two type of activities are considered together, virtually equal percentages of both older Vietnames men and women are active in either what conventionally is thought of as economically productive work or in maintaining the household. Both activities are likely to be valued by their families, especially when the elderly persons areliving together with younger generation family members. Thus, it is not clear whether the gender difference in the types of activities that older men and women are engaged in should be considered an advantage or disadvantage for either sex. In any event, the results make clear that many older Vietnamese men and women are not simply dependents but making useful contributions to the family's ability to sustain themselves. This, is turn is likely to contribute to stability in living arrangements, even as Viet Nam is undergoing a major transformation of its economy.

Endnotes

1. Urban-rural residenc e is measured in terms of current residence and does not reflect changes of residence over the lives of the older persons.

2. For example, based on the combined results of two regional surveys of persons aged 60 and over, 53 per cent of men over 60 compared to only 6 percent of women who were widowed or divorced some time in the past have married for a second time (Friedman and others, 2002).

3. Examination of the percentage economically active by single years of age in the 3 per cent sample of the 1999 census does not reveal particularly sharp declines associated with age 55 for women or age 60 for men (results not shown).

4. The index of housing quality is constructed by summing scores for type of houde (ranging from 0 for least permanent to 3 for most permanent), access to electricity (0 if no access and 2 for access), water supply (2 for piped water, 0 otherwise), type of toilet (ranging from 0 for no toilet to 2 for flush toilet).

5. Living arrangements for the elderly were identified from the household size and the recorded relationships of each household member in relation to the household had. An older person was considered to be co-resident with a child whenever al older head of household or spouse of head resided with a child, or when an older person was identified as a parent of a head of household.This approach is likely to yield slightly downwardly biased estimates of the true co-residency rates, since elderly who are neither head nor parent of head are never considered to be co-resident even when sone in deed are .

References

Bui The Cuong, Si Truong Anh, Daniel Goodkind, John Knodel, jed friedman (2002). "Vietnamese elderly amidst transformations in social welfare policy", in David Phillips ed., *Ageing in the Asia-Pacific Regions: Issues and Policies (London,Routledge).*

Clark, Robert and R i c hart Anker (1993). "Cross-national analysis of labor force participation of older men and women", *Economic Development and Cultural change* 41: 489-511.

Cowgill, Donald O.(1986). *Ageing around the World* (Belmont, CA, Wadsworth Pub. Co.)

Editor, Gender Dialogue (2001). "The invisible majority: what feminist economics can off er", 1(5): 1-4.

Friedman, jed, Daniel Goodkind, Bui The Cuong and truong Si Anh (2001). "Work and retirement among the elderly in Viet Nam", *Research on Ageing 23:209-232.*

Friedman, jed, John Knodel, Bui The Cuong and Truong Si Anh (2002). "Gender and intergenerational exchanges in Viet Nam" Paper presented at the 2002 Annual Meeting of the Population Association of America, Atlanta, 9-11 May 2002.

Hashimoto, Akiko, Hal Kendig and Larry C. Coppard (1992). "Family support to the elderly in international perspective", in Akiko Hashimoto, Hal Kendig and larry C. Coppard eds., *Family support for the Elderly The International Experience* (New York, NY, Oxford University Press).

Hirschman, Charles, Samuel Preston and Vu Manh Loi (1995). "Vietnamese casualties during the American War: a new estimate", Population and Development Review 21:783-812.

Knodel, John, Jed Friedman, Truong Si Anh and Bui The Cuong (2000). "Intergenerational exchanges in Vi e t Nam: family size, sex composition, and the location of children", Population Studies 54(1):89-104.

Knodel, John, Napaporn Chayovan and Siriwan Siriboon (1996). "Familial support andthe life course of Thai elderly and their children", in Tamara

Hareven, ed., Ageing and Generational Relations: Life Course and Cross-cultural Perspectives (New York, Aldine de Gruyter).

Truong Si Anh, Bui The Cuong, Daniel Goodkind and John Knodel (1997). "Living arrangements, patrilineality and sources of support among elderly Vietnamese", Asia-Pacific Population Journal 12(4):69-88.

United Nations (2001a). World Population Prospects: The 2000 Revision. Vol. I: Comprehensive Tables (New York, United Nations).

(2001b). World Populaion prospects: The 2000 Revision. Vol. II: Sex and Age (New York, United Nations).

(2002). International Plan of Action on Ageing 2002 (advance unedited copy).

World NGO Forum on Ageing (2002). Final Declaration and Recommendations, Madrid.

9

Evolution of Population Concerns: Reflections from the Asian and Pacific

The United Nations Seminar on Population in Asia and the Far East, held at Bandung, Indonesia, in 1955, focused attention on increasing population trends within the region covered by the Economic Commission for Asia and the Far East (ECAFE). The Seminar realized that the current rising population growth rates largely negated or probably even retarded the effects of national socio-economic programmes that provided an environment conducive to lowering birth rates. Interest in the region's population gains was further stimulated by the establishment of the Demographic Training and Research Centre at Bombay, India, jointly operated by the United Nations and the Government of India. At the Centre's inaugural conference it was suggested that the United Nations convene a regional conference on population. That proposal was taken up by the Commission in its resolution 28 (XV) of 13 March 1959 requesting the secretariat to organize an Asian population conference where experts could examine the major problems of planning for economic and social development arising from current and prospective trends in population growth, composition and geographic destribution. Consequently, in 1963, the First Asian Population Conference (APC) was held at New Delhi, with the Government of India providing host facilities. APC was established as a statutory organ of the Commission to be convened every 10 years to consider all aspects of population questions and, of their impact on economic and social development as mandated in Commission resolution 74 (XXIII) of 17 April 1967.

The Second APC, hosted by the Government of Japan, was held at Tokyo in November 1972. In 1974, the name of ECAFE was changed to Economic and Social Commission for Asia and the Pacific (ESCAP). Five years later, in line with its enlarged scope, the Commission decided that APC should thereafter be referred to as the Asian and Pacific Population Conference (APPC). The third and Fourth APPCs were convened at Colombo in September 1982 and at Bali, Indonesia, in August 1992, respectively. The most recent APPC was held as Bangkok in December 2002. Today, half a year after the Fifth APPC, it seems appropriate to reflect on the evolution of issues and opinions since the 1963 Conference.

The following paragraphs will describe the development of the Conferences in terms of participation, organization and especially the debate on emerging issues in response to the changing demographic scene. The population growth pattern and the general locale that prompted the discussions during the first and subsequent Conferences will be set forth. The role of the United Nations, especially ESCAP, in placing population issues on the agendas of Governments across the Asian and Pacific region will also be portrayed.

Organization

Purpose

The first APC provided a forum where experts examined the major problems of planning for economic and social development arising from present and prospective trends in population growth, composition and distribution. During the Second APC, participants arrived at a better understanding of the central role of population in achieving development goals. Governments in the region were assisted in ascertaining and applying the most effective means of influencing population trends and patterns in order to hasten the attainment of the Second United Nations Development Decade goals. A further understanding of the two-way interrelationships between population and development and the need to consider relevant factors fully in the formulation and implementation of policies and programmes to achieve overall national development goals were the aims of the Third APPC. The Fourth APPC enabled Governments in the region to understand clearly the strategic value of formulating multidisciplinary policies and programmes, to realize the need to integrate research and evaluation into programme planning and implementation and to appreciate the role of population data and information in policy formulation and programme implementation. Progress made in implementing the recommendations contained in the Bali Declaration, the Programme of Action of the International Conference on Population and Development (ICPD), the five-year reviews and appraisals of the Bali Declaration and the ICPD Programme of Action, the Platform for Action of the Fourth World Conference on Women and the Millennium Declaration adopted at the United Nations Millennium Summit was reviewed during the Fifth APPC.

Participation

Participation in the Conferences more than doubled from some 20 members and associate members in the ECAFE region in 1963 to 42 ESCAP members and associate members in 2002. Selected non-governmental organizations (NGOs) and foundations were invited to attend the First APC. In attendance were the trainees and staff of the Bombay Demographic Training and Research Centre.

In addition to the 21 ESCAP members and associate members, United Nations bodies, United Nations specialized agencies and NGOs, 38 experts in demography and related disciplines were appointed as resource persons to assist in the Second APC, held in 1972. A decade later, 32 members and associate members of the Commission took part in the Third APPC together with representatives of United Nations bodies, intergovernmental organizations, NGOs and observers from various organizations in the region. In Bali, the Fourth APPC changed in format with two different segments: senior officials from 36 members and associate members of ESCAP gathering first for six days, followed by a two-day meeting of ministers from 40 members and associate members of the region. Forty-two members and associate members sent their senior officials to the Fifth APPC while 26 ministers from 23 countries were present during the ministerial meeting. A large number of representatives from United Nations Headquarters, United Nations bodies, United Nation specialized agencies as well as intergovernmental organizations and NGOs registered for these last two Conferences.

Opening addreses

Heads of State have usually inaugurated the Conference. In his opening address, Prime Minister Jawahaeral Nehru stated that the New Delhi Conference was the first to deal with subjects that were highly important to the world at large and to Asia in particular. The ESCAP countries and areas faced a race between the growth rates of the economy and that of population, he explained, hoping that the Conference would initiate a combined approach to common problems in the region with assistance from non-Asian countries.

Inaugurating the Second APC, the Japanese Vice-Prime Minister Takeo Miki stressed that Asia was the focal point of the world population problem and anticipated that the 1970s would be for Asia an age of action closely tied to policy. He counted upon the Second APC to provide momentum for the attainment of the Second United Nations Development Decade objectives.

The President of Sri Lanka, J.R. Jayewardene, observed in front of the representatives gathered for the Third APPC that Asian and Pacific countries experienced similar demographic problems where the solution applied in one situation could be adapted in another with modifications to suit local social, political, cultural and economic needs. He perceived great scope for regional cooperation in the population field among ESCAP countries and areas. The Prime Minister of Sri Lanka, R. Premadasa, urged the Third APPC to seriously consider adopting a regional population plan of action.

The Minister of State for Population and Environment of Indonesia, Emil Salim, speaking to the senior officials assembled at Bali for the Fourth APPC, stressed that the adoption of a participatory approach to cover the broadest possible range of issues would be most appropriate for reconciling population concerns, environmental factors and development objectives. In inaugurating the Meeting of Ministers, President Soeharto of Indonesia remarked that development not merely dealt with econimic growth and related issues, rather it concerned people and whether they could live decently and prosperously. Future generations in the region might have a better quality of life if the resolutions and recommendations of the Fourth APPC were implemented.

Sudarat Keyuraphan, Minister of Public Health of Thailand, in her address to the Senior Officials Meeting at Bangkok, observed that the strategies and approaches introduced in earlier APPCs and ICPD by providing specific goals and a focused framework within a specific time frame would help to reduce poverty and improve the people's quality of life. The best practices or lessons learned from neighbouring countries could provide valuable models for this purpose and strengthen partnership through South-South cooperation. Inaugurating the Meeting of Ministers, Thaksin Shinawatra, Prime Minister of Thailand, stated that the recommendations emerging from the discussions during the Senior Officials Meeting provided the ministers with important guidelines for interventions and policies to promote informed choice, create opportunities, reduce poverty and improve the welfare and quality of life of people in the region.

The Secretary-General of the United Nations, the Executive Secretory of the Commission and the Executive Director of the United Nations Population Fund (UNFPA) also gave opening statements or had their messages read before the Delegations. To draw attention to the 1974 United Nations World Population Conference (WPC), Antonio Carrillo-Flores, WPC Secretory-General, stated that the Second APC paved the way for the 1974 WPC. In the same manner, speaking to the senior officials assembled in Bali in 1992, the Secretory-General of the 1994 ICPD elaborated on the policy agenda for the future, observing that the APPCs had come to symbolize leadership in the population and development field.

Agenda

The agendas of the five Conferences varied from simple consideration of the regional demographic situation and the economic and social implications of prospective population trends in 1963 to issues related to the themes adopted at the Conferences that followed. Recurring topics for the first four Conferences were the demographic situation and future outlook, research and training and information dissemination. The first APC participants unanimously adopted a resolution inviting Commission members to adopt a positive population policy related to their individual needs, keeping in mind the Conference recommendations relating to national population policies when formulating and executing their general socio-economic development policies and plans.

Family planning programmes and the ecological implications of rural and urban change were two new topics introduced at the Second APC. Held during the Second United Nations Development Decade, the Conference adopted a Declaration of Population Strategy for Development containing recommendations ranging from labour utilization to land reform, from pollution to planning mechanisms and from contraception to construction.

Under the theme "An integrated approach to population and related developmental issues", representatives at the Third APPC reviewed the progress made by members in implementing the recommendations if the World Population Plan of Action approved at Bucharest in 1974 and considered actions to be taken in the future. The formulation and implementation of integrated population and development policies and urbanization and the growth of cities were added to the agenda along with the evaluation of integrated family planning/family welfare/family health programme schemes and strategies. With the Commission enlarged to embrace the Pacific countries and areas, the population problems of small island States gained prominence. In response to the urging of the Prime Minister of Sri Lanka, a regional population plan of action, the Asia-Pacific Call for Action on Population and Development, was adopted by the delegations during the plenary session.

The theme chosen for the Fourth APPC was "Population and sustainable development: goals and strategies into the twenty-first century". The agenda included a discussion of the socio-economic implications of population ageing as well as human resources development and poverty alleviation issues. After examining the population situation and outlook and noting the substantial progress achieved by the region-s countries in responding to the Asia-Pacific Call for Action on Population and Development adopted at the previous APPC, the meeting of ministers adopted the Bali Declaration on Population and Sustainable Development.

The theme of the Fifth APPC, "Population and poverty in Asia and the Pacific", emphasized the need to re-evaluate the links between population and development and to crystallize and revitalize the thinking on the links between population and poverty in the light of the United Nations Millennium Declaration adopted in 2000. To highlight the theme, the first agenda item taken up was population and poverty in Asia and the Pacific. Adolescent reproductive health, HIV/AIDS and poverty, gender equality and development behavioural change communication and advocacy as tools for population and development and poverty reduction were new topics covered in the Bangkok agenda. The senior officials strongly reaffirmed their commitment to the ICPD Programme of Action, which continued to serve as their guide in undertaking their reproductive health programmes. Future activities to advance the Bali and ICPD agendas to reflect realistically the needs of the region's countries and their expectations from international partners towards meeting those needs are embodied in the Fifth Asian and Pacific Population Conference Plan of Action on

Population and Poverty adopted by the meeting of ministers after a vote.

The debates

Knowledge and understanding of the demographic situation and population problems of most countries in the region were still rudimentary at the time of the First APC despite progress made since the 1955 Bandung Seminar. In 1963, only a few Governments recognized the implications of high population growth rates. Only five administrations in the region had official population policies. The region's population totalled about 1.7 billion. Recognizing the role of demographic factors in economic and social development, the representatives stressed that moderation of population growth was a matter of great urgency and famiily size limitation should be accorded the highest possible priority in development programmes. Industrialization, land reform and other programmes were recognized to have accelerated socio-economic development. The Conference agreed that rapid population growth in many of the region's less developed countries was impeding socio-economic progress and threatening the success of efforts to reach satisfactory levels of living within a tolerable length of time. The Conference called on the United Nations and its specialized agencies to expand the scope of their technical assistance. The Commission was requested to: (a) strengthen its regional advisory services in the demographic field; (b) increase opportunities for qualified students from countries in the region to obtain fellowships for advanced studies in demography and related fields; (c) strengthen its secretariat assigned to work on population matters so as to ebable it to render effective services to government agencies and institutions working in this field; (d) compile and analyse statistical data and other information on the demography of countries in the region, and prepare reports for publication on various aspects of the demographic situation and prospects in the region and the interrelation of population trends with social and economic development; and (e) arrange for fundamental research on population questions to be carried out by universities and research institutions within the region in coordination with the Asian Institute for Economic Development and Planning and other regional demographic training and research facilities.

In 1972, the region's population had risen to 2.1 billion. Fifteen member countries had official population policies and another 10 were actively supporting family planning programmes. Against this backdrop, the Second APC considered the need to formulate population policies and programmes as integral parts of the social and economic development process and recognized the two-way relationship of population with socio-economic development.The delegations stressed that reducing infant and maternal mortality, achieving full and productive employment, abating excessive migration flows to the larger cities and improving the status of women ensured a more equitable distribution of opportunity and income. Governments seeking to fulfil the ideals of their people and their national goals through population policies and programmes should: (a) provide information, education and services for all their citizens as early as possible; (b) encourage smaller families in rural and urban areas through intensive information, education and communication efforts together with the enactment of appropriate socio-economic measures; (c) consider establishing population commissions or other bodies having multidisciplinary and multidepartmental representation to assess the current status and future needs in the population and family planning fields; (d) ensure coordination among various agencies at all levels in order to expedite action on integrated development policies and plans; (e) provide essential training facilities to improve management and planning skills, and promote comprehensive and innovative population policies to increase population and family planning programme administrative capabilities; (f) encourage the development of new communication tools and utilization of existing ones so that knowledge might be shared at all levels of society; and (g) include provisions in population policy and programmes to ensure that all pertinent information reached policy makers, opinion leaders and socio-economic planners.

With a population exceeding 2.5 billion in 1982, the ESCAP region witnessed significant declines in fertility and mortality. However, population growth rates were higher than desired in 16 countries while 10 still had life expectancies of 50 years or under. Sixteen countries had fertility reduction policies and an even greater number supported family planning programmes. At the Third APPC, participants pointed out that most ESCAP countries and areas recognized the integrated approach. However, that approach had included maternal and child health since the early 1970s and more recently other programmes such as those related to the status of women had been added. While population programme managers were willing to involve other development sectors, corresponding responses had not always been forthcoming from the other sectors. The problem centred on how to design a coordinated approach to population and development policies so as to obtain the support of other sectors. The slow progress of integration was due both to the limited knowledge base relating to diverse population processes and to a likelihood that planning structures and approaches had become rigid, thus precluding the needs of population planning being taken into account. Population programmes had to be accorded an appropriate place in a Government's political and administrative structure. High-level population units had to be established within development planning organizations responsible for integrating population policies and programmes with related social and economic development policies and programmes. The concept of integration and the policies relating to integration of family planning services with other programmes had also to consider the programme recipients' viewpoint. An effective monitoring system needed to be established to undertake systematic and periodic evaluation of integrated population policies and programmes. Programmes that resulted in diminishing demand for large families should be given priority with a view to creating a socio-economic environment conductive to reducing the population growth rate.

Although considerable progress has been made in the matter of implementing population programmes, a wide gap exists between current fertility and mortality levels and fertility and mortality goals. For the first time, the 1982 APPC included population goals in its Asia-Pacific Call for Action. Existing targets and goals for reducing birth and death rates must be reviewed and modified to attain low levels as early as possible and attain a replacement level of fertility by the year 2000. Towards that end, the necessary information, education and a variety of means to practice family planning freely, effectively and in accordance with their cultural values and religious beliefs should be available and accessible to all couples and individuals. Family planning services should be strengthened though the involvement of local population and local institutions in planning, funding and implementing family planning information and services. Programme personal should be reoriented to make family planning programmes more sensitive and responsive to local values and individual needs.

The small island countries and areas of the ESCAP region, because of their size, are economically, socially, environmentally and even demographically vulnerable. Thus, particular attention is required to protect their demographic and cultural viability. This is especially true for those countries subject to emigration. Hence, small island countries and areas, particularly those subject to emigration, were enjoined to formulate social, economic and population policies that would maintain their demographic and cultural viability.

A revolution in thinking about population issues had occurred in the ESCAP region since 1963. Many Governments had launched ambitious programmes with the result that the average annual population growth rate for Asia and the Pacific was just over 1.7 per cent in 1990 with a population numbering around 3.3 billion. The delegations to the Fourth APPC saw that high population growth and density in many countries had caused various environmental and related problems: continuing depletion and degradation of vital natural resources, the persistence of poverty among the rural population and a growing rural-urban income gap, increasing and competing demands for land, water and forests by the non-agricultural sectors and growing urban population, and deteriorating environmental quality owing to unregulated industrial and urban growth. To overcome those problems, the policies and strategies formulated should include development of environmentally friendly technology, reforestation, improvement of air and water quality, waste recycling and the phasing-out of environmentally harmful technology, improving environmental organization, administration and management, as well as appropriate laws and effective law enforcement.

The Bali Conference was concerned that the growing threat to the environment and urban infrastructure posed by rural-urban migration and by the high rate of natural increase in the urban population required effective monitoring of trends and family planning strategies that took account of the population impact. A comparatively new phenomenon in an increasing number of countries of the region was the growing quantum of female migration, including migration of single women. A better understanding of the demographic, economic and social implications of such migration was essential. The management of metropolitan cities was another issue that deserved high priority. In several countries, the growth rate of large cities had slackened. Small cities were suffering from stagnation and obsolescence while medium-size cities were expanding rapidly. Spatial implications and environmental consequences of major sectoral policies should be fully assessed as part of the national development planning process to achieve balanced urbanization, keeping in mind the objective of reducing rural-urban disparities, regional disparities within countries and the need to protect the environment. To cope with rapid urbanization, Governments should create a favourable climate for private sector investment in smaller towns and cities and provide the required support mechanisms, such as physical and social infrastructure and advantageous fiscal and monetary policies.

The Bali Conference was also concerned that while the proportion of older persons remained low in many ESCAP countries, the absolute number of older persons was swelling. The trends and patterns in population movements had further added to the ageing of rural areas, as those who migrated to urban areas tended to be young and able, leaving behind the elderly to attend to farming and other agricultural pursuits, thus adversely affecting agricultural production. Hence, migration had to be closely monitored and redirected by creating job opportunities and other incentives for the young to remain in rural areas. The Conference stressed the need to create awareness of ageing issues and provide the necessary incentives for families to continue caring for their elderly. Emphasis was laid on strengthening community support through the formation of voluntary and mutual aid organizations; encouraging communities to provide the necessary services for elderly care and integrating older persons into all aspects of development; establishing appropriate home industries that enabled the elderly to work at their own pace; and initiating training programmes to improve the productivity of the elderly and their continued participation in the advancement of new technologies and industries.

The population of countries and areas comprising the ESCAP region reached 3.7 billion in the year 2000, i.e., double the population 40 years earlier, and accounting for approximately 62 per cent of the world's population. Fertility levels were diminishing in almost all countries of the region because of family planning services provided under government programmes, among other factors. The Fifth APPC noted that many developing countries in the region were characterized by overpopulation, poverty, malnutrition, poor health and inadequate and unsustainable health-care financing. While economic growth was essential for development and poverty reduction, lowering fertility and population growth rates was equally important in that regard. There was increasing evidence to indicate that the alterations in age structure taking place in most countries could contribute significantly to economic growth if appropriate policies were put in place such as pro-poor economic and social policies that promoted choice; enhanced the development of, access to and utilization of resources; improved gender equity and equality; and increased access to reproductive health, including family planning.

Adolescent reproductive health information and

service programmes were still in the early stages of development, were too narrowly focused and were not adequately available to adolescents in general and unmarried adolescents in particular, with young people not often involved in programme planning and development. The Conference strongly supported the right of young people to adolescent reproductive health, especially as a means for preventing unwanted pregnancies, ab ortion and the spread of HIV/AIDS. The delegations observed that where social, cultural or religious barriers existed to prevent young people from obtaining information on sexual matters at home, sex education and training in life skills should be provided for young people in and outside the school systems, especially in view of their exposure to conflicting forms of information on sexual matters through the media, pornographic sites on the Internet and the popularity of its unmoderated electronic "chat rooms". Behavioural change communication, advocacy and education programmes should be implemented to raise awareness and enhance communication with parents, families, teachers, religious and community leaders, service providers and other adults, peer groups and mass media on improved reproductive health adolescents.

Many Asian and Pacific countries assessed the existing policy environment and resource base for mainstreaming gender concerns, established national machineries and focal points and developed national plans of action for improving the status of women. While substantial progress had been demonstrated through improved education, health status and labour force participation of females, the gains were unequal among the countries of the region. Although the gender gap had narrowed somewhat in terms of gross enrolment at the primary level, the female disadvantage persisted at the higher educational levels in almost all countries and areas of the region. The share of female wage employment in the non-agricultural sector was low and the proportion of seats held by women in parliaments remained under 10 per cent, on average. Emerging issues in the region included the marginalization of female employment, the rise in poor female-headed households, increase in girl-child labour and trafficking of women and children. Governments in cooperation with civil society organizations and the international community were urged to reduce the marginalization of women in employment through policies and programmes that addressed gender-based discrimination and also reduced tha negative impact of globalization on women's employment while recognizing its positive impact in empowering women and augmenting opportunities in decision-making. Exploitation of children could be eliminated through vigorous policy actions and their effective implementation. Awareness of gender-based violence should be increased, relevant laws simplified and law enforcement officials trained to ensure the effective enforcement of adequate and appropriate legislative and programmatic responses to violence against women and exploitation, including trafficking. Policies should be formulated to promote greater male involvement and participation in improving gender equality, equity and empowerment of women.

Role of the United Nations, ECAFE and ESCAP

As its 1964 session, the Commission unanimously adopted resolution 54 (XX) of 17 March 1964, in which it requested the secretariat to expand its activities in particular fields of work relating to the population problems of the region. Subsequently, the Economic and Social Council adopted resolution 1048 (XXXVII) in August 1964, commending ECAFE for organizing the First APC and drawing the attention of the General Assembly to the Commission's resolution.

ECAFE continued to be the focal point among countries and areas in the region in the population dialogue and in population information dissemination. The Commission members welcomed the secretariat's work in family planning and in the relationship between population and agricultural change.

The secretariat played a central role in initiating debate on population and development issues in the region, providing the forum for the region's developing countries to address them and assisting those countries through its regional programmes, advisory services, training and information dissemination activities. The Bali Conference called upon ESCAP to continue to play a pivotal role in assisting members and associate members in implementing their population and development policies and programmes.It recommended that ESCAP fully incorporate the population dimension into the focus of three thematic committees: regional economic cooperation, environment and sustainable development and poverty alleviation.

The capacity of the United Nations system to provide assistance to countries was increased as a result of the establishment of the United Nations Fund for Population Activities (UNFPA) in 1967. Its resources through voluntary contributions from countries grew from US$ 7 million in 1970 to nearly US$ 40 million in 1972. Those funds were available for projects related to all aspects of population, including family planning programmes in developing countries. The extension of the UNFPA system of country coordinators,together with the United Nations Development Programme's newly instituted system of country programming, helped to prevent duplication of effort and of measures that were not mutually supporting. UNFPA had taken steps to increase its administrative capacity to respond more effectively to requests for assistance from Commission members for the design and implementation of their population policies in accordance with national priorities, working closely with government officials to ensure effective coordination and harmonization of population activities and to develop fully national capacity for self-reliance. UNFPA assisted ESCAP in playing an enhanced role in helping developing countries in the region to shape their future population policies and programmes.

Since 1990, the ESCAP region has been the second-largest recipient of population assistance after sub-Saharan Africa. According to UNFPA, final expenditures for population assistance in the region increased from US$ 211.5 million in 1990 to US$ 389.3 million in the year 2000. The bilateral and multilateral channels each accounted for over 30 per cent of funds expended in the region. A total of 39 countries and territories in the region benefited from international population assistance in 2000 with Bangladesh, India and the Philippines as the top three recipient countries. A total of US$ 19.5 million was spent on regional programmes.

Appropriate steps have been taken to reorient the Asian and Pacific regional programme on population and sustainable development with a view to assisting developing countries in the region, paying special attention to least developed countries, in response to the challenges that they face and the need to strengthen national capacity. In that regard, ESCAP staff members have provided technical assistance to a large number of members and associate members of the Commission on a wide range of population and reproductive health issues during the years since the adoption of the resolution 54/4 on 22 April 1998. Such assistance has included policy and programme development, capacity-building, the collection and analysis of data from censuses and surveys, detailed analysis of and research on priority issues, as well as programme monitoring and evaluation of population and reproductive health programmes. Staff members of ESCAP have acted as resource persons for intercountry workshops on population and reproductive health issues organized by the secretariat, the Statistical Institute for Asia and the Pacific, the UNFPA Country Technical Services Team for East and South-East Asia, Chulalongkorn University in Thailand and the Asian Forum of Parliamentarians on Population and Development. A considerable number of seminars, expert group meetings and training workshops have been organized for capacity development in the region on various aspects of population and development and for maximizing the benefits of modern information technologies for processing and disseminating data and information.

Reflections

From the First APC in 1963 to the Fifth APPC in 2002, the Conferences have dealt with population concerns at the regional and global levels. The purposes of the Conferences, the themes, the agenda items taken up during the successive meetings and the resolutions and plans of action adopted by delegations at each Conference all reflected the predominant population and development issues at the time.

What is striking is the strong will and collaboration shown by the Commission's members and associate members in tackling what they perceived to be critical demographic problems and in arriving at pertinent sloutions. The technical and financial support of the United Nations, its specialized agencies and UNFPA, enabled member States to embark on family planning and reproductive health programmes to achieve their population and development goals.

The Fifth APPC revealed the dramatic reversal in thinking of the Government of the United States of

America since the 1994 ICPD. While the United States actively supported the paradigm shift to reproductive health in Cairo, the change of administration in the year 2000 has led to its vigorous campaign against reaffirming the ICPD Programme of Action in toto, objecting to such terms as reproductive health, reproductive health services and adolescent reproductive health in the belief that these terms promote abortion and underage sex. Thus, the United States delegation attempted to substantially revise or to block the adoption of the draft Plan of Action during the Fifth APPC. This caused the other delegations to take a unified stand to reaffirm the ICPD Programme of Action. If the United States remains unaltered in the coming decade, holding a 10-year review and appraisal of ICPD (ICPD+10) or a Sixth APPC would likely be an exercise in futility.

It is imperative that the population community sustain its efforts to keep the population perspective in the forefront of issues such as globalization, environment and sustainable development even if the Plan of Action in these areas ignores population, as was patently obvious at the 2002 World Summit on Sustainable Development held at Johannesburg, South Africa. By reiterating its affirmation of the relevant international conventions, by vigorously lobbying at international forums and by supporting regional collaboration in population and development programmes, the population community underscores the importance of maintaining the population perspective in the discussion of issues germane to genuine development.

10

Asian and Pacific Population Conference: Towards a Repositioning of Population in the Global Development Agenda

The Fifth Asian and Pacific Population Conference, held at Bangkok in December 2002, followed a little more than 10 years after the Fourth Asian and Pacific Population Conference, held at Bali. The Bali Conference was one of the regional conferences leading up to the path-breaking International Conference on Population and Development, held at Cairo in 1994, and was important in the context of providing input into the Cairo Conference, but also in its own right as reflecting the consensus among the Member States making up over 60 per cent of the world's population.

It is well known that the Cairo Conference led to some dramatic shifts in direction in the rhetoric of population and development, as well as in the priorities for and conduct of national population programmes. These shifts in direction had not been apparent at the Bali Conference, which had indeed spelled out a set of population targets in line with sustainable development goals, an approach that came under attack from various sources at Cairo (McIntosh and Finkle 1995:227). The Cairo document, in paragraphs 3.14, 3.25, 3.26,

3.28, 6.3 and 6.4, gives muted support to the need to reduce population growth rates. But the main thrust of the document lies elsewhere. "Population policy becomes a welfarist activity, seeking especially to benefit women. Effects on birth rates are not so much seen as secondary, but as an inevitable - and desired - consequence of women's empowerment" (McNicoll 1995:334).

The emphasis on reproductive health and reproductive rights was a major accomplishment of the Cairo Conference, though the stress on women's empowerment was arguably taken too far in some areas: for example, by stressing gender inequities in access to education while ignoring inequities in access by socio-economic status (Knodel and Jones 1996) and viewing the gender difference in child mortality as "much more crucial than the high level of child mortality, male and female, in poor societies across the world" (Basu 1997:226). Be that as it may, the countries and areas of the ESCAP region, individually and as a group, made concerted efforts to orient their policies and programmes to the new emphases of Cairo. This was evident, for example, in the stress placed on adolescent reproductive health in the report of the high-level meeting held at Bangkok in 1998 to review the implementation of the Cairo Programme of Action and the earlier Bali Declaration on Population and Sustainable Development (ESCAP 1998). Adolescent reproductive health had been ignored in the Bali document.

In the decade that passed between the Fourth and the Fifth Asian and Pacific Population Conferences, the world (and specifically the Asian and Pacific region) had moved on, in terms of both its economic and demographic situations. First of all, the demographic transition in the region had progressed considerably. This can be observed by comparing the total fertility rate and expectation of life at birth in the region at the time of the two Conferences. In 1992, these were about 3.1 and 63 years, respectively. Not only this, but by 2002 there were few countries where fertility had not started to decline. In 1992, real doubts could still be raised about whether any decline had taken place in Cambodia, Nepal or Pakistan. By 2002 they could not.

At the other end of the spectrum, by 2002, some countries where fertility in 1992 was already below replacement level had sunk to even lower levels, and the implications of this low fertility were causing considerable concern. In general, then, demographically the Asian and Pacific region had become even more diverse that it had been in 1992, but with a clear shift towards lower fertility and mortality levels. Although demographic momentum was clearly going to swell population numbers very considerably, the overriding need to lower fertility rates, which had been recognized in the Asian and Pacific Population Conferences of the 1970s and 1980s, and indeed to a lesser though still substantial extent in 1992, was no longer such a priority concerrn in 2002.

In terms of economic development, the decade had seen impressive growth in the Asian and Pacific region, albeit with considerable variation. Populaion and poverty was apprapriately chosen as the theme of the Bangkok Conference, but this did not mean that the incidence of poverty was getting worse. Indeed, a recent Asian Development Bank study of 18 Asian countries, using national poverty lines and survey estimates of consumption, found that the poverty incidence in these countries had fallen from 65 per cent in 1960 to 17 per cent in 2000. The biggest decline came during the last two decades. Major countries in the region - China, Indonesia, Thailand and Viet Nam-have seen major reductions in the incidence of poverty (Jones 2002: 6-9). Though there can be (and are) debates about the exact trends, there can be no contesting the reality of a substantial decline in the incidence of poverty in all these countries. Even the Asian economic crisis, which hit countries including Indonesia, the Republic of Korea and Thailand hard from 1997, was not able to put a major dint in the general reduction in poverty throughout the region. Africa was the continent where poverty increases were matters of grave concern; the Asian and Pacific region was certainly not Africa.

The thrust of the Bangkok Conference

The debate at the Bangkok Conference reflected the continuing vital interest of the countries and areas of the Asian and Pacific region in the interrelationships between population trends and development. Many of these countries had espoused the Programme of Action of the Cairo Conference with a degree of diffidence, recognizing the winds of change that were seemingly unstoppable at that Conference, yet concerned that their continuing strong national emphases on reducing fertility rates through family planning and other measures would be undermined by the new emphasis on reproductive health and reproductive rights. Since that time, debates have continued throughout the region about the degree of compatibility of reproductive health approaches with the aim of lowering fertility, with some protagonists arguing that by diluting family planning resources, the impacts on fertility will weaken, and others making the point that a well-executed reproductive health approach will lower dropout and failure rates and appeal to those younger people whose delayed sexual initiation and longer and effective practice of contraception are crucial to a sustained decline in fertility. However, as noted earlier, demographic trends have reduced the salience of efforts to reduce fertility in many of the Asian and Pacific countries, and for this reason alone, leaving aside changes in the ideology of family planning and reproductive health, reducing fertility is no longer as prominent a concern of the region as it was at the time of the Bali Conference.

There are many issues surrounding reproductive health and reproductive rights, apart from their relation to fertility reduction strategies. At the Cairo Conference, certain of the Asian and Pacific countries shared the concern of some other countries that the sections on reproductive health and reproductive rights in the Cairo Programme of Action might have the effect of promoting abortion or adolescent sexual activity. However, many of them were more concerned that the protracted debate over these issues at Cairo served to constrict discussion of the kinds of broader population and development issues that had received considerable attention at the Bali Conference. On this score, history repeated itself in Bangkok. An inordinate proportion of the time of the drafting committee was taken up with the concerns of the United States of America delegation about language contained in the Cairo Programme of Action, which according to that delegation, tended to promote abortion and adolescent sexual activity. In the event, the Asian and Pacific countries stood firm in supporting the language of the Cairo Programme of Action (the cohesion of such a diverse group of countries in doing so being one of the most striking features of the Conference), but at the cost of minimizing the time and intellectual effort that could be devoted to other important aspects of the Plan of the Action.

It is clear that as time has moved on, the Cairo consensus has become entrenched in Asian and Pacific countries' approaches to population issues, and nowhere is this seen better than in these countries' determination to adhere to the language contained in the Cairo Programme of Action in the Plan of Action finally agreed to at Bangkok. Country delegation after country delegation, in statements from the floor, indi cated their conviction that the Cairo consensus did not in any way promote abortion or adolescent sexual activity.

Though the debates in Bangkok were focused heavily on this issue, if we examine the Plan of Action on Population and Poverty that was adopted by consensus at the conclusion of the Conference, it does have a great deal to say about population and development. In this sense, it will serve as a benchmark for policy emphases for some time.

What are the main emphases of the Plan of Action? First of all, in terms of overall directions, the preamble emphasizes the centrality of poverty eradication concerns and recognizes that sustainable development requires an appropriate balance between economic growth, poverty, resources and environment. The preamble recognizes the importance of human capital and in that context refers to the special need to address women's disadvantage and marginalization. Human rights are recognizes as central to development and population policies are seen as an integral component of development policies and planning. The preamble then indicates that these concerns are in line with previous consensus by the international community by affirming a commitment to the principles and recommendations adopted in Bali, Cairo, Beijing (Fourth World Conference on Women), five-year review reports on Bali and Cairo, and finally the Millennium Declaration.

As for the strategic recommendations of the Plan of Action, these are set out under 12 headings:

- Population, sustainable development and poverty
- International migration
- Internal migration and urbanization
- Population ageing

- Gender equality, equity and empowerment of women
- Reproductive rights and reproductive health
- Adolescent reproductive health
- HIV/AIDS
- Behavioural change communication and information and communication technology
- Data, research and training
- Partnerships
- Resources

In the end, the reader of the document will find it to be carefully worded, reflecting current consensus about principles and broad directions for action in these important areas, and not distorted by the highly skewed amounts of time spent in debating and discussing certain sections. In this respect, it reflects the considerable work that had gone into drafting the document, large sections of which were able to be adopted by consensus without need for lengthy discussion.

The difficulty of reaching a consensus at Bangkok actually reflected, not divisions within the ESCAP members, but rather their determination to maintain the commitment to the principles and recommendations or earlier Conferences, most notably the Cairo Conference, when that was challenged by one delegation. The publicity given to this issue was described in a statement by the Asian Forum of Parliamentarians on Population and Development as creating "such hype that population has received new energy". Is this just hyperbole, or will a new impetus be given to population concerns as a result of the Bangkok Conference? It is really too early to judge, and a balanced assessment will need to be based on the actions of individual countries, groupings of countries and doner agencies over the coming years. Nevertheless, it is appropriate at least to look for "straws in the wind" at this stage.

What is the general outlook for the field of population now?

The 10-year review and appraisal of ICPD, also known as ICPD+10, is due to be held in 2004. If it is indeed held, the context will be different from that of the Cairo Conference. One of the key differences is that population growth rates are slowing quite generally throughout the world. Not only this, but many countries are now very concerned about excessively low fertility, which will lead in time to a significant downward spiral in population size unless fertility rates can be raised.

The steam has really gone out of the population issue as conventionally understood. Though world population is still expected to grow from the current 6.2 billion to somewhere between 7.3 and 10.4 billion by 2050, the growth will be at ever-decreasing rates. There is now said to be a 60 per cent probability that the world's population will not exceed 10 billion people before 2100 (Lutz, Sanderson and Scherbov 2001: 543), a far cry from earlier projections which suggested the likelihood of considerably larger populations (see also Bongaarts and Bulatao, eds. 2000). Though the need to lower birth rates is still of critical importance in some countries, particularly in Africa and South Asia, nobody seems to doubt any more that these declines will take place.

Popular attention, as guided by the emphases in the news media, has turned to issues that are considered more pressing, in particular, issues of environmental sustainability and poverty. Donor agencies, foundations and universities have likewise moved on to issues that they see as more on the "cutting edge", matters including environment and poverty, and post-11 September terrorism. Some of them see illegal migration and refugee movements, both of them "population issues",- as issues of considerable moment.

The general understanding that population issues are a thing of the past is unfortunate for two reasons. First, population and development issues are just as important for countries with low fertility as they are for countries with high fertility. Dealing with changing age structures and declining populations presents formidable intellectual and planning challenges. Secondly, there are important population dimensions of the issues that are currently given greatest prominence (see, for example, Geist and Lambin 2002 on population and the environment), but these dimensions are insufficiently recognized by the agencies dealing with them (for example, population was effectively ignored at the World Summit on Sustainable Development, held at Johannesburg in 2002).

In other words, academics, planners, international agencies and NGOs concerned with population and development issues have not "sold" the population field very effectively, and we are now suffering the consequences. Thirty or 40 years ago, when population growth appeared almost out of control, it was easy to see population as an area of crucial importance. But at that time, most university population programmes, international agencies and foundations dealing with population issues were content to ride the wave of popular concern, without devoting enough attention to educating the public to the crucial demographic dimensions of planning issues, whether in circumstances of rapid population growth or of slower or even negative population growth. Perhaps the greatest indictment of population researchers and planners is that we have been too ready to espouse one-dimensional notions of the adverse impacts of rapid population growth on development, without acknowledging that population trends - and the way in which they impact on society and development - are influenced by the complex sociocultural and political settings in which they occur.

It is somewhat ironic that we are now claiming that population itself is being left out of the equation by those from other disciplines when assessing the causes of poverty or environmental degradation.

Trends in institutional and financial suport

What does the flow of international development assistance indicate about the importance of the field of population nowadays? Is population being marginalized in the broad context of development assistance?

First, it needs to be noted that the agreed international goals for official development assistance (ODA), i.e., a proportion of 0.7 per cent of the GNP of the wealthy countries, have never been reached, or indeed ever approached. Although reiterated in the Millennium Declaration adopted by the Member States of the United Nations at the Millennium Summit in September 2000, the lack of demonstrated will to reach this goal in practice, at a time of rising expenditures on armaments and security, is one of the most depressing facts of our time. "Compassion fatigue" appears to have become a permanent state of enervation in the wealthier countries. The specification, in the Monterrey Consensus adopted at the International Conference on Financing for Development in 2002, of the need for the adoption of sound policies and good governance in developing countries to ensure the effective use of ODA implicity acknowledges one of the reasons for such "compassion fatigue." Unfortunately, it does not necessarily follow that improvements in this direction by the developing countries will loosen the purse strings in developed countries.

As for population activities specifically, many attempts were made, even before Cairo, to come up with estimates of the costs of population programmes. Estimates of global resources needed in the year 2000 ranged widely, between US$ 600 million (for just contraceptive commodities) to US$ 11.5 billion (Zeitlin, Govindaraj and Chen 1994). This highlights one of the problems in tracking how much has really been devoted to meeting the goals of the Cairo Conference: the boundaries of population spending are very hard to define, once broader reproductive health becomes the key objective, and even more so if recognition is given to the demographic impacts of spending on broader areas such as education.

The ICPD Programme of Action specified the financial resources, both domestic and donor funded, believed necessary to implement a wide-ranging population and reproductive health package. For the year 2000, the estimate was US$ 17 billion (US$ 11 billion in the ESCAP region), rising to US$ 18.5 billion by 2005. Approximately two thirds were expected to come from domestic sources and one third from the international donor community (UNFPA 2002). Subsequent UNFPA monitoring of international population assistance and domestic spending for population activities shows that financial constraints remain one of the chief obstacles to the realization of the ICPD objectives. According to UNFPA estimates, the total sum generated in 1999-2000 was about US$ 11 billion, with international population assistance funds (which reached only about 46 per cent of the target) falling further short of the target than domestically generated funds (UNFPA 2002). Given the ESCAP region's large share of total required funds, it is clear that the relative shortfall within the ESCAP region must be of the same general order of magnitude as the overall shortfall.

Such broad-grained estimates of funding shortfalls are really of questionable relevance when the complex determinants of population trends are recognized. What other points can be made about the relative importance accorded population issues, especially in the Asian and Pacific region, in the post-Bangkok Conference world?

It would be easy to seize on the downgrading of population activities in ESCAP (already in train before the Bangkok Conference), as well as a shrinking of resources provided by UNFPA, as signs that population issues are no longer as high up on the priority list of development issues as they once were. However, the Asian Development Bank and the World Bank seem to be continuing a substantial level of support for population projects. Although the United States Government cut off support for UNFPA in 2002, this does not mean that it is reducing its support for population programmes, but just redirecting it to other ways of financing those population activities that meet its ideological conditions.

The situation regarding population data is a mixed bag. On the plus side, demographic and health surveys have provided many Asian countries with a sound basis for assessing trends in the determinants of fertility and mortality, for many of them at more than one date, but few Asian and Pacific countries can track annual changes in fertility and mortality from vital registration data. And the problems faced by many countries of the region with their 2000 round of population censuses seem to reflect not only country-specific issues such as the impact of governmental decentralization in Indonesia and the Philippines, but also a squeezing of funds which, even in these times of financial stress, reflects the lowly place in the financial priorities spectrum accorded population data. Population data received more attention when it seemed crucial to know just how rapid population growth rates were, and whether efforts to bring them down were succeeding.

What might be done to follow up on the Plan of Action adopted in Bangkok?

There is an urgent need to reposition population in the global development agenda. In doing so, the first point to make is that people's welfare is the ultimate objective of all development planning. Therefore, we need to know who those people are in the aggregate - what are their characteristics, and the trends in the composition of this population. The second point is that there are demographic components of all aspects of development planning - in all settings, not just those where rapid population growth is seen as a problem. The difficulty of showing precisely how population dynamics are implicated in the key issues of current concern, such as poverty and the environment, should be seen as a challenge to the demographic community rather than a reason to be silent. It behoves the population community in the region to use its influence in a range of settings - government deliberations, planning meetings, seminars and through the media - to drive home the point that population matters.

This implies the need for a good understanding of demographic trends, which in turn implies the need for good data and good research. Increased spending on demographic data collection is vital, as is adequate support for demographic programmes in universities, including programmes emphasizing interactions between demographic and socio-economic trends. Adequate data and research capacity should be seen as the building blocks for an effective understanding of population issues.

Finally, the Cairo emphasis, reiterated at Bangkok, requires continuing attention to reproductive health issues. There are still a tragically large number of people having children they do not want, and also some who are not able to have children they would like to have. There are unconscionably high maternal mortality rates in many Asian and Pacific countries, and millions whose lives are blighted by non-life threatening sexually transmitted diseases and reproductive tract infections. In this context, unmet need and a balanced understanding of its causes should remain a key pillar of family planning approaches (Sinding and others 1994; Casterline and Sinding 2000). Pilot projects are needed to test reproductive health approaches that work, but perhaps even more necessary at this stage is analysis of ways to scale up successful pilot or experimental projects to the larger programmatic settings in which reproductive health services will be provided, beset by the usual problems of large-scale bureaucracies (Simmons, Brown and Diaz 2002). To bring effective reproductive health facilities to poorer countries requires money, planning and changed attitudes on the part of both those who determine government budgets and many health providers. Serious and imaginative attention to these issues will not only ensure lower population growth rates in countries where these remain troublingly high, but will also have major benefits for quality of life.

References

Basu, Alaka (1997). "The new international population movement: a framework for a constructive critique", *Health Transition Review*, vol. 7, Supplement 4.

Bongaarts J. and R. Bulatao, eds (2000). *Beyond Six Billion: Forecasting the World's Population* (Washington, The National Academies Press).

Casterline, John B. and Steven W. Sinding (2000). "Unmet need for family planning in developing countries and implications for population policy", *Population and Development Review*, vol. 26, No. 4, pp. 691-723.

ESCAP (1998). *Asia-Pacific Population Policies and Programmes: Future Directions - Report, Key Future Actions and Background Papers of a High-level Meeting,* Asian Population Studies Series No. 153, (United Nations publication, Sales No.E.99.II.F.4).

Geist, Helmut J. and Eric F. Lambin. (2002). "Proximate causes and underlying driving forces of tropical deforestation", *BioScience*, vol. 52, No. 2, pp. 143-150.

Jones, Gavin W. (2002). "Population and poverty in Asia and the Pacific", paper presented at the Fifth Asian and Pacific Population Conference, Senior Officials Segment, Bangkok, 11-14 December.

Knodel, John and Gavin W. Jones (1996). "Post-Cairo population policy: does promoting girls' schooling miss the mark?", *Population and Development Review*, vol. 22, No. 4. pp. 683-702.

Lutz, Wolfgang, Warren Sanderson and Sergei Scherbov (2001). "The end of world population growth", *Nature*, vol. 412, pp. 543-545.

McIntosh, C. Alison and Jason L. Finkle (1995). "The Cairo Conference on Population and Development: a new paradigm?", *Population and Development Review*, vol. 21, No. 2, pp. 223-260.

McNicoll, Geoffrey (1995). "On population growth and revisionism: further questions", *Population and Development Review,* vol. 21, No. 2, pp. 307-340.

Simmons, Ruth, Joseph Brown and Margarita Diaz (2002). "Faciliatating large-scale transitions to quality of care: an idea whose time has come", *Studies in Family Planning*, vol. 33, No. 1, pp. 61-75.

Sinding, Stephen W., John A. Ross and Allan G. Rosenfield (1994). "Seeking common ground: unmet need and demographic goals", *Interna-*

tional Family Planning Perspectives, vol. 20, No. 1, pp. 23-29.

UNFPA (2002). "Resource mobilization in the ESCAP region", paper presented at the Fifth Asian and Pacific Population Conference, Senior Officials Segment, Bangkok, 11-14 December.

Zeitlin, Jennifer, Ramesh Govindaraj and Lincoln C. Chen (1994). "Financing reproductive and sexual health services", in Gita Sen, Adrienne Germain and Lincoln C. Chen, eds., *Populaion Policies Reconsidered: Health, Empowerment, and Rights* (Harvard, Harvard University Press).

11

Knowledge of Sexual Health Issues among Unmarried Youths

Early and universal marriage has traditionally been the norm in Nepalese culture, although the practise of delayed marriage appears to be on the increase. In 1961, nearly 75 per cent of young women aged 15 to 19 years were married; this figure declined to just under 50 per cent by 1991 and to a low of 40 per cent in 2001 (Mehta 1998; Khanal 1999; NDHS 1996 and 2001). This, along with the advent of reducing age at first menarche due to improved nutritional status, has led to an increase in the window of opportunity for premarital sexual activity to occur.

Owing to social and cultural taboos and inhibitions, sexual health research in Nepal remains restricted to a small number of studies; for young people, especially those who are unmarried, this is particularly pertinent. Further, much of the hitherto limited research with young people remains unpublished.

Findings from studies which have investigated premarital sexual behaviour among high school and college students have found rates of activity to vary from 11 per cent among students in Pokhara to 14 per cent among Kathmandu students[2] and 16 per cent among students[2] in Palpa District (Limbu 2001; Prasai 1999). Among young unmarried men and women aged 14 to 19 years working in factories in the Kathmandu Valley, 20 per cent and 12 per cent of the men and women respectively reported having experienced sex (Puri 2002). Further, studies of single men in the border towns of Nepal found activity rates of 10 per cent among a sample aged 15 to 19 years and about 50 per cent among a slightly older sample aged 18 to 24 years (Mehta 1998; Tamang and others 2001).

Although the use of modern contraceptives in Nepal has risen steadily over the last two decades, levels still remain low (NDHS 2001; Pradhan and others 1997). For example, among currently married women, ever use and current use of a modern method stand at 50 and 35 per cent respectively. The use of condoms also remains particularly low at only 3 per cent for current usage and 12 per cent for ever use, rising to a high of only 16 per cent among women aged 20 to 24 years (NDHS 2001). Given the perceived problems associated with the discussion of personal sexual behaviour outside of marriage, there is a dearth of information with regard to safer sexual practices during premarital and extra marital sex. A study of condom use during sex with non-regular partners by married and unmarried young men (18 to 24 years), however, found that just over half had used a condom during the last intercourse (Tamang and others 2001). Furthermore, in the light of rising rates of sexually transmitted infections (STIs) among certain target groups and increasing rates of unplanned pregnencies, leading to maternal morbidity and mortality from unsafe abortions, it would appear that safer-sex practices during premarital and extramarital relations are infrequently being adhered to (Dahal 1999;

Furber and others 2002; Mehta 1998; UNFPA 1996).

Data collected during the demographic and health surveys as well as from small-scale surveys indicate that awareness of condoms, HIV/AIDS and other STIs appears to be rising among the general population, mainly owing to extensive media campaigns (NDHS 1996 and 2001; Mehta 1998; Pradhan and others 1997). In 2000, the Nepal Adolescent and Young Adults Survey (NAYA) questioned both married and unmarried young people (aged 14 to 22 years) regarding their awareness of contraception and HIV/AIDS. Their results showed that 93 per cent of young people had heard of HIV/AIDS and 95 per cent were aware of condoms (Neupane and Nichols 2002; Aryal and Nichols 2002).

For many young people in Nepal, however, especially those who are unmarried, social and cultural norms impose barriers to the transfer of sexual health information. Consequently, countless remain ignorant of even the basic knowledge required for safer sexual behaviour. For example, when the comprehensiveness of knowledge was tested during the NAYA survey, among those young people who had ever heard of HIV/AIDS, only 36 per cent were able to cite all three of the following measures to reduce or avoid the possibility of exposure: avoiding sex with a prostitute, using a condom during sex and having one steady partner (Neupane and Nichols 2002). Further, among young people who were aware of condoms, 1 in 10 did not know they could be used to protect against pregnancy, including 1 in 6 married young women.

Evidence from other country settings shows that sex education delivered in school can make a positive contribution to children and young people's knowledge and personal and social development, helping to prevent negative health outcomes such as unintended pregnancies and STIs. It contributes to preparing pupils for the opportunities, responsibilities and experiences of adult life and, when linked to confidential sexual health services, is shown to delay the onset of sexual activity. To achieve sustainable change, however, it is necessary to focus on young people before they become sexually active, before myths become deep-rooted and unsafe patterns of sexual behaviour are established (Kirby 2001; Grunseit and others 1997).

Nepal's education policies over the last 30 years, including the provision of free education up to secondary level, scholarship programmes for girls and the launching of the Education for All campaign, have greatly increased school attendance and raised the educational status of both males and females. In 1998, Nepal had 58,000 trained and 72,000 untrained teachers teaching more than 4.8 million students in 34,000 primary and secondary schools (Nepal 1998). Schools therefore have the potential to act as a key resource in the struggle to achieve optimal sexual health among Nepal's young people.

The present secondary school education curriculum includes health, population and environmental education as a compulsory subject in classes 9 and 10; topics covered include reproductive health, family life education and safe motherhood. Additionally there are two optional cources on health education and population education. Anecdotal evidence suggests, however, that classes, where they are taught, tend to be biomedical in focus, teaching methods tend to be didactic and time allocation is limited. To date, insufficient research has focused on investigating the quality of sexuality education within the school context in Nepal, although some pilot work has been undertaken (Prasai 1999).

In the light of the need to provide high-quality

sex education in schools, the Department for International Development (DFID)-funded Safe Passages to Adulthood programme (based at the University of Southampton, United Kingdom) funded the local non-governmental organization, The Society for Local Integrated Development Nepal (SOLID Nepal) to investigate the challenges facing Nepal in its development of a more comprehensive sex and sexuality education curriculum in secondary schools. Using a combination of qualitative and quantitative research techniques, information was gained on young people's, teachers' and parents' knowledge, experiences and attitudes towards school-based sex education, perceived barriers to improving the curriculum and opportunities for change. This paper presents some of the findings from the questionnaire survey conducted among high school students, in particular, the sections focusing on sources of information and current knowledge of sexual health matters.]

Methodology

The research consisted of a quantitative self-completion questionnaire distributed among young people attending school in classes 8,9 and 10. Section 1 covered basic demographic questions including age, sex, family composition, parental education and employment status, ethnicity, religion and, as measured by provision of household amenities and assets, socio-economic status. Section 2 asked respondents about their current sources of information about sexual and reproductive health and assessed knowledge. Section 3 asked pupils' views and attitudes concerning a series of health and sexuality issues, and section 4 focused on the sex and sexuality education the respondents had received at school, including issues discussed, teaching methods used, quality of teaching, improvements that could be made and other relevant issues. This paper explores factors that influence young people's sexual health knowledge.

Three districts, out of a total of 75 in Nepal, were purposively selected for distribution of the questionnaire; Dhading, Morang and Lalitpur. The sites were selected to represent regions of differential development, urban, semi-urban and rural settings and cultural and ethnic diversity.

Dhading district is located in the Central Development Region of Nepal and borders China. The district consists of remote communities with limited access to electricity and telephones. Road access is poor with the only motorable road linking the district headquarters with Kathmandu being five hours' drive away. Morang district is located in the Terai in the Eastern Development Region bordering India. Electricity and telephones are available here, although not comprehensively. Finally, Lalitpur is the second biggest city of Nepal and located within the Kathmandu Valley. It is located in the Central Development Region and is one of the most urbanized cities. Communication facilities are extensive and include national and international television, fax, telex and the Internet. Residents in Lalitpur are widely exposed to the tourist trade and the district has a diverse cultural mix.

Owing to political, access and communication barriers it was not possible to undertake a fully random sample of schools in the selected areas. Therefore, purposive sampling techniques were employed. Suitable high school educational establishments in the three sites were contacted by the research team and invited to participate in the research. From those who agreed, three schools in Lalitpur, two in Morang and one in Dhading were chosen and issued with questionnaires to be distributed among pupils in the target classes. The final selection of schools was proportionate to the number of secondary schools in each district and all, except one in Lalitpur, were government-run[3].

The questionnaires were based on an appropriately adapted version of a questionnaire previously used in another country context to examine quality of sex education. Following pre-testing, 1,200 questionnaires were distributed in the six educational establishments. After obtaining written consent and giving oral instructions on how to complete the questionnaire, forms were filled in under the supervision of a researcher in examination conditions. The respondents were provided with a pen and an envelope in which to seal their answers and a post-box was used for collection to maintain confidentiality and anonymity. The questionnaires were in both the English and Nepali languages.

Testing of sexual health knowledge

Section 2 of the questionnaire explored young people's knowledge of sexual health matters through the use of 16 true/false statements. The statements fell into four categories; reproductive health, STIs and HIV/ AIDS, myths and contraception.

The five statements in the reproductive health category were "It is possible for a women to get pregnant before she has her first period", "There are times in a woman's menstrual cycle when she has a greater chance of becoming pregnant", "A women will not get pregnant if she has sex standing up", "Sexual intercourse whilst pregnant harms the foetus", and "A girl's hymen doesn't tear without sexual intercourse."

The five statements categorized as STIs and HIV/ AIDS were "If used properly condoms can protect against HIV", transmission. A person who looks strong and healthy can have HIV "A person can get AIDS through mosquito, flea and bedbug bites", "There are diseases caught by having sex that can cause a woman to be unable to have a baby" and "A person with an STI can sometimes show no symptoms".

Two statements featured in the mythical grouping, "Masturbation causes serious damage to health" and "A man needs to have sex regularly to maintain his masculinity". Finally, four statements were grouped under the heading of contraception: "The contraceptive pill works just as well even if the women has been sick or had diarrhoea", "Men can have a contraceptive injection (birth control injection) every couple of months to prevent getting a woman pregnant", "Condoms can be used more than once" and "Condoms should not be removed from the penis whilst it is still stiff/hard".

Analytic techniques

The responses of the young men and women to each of the individual 16 knowledge statements were examined and differences between the two sexes identified. Those giving a response of "don't know" were not excluded from the analyses but coded as giving an incorrect answer. Each respondent was allocated four knowledge scores dependent on how many questions they correctly answered in each of the categories, a score of 0 for every incorrect answer, and of 1 for each correct one.

Binary logistic regressions, one for males and one for females, were then fitted to the data to identify the significant factors predictive of correct knowledge. The models were built using both forward and backward conditional stepwise selection procedures; factors were added below the 5 per cent significance level and removed once they became insignificant above that level. Interactions between the variables were also tested for.

Results

Description of the sample

The six educational sites yielded a total of 1,059 completed questionnaires (88 per cent completion rate), 55 per cent of which were returned by young men. Selected demographic characteristics of the sample are displayed in table 1. The results displayed in table 2 illustrate the vast differentials in access to modern amenities experienced by the respondents in the purposively selected three districts (a consequence of the sampling strategy employed). In Dhading, no respondents reported having electricity in their homes, compared with 53 and almost 100 per cent of respondents in Morang and Lalitpur respectively. Table 2 also highlights the differences between the three districts in the educational status of pupils' parents. In both Dhading and Morang, approximately two thirds of mothers were illiterate and, among women who had received some schooling, very few had attended beyond primary school. In Lalitpur, though, just over 40 per cent of mothers had continued education after obtaining their school leaving certificates (SLC). Among fathers, education attainment was at a similar low level in Dhading and Morang, whereas in Lalitpur a much greater proportion of fathers had attained a qualification beyond SLC.

Table 1. Percentage distribution of respondents by selected demographic characteristics

Variable	Grouping	Percentage	N
Sex	Male	54.8	580
	Female	45.2	479
School class	8	11.1	118
	9	52.6	557
	10	36.3	384
Age	14 and under	16.6	176
	15	27.3	289

	16	32.7	346
	17	12.6	133
	18 and above	10.9	115
District	Dhading	17.3	183
	Morang	31.4	333
	Lalitpur	51.3	543
Ethnicity	Brahmin/Chhetri	42.6	451
	Newar	23.5	249
	Rai/Limbu/Sunuwar	10.7	113
	Others	23.2	246
Religion	Hindu	88.7	939
	Buddhist	7.4	78
	Others	2.8	30
	No religion	1.1	12

Table 2. Per entage distribution of respondents by selected socio-economic educational indicators

Indicators	Dhading	Morang	Lalitpur
Socio-economic:			
Drinking water	91.3	91.9	96.1
Electricity	0.0	52.6	99.6
Radio	89.7	62.5	98.9
Freezer	0.0	9.3	76.2
Motorbike	0.0	8.4	52.5
Car	0.0	1.8	22.8
Telephone	0.0	3.9	80.7
Computer	0.0	1.5	47.1
Mother's education:			
Illiterate	66.7	67.6	23.9
Informal	19.7	11.1	7.0
Primary	9.3	14.7	6.3
Some secondary	1.6	5.1	5.3
SLC	0.5	1.5	16.2
Above SLC	2.2	0.0	41.3
Father's education:			
Illiterate	33.3	33.3	9.0
Informal	18.6	9.3	6.8
Primary	27.9	28.2	8.5
Some secondary	7.7	15.0	3.7
SLC	4.9	9.6	7.9
Above SLC	7.7	4.5	64.1

Sources of information

All respondents were asked in the questionnaire who or what were their main sources of information regarding reproductive health (i.e., reproductive system, menstruation, pregnancy, contraception) and HIV/AIDS and other STIs. As issues stated in table 3, the most important sources of information for young people concerning general reproductive health issues were teachers, books, radio and television. Roughly half of the respondents also reported friends of the same sex and health workers as important sources, and young women frequently cited their mother and sister(s) as key resources for reproductive health knowledge.

The main difference found between young people's sources of information concerning reproductive health and STIs and HIV/AIDS was the role of the immediate family (see tables 3 and 4). Although mothers of young women appeared to be a central source regarding reproductive health knowledge, they did not appear to play such an important role in the provision of information on HIV/AIDs and STIs, for which fathers seemed to perform a somewhat increased role.

Table 3. Percentage of young men and women reporting various sources of information regarding reproductive health (reproductive system, menstruation, pregnancy, contraception)

Indicators	Male	Female	
Mother	15.7	61.9	***
Father	18.8	12.3	*
Brother (s)	16.0	8.4	***
Sister (s)	6.8	40.7	***
Other family members	13.8	17.8	
Grandparents	9.0	15.0	*
Friends of the same sex	49.2	54.0	
Friends of the opposite sex	12.7	7.9	*
Teachers	79.4	79.5	

Health workers	49.7	50.0
Television	50.6	55.8
Cinema	34.1	31.5
Radio	66.5	64.6
Books/magazines	65.4	68.2

*p<0.05 **p<0.01 ***p<0.000

Variations between the three districts in young people's sources were investigated, with a number of significant differences being found. Young people whose homes were supplied with electricity were more likely to cite radio and television as major sources, as would be expected. Further, young women in Lalitpur were significantly more likely to report their mothers as a source of information regarding reproductive health issues (69 per cent) than their counterparts in the other two districts (Dhading:60 per cent, Morang: 44 per cent); possibly owing in part to the concentration of more highly educated mothers in Lalitpur district.

Delivery of sex education in school

Section four of the questionnaire focused on pupils' experiences of the sex and sexuality education they had received at school. To monitor which subjects were actually being covered during sex education classes, the pupils were presented with a list of 11 topics and asked if they had received instruction on each. As shown in the figure over three quarters of the pupils in class 10 said they had definitely received instruction about the physical and mental changes which occur during puberty, the reproductive systems of both men and women, the menstrual cycle, HIV/AIDS and STIs. However, just over a third reported having been taught how to protect themselves from pregnancy (contraception) and under five per cent reported having been taught about relationships.

As expected, satisfaction with the issues covered increased significantly as pupils progressed through the school system. Only 15 per cent of pupils sampled in class 8 felt that their health education classes had covered all the sexual health issues they wanted to know about, compared with 28 per cent in class 9 and 40 per cent in class 10. Furthermore, variation was evident between the pupils in each of the six schools. In class 10, students' satisfaction in the different schools ranged from a high of 51 to low of 30 per cent.

Fig. Percentage of respondents in class 10 reporting having received teaching on selected sex education topics at school

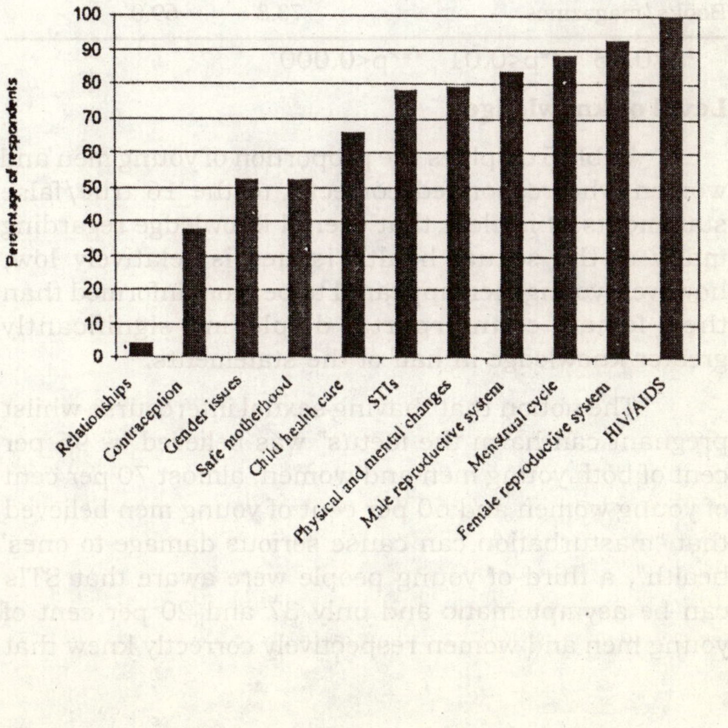

Table 4. Percentage of young men and women reporting various sources of information regarding STIs and HIV/AIDS

Indicators	Male	Female	
Mother	8.7	29.9	***
Father	11.9	21.4	***
Brother (s)	17.0	11.3	*
Sister (s)	7.1	32.3	***
Other family members	15.6	19.2	
Grandparents	7.3	13.7	*
Friends of the same sex	46.1	44.1	
Friends of the opposite sex	14.6	8.6	*
Teachers	83.1	77.4	*
Health workers	55.0	56.7	
Television	58.6	62.7	
Cinema	42.9	41.4	
Radio	69.9	68.4	
Books/magazines	73.8	69.0	

*p<0.05 **p<0.01 ***p<0.000

Level of knowledge

Table 5 displays the proportion of young men and women who responded correctly to the 16 true/false statements. It is clear that overall knowledge regarding many of the sexual health issues is relatively low; however, young men appeared to be more informed than their female counterparts, displaying significantly greater knowledge in half of the statements.

The notion that "having sexual intercourse whilst pregnant can harm the foetus" was believed by 95 per cent of both young men and women, almost 70 per cent of young women and 60 per cent of young men believed that "masturbation can cause serious damage to ones' health", a third of young people were aware that STIs can be asymptomatic and only 37 and 20 per cent of young men and women respectively correctly knew that condoms need to be removed from the penis while it is still hard.

Greatest knowledge existed with regard to HIV/ AIDS. For example, 73 per cent of men and 60 per cent of women correctly knew that condoms could be used to protect against HIV infection and 71 and 73 per cent of young men and women respectively were aware that "individuals carrying the infection can look strong and healthy".

Table 5. Percentage of respondents correctly responding to each true/false knowldege statement

Knowledge statement		Male	Female	
Reproductive health				
There is the possibility that a woman can get pregnant before she has had her first period.	True	7.2	4.4	*
A woman will not get pregnant if she has sex standing up	False	21.0	14.4	*
There are times during a women's menstrual cycle when she has a greater chance of becoming pregnant if she has sex.	True	50.7	39.5	***
A girl's hymen doesn't tear without sexual intercourse	False	36.0	39.5	
Sexual intercourse whilst pregnant harms the foetus	False	5.0	5.0	
STIs and HIV/AIDS				
If used properly condoms can protect against HIV transmission	True	73.4	60.1	***
There are diseases caught by having sex that can cause a woman to be unable to have a baby	True	58.8	53.4	
A person who looks strong and healthy can have HIV	True	71	72.7	
A person can get AIDS through mosquito, flea or bedbug bites	False	41.9	45.1	
A person with an STI can sometimes show no symptoms	True	31.7	36.3	
Myths				
Masturbation causes serious damage to health	False	40.7	30.5	**
A man needs to have sex regularly to mâintain his masculinity	False	39	43.2	
Contraception				
The contraceptive pill works just as well even if the woman has been sick or had diarrhoea	False	22.4	23.2	
Men can have a contraceptive injection (birth control injection) every couple of months to prevent getting a woman pregnant	False	27.9	20.0	**
Condoms can be used more than once	False	57.8	47.6	**
Condoms should not be removed from the penis while it is Still hard/stiff	False	37.1	20.2	***

*p<0.05 **p<0.01 ***p<0.000

Table 6. Mean scores for each knowledge category by gender and school site

School Site	Reproductive health (0-5)	STIs and HIV/AIDs (0-5)	Myths (0-2)	Contraception (0-4)
Males				
Dhading (1)	0.77	1.99	0.95	1.59
Morang (1)	1.39	2.84	0.66	1.34
Morang (2)	1.22	2.61	0.63	1.54
Lalitpur (1)	1.30	3.41	0.90	1.34
Lalitpur (2)	1.11	2.26	0.82	1.56
Lalitpur (3)	1.38	3.32	0.89	1.45
Sig	0.000	0.000	0.001	0.317
Famales				
Dhading (1)	0.71	1.71	0.86	1.06
Morang (1)	1.36	2.12	0.51	1.05
Morang (2)	1.53	2.47	0.43	1.40
Lalitpur (1)	0.96	3.44	0.79	1.07
Lalitpur (2)	0.97	1.79	0.79	1.24
Lalitpur (3)	1.09	3.44	0.78	1.09
Sig	0.000	0.000	0.003	0.556

Table 6 displays the school-level mean scores for both men and women in each of the four knowledge categories. As shown, significant differences in knowledge between the six sites were apparent for all topics except that of contraceptive knowledge.

The maximum possible knowledge score in the reproductive health category was 5. No pupil received full marks and only eight pupils correctly answered four out of the five questions; 64 per cent of young men and 73 per cent of women scored less than two. General knowledge regarding contraception was also found to be low, with only 3 and 2 per cent of men and women, respectively, correctly answering all four questions as compared with 19 and 34 per cent respectively not getting any of the answers correct. More encouraging were the scores for STI and HIV/AIDS knowledge. Overall, 9 per cent of men and women correctly answered all five questions and only 15 per cent of men and 20 per cent of women scored less than two.

Determinants of knowledge

It would appear that success, to a certain degree, has been achieved in the delivery of health messages concerning HIV/AIDS, the statements "individuals with HIV/AIDS can look strong and healthy" and "when used properly condoms can protect against HIV" (the two highest-scoring statements) were therefore selected as dependent variables in the logistic regressions performed to identify factors associated with increased knowledge.

When used properly condoms can protect against HIV

Factors found to be predictive of young people's knowledge concerning the use of condoms to protect against HIV are displayed in table 7. As shown, young men who live in Morang have a little over seven times the odds of knowing that condoms protect against HIV as young men who live in Dhading district; likewise, young men in Lalitpur have 1.8 times the odds. Similar findings are evident among the young women, where odds are increased by about 21 and 6 times in Morang and Lalitpur, respectively. As a young person progresses through the school system, knowledge is found to increase significantly. Young men and women in class 10 are 3.1 and over 10 times, respectively, as likely to have correct knowledge about condoms than their peers in class 8, after controlling for all other factors. School type also appears to impact on levels of knowledge. Students attending the privately run school were found to have up to 3 times the odds of correct knowledge as similar students attending State-run establishments.

Other factors found to be significant in the male model included the cited sources of information regarding HIV and topics covered during sex education classes delivered at school. As illustrated in table 7, young men who reported their brothers, television and magazines/books as main sources of information on

HIV/AIDS were roughly 2 to 3 times as likely in each case to correctly know that condoms can protect against HIV is used properly as those who did not cite each as sources. Finally, young men who had received basic sex education at school (the physical and mental changes that occur at puberty, the male reproductive system and safe motherhood) had significantly greater odds of knowldege than those who had not attended classes, after all other factors had been controlled for.

Additional significant knowledge predictors in the female model included religion, father's educational level, sex education received at school, and television and books as main sources of HIV/AIDS information.

Table 7. Odds ratios from logistic regression analyses predicting the effects of various characteristics on the likelihood of correct knowledge

Characteristic		Odds ratio	
Men			
District	Dhading	1.00	
	Morang	7.42	***
	Lalitput	1.79	
Class	8	1.00	
	9	1.87	
	10	3.14	**
Source of HIv information	Brother	3.05	*
	Television	2.33	**
	Books/magazines	2.29	**
Sex educationreceived	Physical and mental change	2.04	*
	Male reproductive system	2.57	**
	Safe motherhood	2.44	**
Type of school	Public	1.00	
	Private	2.47	*
Constant		0.03	
Df		11	
-2 Log likelihood		469.70	
Woman			
District	Dhading	1.00	
	Morang	21.26	***
	Lalitpur	5.82	***
Class	8	1.00	
	9	5.79	**
	10	10.19	**
Religion	Non-Hindu	1.00	
	Hindu	0.33	*
Father's education	Illiterate	1.00	

	Primary/Informal	2.92	*
	Secondary/SLC	1.32	
	Above SLC	3.98	**
Source of HIV information	Television	1.98	*
	Books/magazines	3.49	***
Sex education received	Physicial and mental changes	5.39	***
	The menstrual cycle	0.32	*
type of school	Public	1.00	
	Private	2.94	*
Constant		0.007	***
Df		13	
-2 Log likelihood		355.54	

*p<0.05 **p<0.01 ***p<0.000

Young women who practised Hinduism were significantly less likely to respond with the correct answer and, after controlling for all other factors, young women with more educated fathers were more likely to respond correctly. For example, women whose fathers were educated above SLC level had almost 4 times the odds of being correct as those with illiterate fathers.

The sources of information which were found to significantly impact on knowledge among young women concerning the use of condoms as a protection against HIV included television and magazines/books, which increased the odds by 2.0 and 3.5 times respectively. As with young men, young women who reported basic sex education teaching at school (physical and mental changes at puberty) were significantly more likely to have correct knowledge; however, after controlling for all other factors, young women who had received teaching on the menstrual cycle were 68 per cent less likely to respond correctly (although this finding was only just significant at the 5 per cent level).

People who have HIV/AIDS can look strong and healthy

Factors found to be predictive of young men's and women's knowledge concerning the appearance of individuals infected with HIV are displayed in table 8.

Father's level of education appeared to be a

significant predictor of correct knowledge among the young men sampled. For example, young men whose fathers were educated to degree standard had 2.3 times the odds of providing a correct response as young men who had illiterate fathers. Furthermore, young men who reported books and television as a main source of information regarding HIV/AIDS had roughly twice the odds of knowing that people infected with HIV can look strong and healthy as those not accessing such sources. Young men who rely on teachers as an informative source were, however, found to be significantly less likely to respond correctly.

Having received basic sex education at school (physical and mental changes during puberty and the male reproductive system) was also found to be significantly associated with odds of correct knowledge; however, unlike the previous model, receiving safe motherhood education at school this time decreased the odds by 43 per cent, after controlling for all other factors.

Table 8. Odds ratios from logistic regression analyses predicting the effects of various characteristics on the likelihood of correct knowledge regarding the healthy appearance of individuals infected with HIV

Characteristics		Odds ratio	
Man			
Father's education	Illiterate	1.00	
	Primary/Informal	0.80	
	Secondary/SLC	2.80	**
	Above SLC	2.31	**
Source of HIV Information	Teachers	0.55	*
	Television	2.22	**
	Books/magazines	2.39	***
Sex education received	Physical and mental changes	1.71	*
	Male reproductive system	2.51	**
	Safe motherhood	0.57	**
constant		0.50	
Df		9	
-2 log likelihood		602.15	
Women			
Mother's education	Illiterate	1.00	
	Primary/informal	1.06	
	Secondary/SLC	5.49	**

	Above SLC	2.16	(10%)
Source of HIV information	Books/magazine	2.43	***
Sex education received	Male reproductive system	1.89	*
	Relationships	4.13	*
Number of amenities/	0-2	1.00	
Household assets	3-5	0.92	
	6-7	2.90	**
	8-10	1.90	(10%)
Constant		0.44	
Df		9	
-2 Log likelihood		458.13	

*p<0.05 **p<0.01 ***p<0.000

Among the young women, mothers' education appeared to be a good predictor of knowledge; young women whose mothers had completed secondary education or higher had significantly raised odds of correct knowledge. The use of written literature as a source of HIV/AIDS information provided young women with significantly increased knowledge, and young women who reported receiving some basic sex education including the teaching of male reproductive system and the role of relationships were roughly 2 and 4 times as likely to know that HIV-infected individuals can look healthy as similar young women not receiving such instruction. Finally, level of social-economic deprivation, as measured by the number of amenities in the household, significantly impacted on the likelihood that a young women knew that people with HIV can look strong and healthy, with young women living in more affluent households displaying greater awareness.

Discussion

In the context of a global decline in age of sexual maturation and rising age of marriage, the window of opportunity for young people to engage in premarital sexual relations is opening. Social taboos and inhibitions have in the past limited the study of Nepalese young people's sexual knowledge, attitudes and behaviour, however, with the advent of HIV/AIDS and increasing prevalence of STIs there has been a realization of the need to provide young people with information and skills to reduce their vulnerability to negative sexual health outcomes.

The results presented here are from a sex and sexuality education survey distributed among young people at secondary school. It forms part of a much larger study looking at the barriers and opportunities to developing a more comprehensive sex education curriculum. It is recognized that the analyses are based on a relatively small proportion of young people in Nepal and include only those attending school. Also, the purposive sampling techniques employed mean that the final respondent sample is not truly representative of all young people in school classes 8, 9 and 10. Nevertheless, the results highlight several key issues which merit further attention and have a direct bearing on health promotion and school curriculum development activities.

With regard to young people's sources of information about sexual health issues, the results from this study clearly show that schools play an important role in informing young people about sexual health matters. However, on examination of the topics that are being covered in class, it is apparent that the more easily taught, less challenging, factual and biological issues are fairly consistently being covered, whereas the broader issues such as feelings and relationships are often being overlooked. Although it is crucial that young people be given the basic facts on such things as the male and female reproductive systems, the menstrual cycle, HIV/AIDS and methods of contraception, unless these are provided in conjunction with the skills training to enable young people to communicate their wishes and desires effectively, it is unlikely that the knowledge gained will lead to effective behaviour change.

This study found in-depth knowldege regarding many sexual health issues to be low among both young men and young women in Nepal, with the exception of particular knowledge concerning HIV/AIDS. Although young men appear to be better informed than young women, myths about masturbation and virility remain widespread and detailed knowledge regarding contraception remains sparse.

The results of the modelling, which attempts to identify factors predictive of HIV/AIDS knowledge, show that awareness regarding the use of condoms to avoid exposure to HIV infection improves as pupils move up through the school classes; however, clear disparities are evident between the districts and schools sampled. Young people living in the most remote district, Dhading, with little access to modern media, have significantly reduced levels of knowledge, compared with young people living in the more developed districts of Morang and Lalitpur, after controlling for all other factors. Furthermore, pupils, and in particular female students, in Morang district, appeared to be better informed than their counterparts in Lalitpur. This unexpected outcome, given the relative levels of social deprivation and modernization in the two districts, could possibly be explained by the presence of a Healthy Schools Programme in Morang, run by PLAN International. Although the initiative is not being implemented in the specific schools included in this particular study, the information that is being provided by the programme could possibly be filtering into the wider community and thereby increasing overall knowledge.

Parental education, rather than district of residence, was found to be a much greater predictor of knowledge regarding the healthy appearance of individuals infected with HIV. This finding could purely be a reflection of the differential levels of development in the three regions; alternatively, it might be that more educated parents, having greater awareness of the impact that HIV can have on an individual's health, subsequently transfer correct knowledge to their children.

In all the models, the detrimental effect of social deprivation on young people's level of knowledge is highly evident along with the positive impact that exposure to visual media messages and access to informative sources of literature can have. In every instance, young people who cite television and magazines/books as main sources of information of HIV have substantially increased odds of correct knowledge. Finally, but by no means least, young people who have received basic sex education at school are, in general, better informed as a result, even after controlling for all other factors including age, district, social deprivation and exposure to media.

Although this research, on which further work is required, leaves a number of key questions unanswered, it is clear that if the desired shift in behaviour to reduce HIV/AIDS and STI prevalence and the number of unwanted pregnancies is to be achieved, we need to take a multifarious approach to delivering knowledge to tackle the issues. Appropriately designed and relevant educational activities need to be targeted, not only at young people, but also at the parents and elderly persons from whom they seek information and guidance. The results of this study would indicate that media messages delivered via visual means are effective; however, many people in Nepal do not have access to such amenities so alternative means of transferring messages need to be explored. Since many people are also illiterate, this is not a simple task.

Although Nepal has incorporated sex and

sexuality education into its national curriculum, it is still very much in its infancy and requires further monitoring and evaluation. Nevertheless, given the relatively short period of time that the programme has been running, the results presented here clearly show the potential that schools have to contribute to improved learning about sexual and reproductive health matters. Detailed and comprehensive knowledge among many young people, and in particular young women, appears to be remain low, emphasizing the need for further curriculum and teacher training material development with a shift away from superficial biological coverage towards a more inclusive programme.

Endnotes

1. Age and sex distribution unspecified.

2. Classes are organized by level of ability not by age; however, ages of the sample ranged from a low of 12 to a high of 22 with 87 per cent aged between 14 and 17 years.

3. All schools, whether government-run or private, are obliged to cover the same curriculum.

4. Factors tested in the model included: district, school site and type, age, class, ethnicity/caste, religion, importance of religion, sources of HIV/AIDS information, topics covered during school sex education classes, highest educational level of mother and father, and level of socio-economic deprivation.

5. Each of these 11 topics are listed in the curriculum handbook.

6. A child-focused, non-profit developmental organization aiding deprived children in developing countries.

References

Aryal, R. H. and D. Nichols (2002). *Birth Planning among Urban Youth in Nepal: Awareness, Knowledge, Perceptions and Practice,* NAYA report series No. 13 (Kathmandu, Family Health International).

Dahal, G. P. (1999). "An insight on the recommendations of the ICPD Programme of Action: emerging challenges to implement reproductive health policy in Nepal", *FPAN Journal of Reproductive Health,* vol. 1, No. 1, pp. 32-44.

Furber, A. S., J. N. Newell and M. M. Lubben (2002). "A systematic review of current knowledge of HIV epidemiology and of sexual behaviour in Nepal", *Tropical Medicine and International Health,* vol. 7, No. 2, pp. 140-148.

Grunseit, A. and others (1997). "Sexuality education and young people's sexual behavior: a review of studies", *Journal of Adolescent Research,* vol. 12, No. 4, pp. 421-453.

Khanal, H. (1999). "Adolescent reproductive health in Nepal", *FPAN Journal of Reproductive Health,* vol. 1, No. 1, pp. 45-53.

Kirby, D. (2001). *Emerging Answers: Research Findings on Programs to Reduce Teen Pregnancy* (Washington, National Campaign to Prevent Teenage Pregnancy).

Limbu, R. (2001). "Nepal: let's talk about sex", Inter Press Service, 12 October.

Mehta, S. (1998). Responsible Sexual and Reproductive Health Behaviour among Adolescents (United Nations Population Fund).

Nepal (1998). Ministry of Education, Department of

Education

Nepal Demographic and Health Survey (NDHS) (1996).Demographic and Health Surveys STATcomplier [online].Measure DHS+. Available from: <*http://www.measuredhs.com*>.

(2001). Demographic and Health Surveys STAT complier [online]. Measure DHS+. Available from : <http://www.measuredhs.com>.

Neupane, S. and D. Nichols (2002). *HIV/AIDS and Other Sexually Transmitted Infections in Nepal: Knowledge and Beliefs among Urban Youth*, NAYA report series No. 14 (Kathmandu, Family Health Interrnational).

Pradhan, A., and others (1997). *Nepal Family Health Survey 1996* (Kathmandu and Calverton, Maryland, Ministry of Health of Nepal, New ERA and Macro International Inc.).

Prasai, D. P. (1999). "Effectiveness of sexuality education program in Palpa district of Nepal", *FPAN Journal of Reproductive Health*, vol. 1, No. 1, pp. 6-12.

Puri, M. (2002). *Sexual Risk Behaviour and Risk Perception of Unwanted Pregnancy and Sexually Transmitted Infection among Young Factory Workers in Nepal* (Kathmandu, Centre for Research on Environment Health and Population Activities).

Tamang, A., and others (2001). "Sexual behaviour and risk perceptions among young men in border towns of Nepal", *Asia-Pacific Population Journal*, vol. 16, No. 21, June 2001, pp. 195-210.

UNFPA (1996). *Reproductive Tract Infections including STDs and HIV/AIDS in Nepal* (Kathmandu, UNFPA).

12

Reproductive Health Including Family Planning

Despite occasional efforts to reverse the consensus articulated in the Programme of Action of the International Conference on Population and Development (ICPD), for almost a decade the recommendations contained in this Programme of Action have provided the guiding framework for expanding and reorienting reproductive health programmes in the Asian and Pacific region. Reproductive health in the above-mentioned Programme is defined as "a state of complete physical, mental and social well-being and not merely the absence of disease or infirmity, in all matters relating to the reproductive system and to its functions and processes" (para 7.2). Reproductive health services are viewed as a basic right through which women and men can express their reproductive choices.

The High-level Meeting to Review the Implementation of the Programme of Action of the International Conference on Population and

Development and the Bali Declaration on Population and Sustainable Development and to Make Recommendations for Further Action, which was held at Bangkok in 1998, highlighted the progress that many countries in the region had made in integrating family planning with other reproductive health services and improving the quality of care provided in their family planning programmes. However, the Meeting also noted that major obstacles remained in implementing the recommendations contained in the Programme of Action. Some of the obstacles related to the capacity of the service system to provide expanded services, some to cultural barriers, particularly those related to gender inequality, that limited the reproductive health options of women and some to weak government commitment. The Meeting made a number of recommendations that were designed to manifest further commitment to the ICPD goals and remove obstacles to attaining the goals (ESCAP 1998).

In Asia, there has been continuing debate over the role of national family planning programmes in reproductive health programmes. While national family programmes have undoubtedly contributed to rapidly declining fertility in many Asian countries through allowing couples to achieve their desired family size, the very success of the programmes has resulted in a diminishing interest in using public moneys to fund them. However, the changes in orientation towards family planning and reproductive health that have existed since the late 1980s and that were legitimated by ICPD have provided family planning programmes with new roles and a new purpose.

In this paper several issues are examined. In the first section of the paper, the author summarizes selected aspects of family planning programmes in the region. In the second section, the linkage between family planning and other aspects of reproductive health are examined. The third section of the paper focuses on quality-of-care issues related to reproductive health, while in the final section of the paper new roles for reproductive health programmes are examined.

Family planning programmes in the Asian and Pacific region

Caldwell and others (2002) state that the twenty-first century started with "the greatest number of national family planning programs in position that had ever existed". Asian countries have been leaders in the establishment of family planning programmes and despite the remarkable fertility declines that occurred in most of East and South-East Asia over the preceding decades, the number of programmes continues to grow rather than diminish.

Table 1. Percentage of currently married women aged 15-49 using contraceptives by type of method: nine selected populous countries

Country and year	percentage using contraceptive method			
	Any method	Sterillization	Any modern temporary method	any traditional method
China, 1997	84	41	42	1
India, 1998/99	48	36	7	5
Indonesia, 1997	57	3	51	3
Pakistan, 1995/95	18	5	8	5
Bangladesh, 1999/2000	54	7	36	10
Viet Nam, 1994	65	4	39	21
Philippines, 1998	47	10	18	18
Iran (Islamic Republic of), 1992	65	9	37	20
Thailand, 1993	74	23	50	2

Source : East-West center (2002).

For the entire Asian region, by the year 2000 the total fertility rate (TFR) had dropped to levels that are intermediate between 2 and 3. Well over one half of currently married women in reproductive ages were using contraception, and population growth had slowed appreciably. These changes have been facilitated by the presence of national family planning programmes in most of the countries of the region. There remains, however, significant diversity in the levels and methods of contraceptive use among countries in the region.

In table 1, the contraceptive prevalence rates for nine populous countries in Asia are shown. In several of the countries approximately two thirds or more of currently married reproductive-aged women were using contraceptives. For Pakistan the contraceptive prevalence rate was below 20 per cent. In India there is a particularly high reliance on sterilization, while in countries such as Indonesia and Viet Nam sterilization comprises a small proportion of methods used. Meanwhile, in other countries, traditional methods, primarily the calendar method and withdrawal, contribute a large proportion to overall levels of contraceptive use.

Many of the differences among countries in the levels of contraceptive use and contraceptive method mix can be linked to the evolution of national family planning programmes in the region. Jones and Leete (2002) characterize the 1970s as the "heyday of family planning programmes in Asia." It was during this decade that many countries established their family planning programmes in a context of growing international and domestic concern over the need to reduce fertility. International funding was available for family planning programmes, and a focus on the measurable outcome of achieving targeted lower levels of population growth helped motivate programmes.

The emphasis on achieving fertility decline resulted in family planning programmes in several countries, particularly in South Asia, focusing on permanent methods. Pakistan, a country with a long-established family planning programme, has had difficulty in achieving political support and commitment and this is reflected in low levels of use, and a relatively high proportion of use consisting of non-modern methods. The Philippines is another country where political commitment to family planning has waxed and waned and where the use of non-modern methods is high. In Viet Nam, political commitment to family planning has not been a problem. However, despite recent efforts to broaden contraceptive choice and improve quality of care, it appears that concerns about the quality of services have contributed to relatively high levels of use of non-modern contraceptives.

In many countries with newly established programmes, success was quick in coming. In Thailand, TFR, which had already been declining before the national family planning programme commenced in 1970, declined from over 6 during the latter half of the 1960s to below 4 by the end of the 1970s. Although fertility decline in Thailand has been ascribed to a number of factors (Knodel and others 1987), the flexible approach of the family planning programme and its willingness to respond to interventions successfully piloted by an active non-governmental organizational (NGO) community, helped to facilitate the decline.

Harbison and Robinson (2002) argue that the main reason for the success of family planning programmes in reducing fertility was that they were able to convince the public of the benefits of a small family. In turn, other societal forces contributing to the ideational change favouring fewer children helped to contribute to some family planning programmes being considered as very successful. This argument implies that where family programmes have been able to cater for the emerging needs of women for effective contraception, and where they have in some way been able to help to legitimize those needs, programmes have been successful in attaining the policy objective of lower fertility. The extent to which reproductive health programmes, including family planning, can address the reproductive health needs of women and men will continue to determine their success.

The role of family planning in reproductive health

The centrality of family planning to reproductive health in the post-Cairo era has been reiterated in several international population forums (Khan and others 1998). The provision of quality family planning services provides couples with the ability to choose the timing and number of children they will have. Family planning services undertaken in isolation from other aspects of reproductive health weaken the commitment to providing couples, and particularly women, with the full range of reproductive health services that they require to lead healthy lives. Family planning is a crucial aspect of services since it provides couples with the ability to make choices about their reproductive goals and it is these choices that have implications for health. In much of the region, family planning programmes are the primary organizational structure for implementing policies designed to affect non-contraceptive aspects of reproductive health, so the role of family planning programmes must be recognized and adapted to help to solve reproductive health concerns. Finally, and a fact not recognized by many family planning programmes, women themselves make a link between family planning and their reproductive health. Often this is in terms of the perceived health risk that they feel they will be exposed to if they adopt family planning.

Family planning and mortality reduction

The links between family planning and infant and child mortality are now well established, even if the magnitude of the effect continues to be debated. Over the past decade a number of studies in several Asian countries have demonstrated how the use of contraception, resulting in few children and longer spacing between children, has contributed to improved maternal and child health (Greenspan 1993: Luther and others 1999: Miller and others 1992: Popkin and others 1993). There are a series of interrelated factors that affect the probability of an infant dying. The shorter the interval between births, the higher the parity of the child, and births occuring at the extremes of a women's reproductive career are all associated with higher probabilities of infant deaths. Estimates of the differentials in mortality associated with each of these effects give some indication of the potential for infant mortality decline if contraception was more widely used to space or limit fertility. For example, probabilities of death are up to 2.5 times higher where the birth interval is less than 2 years compared with birth intervals of more than 2 years: the probability of death of an infant or parity 7 or more can be up to 2 times higher than for parities 1 to 3, and women giving birth from age 18 to 34 may be up to 5 per cent less likely to have their infant die compared with mothers aged less than 18, and about 25 per cent less likely compared with mothers aged 35 and over.

Many of the issues that relate infant and child mortality to fertility can also be applied to maternal mortality. Without there being any changes in socio-economic conditions or access to health services, a reduction in fertility would result in a reduction in maternal mortality. This would occur in an absolute sense, with the number of mothers dying declining, and in a relative sense, with the probability of maternal death associated with each birth declining. This latter effect would occur because fertility decline results in a reduction of births occurring to high-risk groups. Based on data from the Matlab in Bangladesh, Fortney (1987) demonstrates that if births at ages of mothers less than

20 and greater than 39 and births of parties greater than 5 were eliminated, the maternal mortality ratio would decrease by 25 per cent while the number of women dying in the age group 15 to 49 would decrease by 56 per cent.

International commitment to Safe Motherhood has increased over the last decade, primarily as a result of the ICPD Programme of Action. There is now a much better appreciation of what are priority interventions and how and where these interventions might be integrated into family planning programmes (Berer and Ravindran 1999).

The indirect effects of family planning on improved morbidity and mortality of mothers and children are harder to document than the direct effects but are probably equally strong. At the societal level, fertility decline can reduce the overall levels of dependency and hence increase the per capita level of resources available for investment in health services for the dependent population. This can also occur at the household level: small families have greater wealth than larger families and hence can devote more resources to improving the health of family members. Access to family planning programmes can also be an entry point for women into the wider healh system. This can lead to better health for women and their families.

A contentious issue that many family planning programmes prefer to avoid is the issue of abortion. Ahman and Shah (2002) estimate that in the year 2000, there were 19 million unsafe abortions and of these, over 50 per cent (10.5 million) occurred in Asia. Unsafe abortion is a major contributor to maternal mortality, with annually over 80,000 deaths of women, the vast majority in developing countries, attributed to unsafe abortions (WHO 1998). The presence of a high level of abortion is one indication of difficulties of women obtaining access to appropriate methods of effective contraception. In many fertility transitions, initial declines in fertility were associated with increases in the incidence of induced abortion. As effective contraception became available, the level of abortion was reduced. In many developing societies, abortion-related deaths are most likely to occur for women in their twenties; therefore, family planning can have a major impct of reducing the risk of maternal mortality at ages where, in the absence of abortion, the risk of materanl mortality is very low. Increases in premarital sexual activity, the difficulty of unmarried women obtaining access to contraception and/or social factors which tend to discourage the use of contraception for the unmarried are also related to increased levels of abortion and attendant mortality risks for young women.

In those areas of the Asian and pacific region where son preference of children is strong, there continues to be the problems of sex-selective abortions (East-West Center 2002). Bairagi(2001), in a study of the effects of son preference in Bangladesh, notes that the effect of son preference of abortion has increased over time and that if foetal sex identification becomes more widely available, the number of abortions of famale foetuses may increase. Other countries in the region where sex-selective abortion has been a concern include China, India and the Republic of Korea. While these countries have combated the problems through legislation banning foetal sex identification, change in the underlying societal values that result in son preference requires more programmatic attention.

Some of the issues not discusssed here, but which deserve fuller treatment, are the effects of family planning on other aspects of a family's life. There is a growing body of evidence that families who limit fertility are able to invest more resources in improving the human capital of their children (better health and education) and in increasing the economic resources of the family. Of course these outcomes are not only a result of the adoption of family planning, but can also be seen as a major motivation for the acceptance of family planning. It is notable that the presence of these relationships is most evident in societies in which the fertility transition is well advanced, suggesting that when couples realize the benefits to their family from limiting fertility, they are quick to practise contraception.

Family planning and reproductive morbidities

In the years leading up to ICPD at Cairo in 1994, evidence emerged of the high levels of reproductive tract infections (RTIs) in developing countries. Bang and others (1989) reported high level of both endogenous RTIs and sexually transmitted infections (STIs) in rural India. Other studies in India have also reported high levels of RTIs (Bhatia and Cleland 1995). Similar results have been reported in other Asian countries such as China and Viet Nam (Kaufman and others 1999; Lein and others 2002).

Since Cairo the provision of RTI/STI services have been seen as an important area of integration with family planning services (Walker 1998). In part this is because methods such as the IUD should not be provided unless it has been determined that the client does not suffer from an RTI. Also, women often see symptoms of RTIs as an outcome of their contraceptive use and hence seek assistance from family planning services when they experience possible RTI symptoms such as vaginal discharge.

The ability of family planning clinics in resource-poor settings to effectively diagnose and treat RTIs requires further investigation. Lien and others (2002), based on their study in Viet Nam, argue that investing in establishing and maintaining diagnostic facilities may not be the most efficient use of resources at the local level. Instead, they provide several alternative options that involve more simplified procedures for diagnosis of RTIs. Kaufman and others (1999) came to similar conclusions based on their study in China. What is clear is that any treatment strategy adopted for RTIs within family planning programmes needs to be based on knowledge of the levels and composition of RTIs within each area.

Even in situations where it is not possible to integrate diagnosis and treatment of RTIs into the operations of family planning programme service delivery points, it is possible to include prevention in programmes. For areas where STIs/HIV are a concern, this could include promotion and distribution of condoms, HIV pre-and post-test counselling and referral. For RTIs, education on recognizing RTIs and appropriate care-seeking behaviour could be provided.

Quality of care in reproductive health services

As part of the demographic argument, and also as a recognition of the human rights and dignity of clients, programmes are now stressing the quality of care provided to clients. It has been shown that where a variety of methods are available, where communication between service provider and client is open and two-way and where service providers are well trained, current users are more likely to continue using contraceptives and to use their chosen method of contraception more effectively. The quality of care framework (Bruce 1990), provides a set of guidelines that programme managers can use to reorient their activities to make them more consistent with the reproductive rights recommendations of the ICPD Programme of Action.

A central component of the Bruce framework is that clients should have a real choice of methods. Ross and others (2002), in a cross-national study, have shown that availability of methods is strongly related to the prevalence of each method and that overall prevalence is related to the overall availability of several methods. Because couples have different contraceptive needs and preferences, and as these needs and preferences vary over their life, a programme should ideally include a range of methods in order to cater for the various inclinations. Where a variety of methods are available to meet the varying needs of clients, one can expect prevalence and client satisfaction to be highest.

Khan, Boon-Ann and Mehta (1998) in their assessment of the quality of care of family planning programmes in the Asian and Pacific region five years after ICPD noted that in many programmes there were a limited number of methods available and that in some programmes where a variety of methods were available, provider biases or method-based incentives reduced choice. While programme managers at the national level have shown clear commitment to broaden effective choice, the understanding of informed choice and indeed the whole concept of quality of care have been shown to be lacking among many providers (Abdullah 1999).

The consequences of a lack of informed choice are low levels of client satisfaction high levels of contraceptive discontinuation and increased numbers of unplanned pregnancies. Johansson and others (1996), in a study of abortion in two villages in Viet Nam, argue that many abortions were related to the limited choice of contraceptives available in the service delivery system. Essentially the only method available was the IUD and many women who had discontinued IUD use because of side effects became pregnant and resorted to abortion.

Informed choice of methods does not simply mean making all methods available. Programmes need to be able to incorporate the new methods into their service delivery system and clients must fully understand the implications of using each method. The inappropriate inclusion of a method into a service delivery system can have adverse impacts on women's health and increase the risk of an unplanned pregnancy. Hull (1998) describes how in an eastern province of Indonesia a lack of knowledge and skill among providers in the removal of contraceptive implants, combined with a related lack of understanding of clients about when removal should occur or even if it should occur, resulted in many women not having the implants removed at the appropriate time.

The difficulties in instituting real informed choice of contraceptive methods is clearly shown in the case of China. China's family planning programme has operated with strict and clearly defined birth limitation rules and within the context of one main method on, the IUD (Attane 2002; Winckler 2002). In the years following ICPD, the Government of China has taken steps to relax some aspects of their programme through promoting aspects of quality-of-care, while retaining population regulations. These steps, which were tentative at first, have now quickened and there are quality of care initiatives in many of the numerous counties in China. One pilot project, designed to introduce informed contraceptive choice, commenced in Deqing county of Zhejiang province in 1995. An assessment of the pilot project in 1998 shows that within the confines of a strict and mandatory policy on the number of births allowed, women are being provided with greater choice of methods and that this results in greater satisfaction for them and has also oriented providers to the importance of women's preferences (Gu and others 2002).

A central component of instituting a client-centred approach to reproductive health services, particularly family planning services, is the removal of targets within family planning programmes. The record of abolition of targets in the family planning programmes of countries in the region is very mixed. Of 25 Asian and Pacific countries and areas responding to an ESCAP questionnaire about their reproductive health programmes in the five years after Cairo, 18 said that their programmes had included quantitative targets and only 4 responded that they had removed those targets after Cairo. India was one of the countries that reported removing programme targets (ESCAP 1998). Murthy and others (2002), based on the results of three case studies in various parts of India, found that experiences varied markedly between their three research sites. In all sites some progress towards eliminating targets was achieved, but the extent of change was limited. Significantly, they note that easing targets did not reduce contraceptive levels and may have resulted in increased use of temporary methods. The findings of this study illustrate the difficulties of changing entrenched practices at lower levels of family planning programmes.

However, attempts are being made within the region to change practices not consistent with the quality-of-care approach. For example, Jain and others (2002) report on a pilot project in the Philippines that used information about the needs of clients, expressed by the clients, to design provider work plans and direct service efforts. This new approach replaced an existing system based primarily on demographic and medical criteria. Unfortunately, this example of a client-centred management approach to providing services is the exception rather than the norm.

Other aspects of quality of care also need to be improved in reproductive health programmes in Asia and the Pacific. Schuler and Hossain (1998), for example, argue that there remain major problems or poor interpersonal communication between providers and clients in the Bangladesh national family planning programme. They recommended that institutional norms, policies and incentives have to follow a client-centred approach if these problems are to be overcome. Koenig and others (2000), in a review of studies that have examined the quality of care under the India Family Welfare Programme, suggest that even though some changes in the Indian Family Welfare Programme were made in 1996 and 1997 to accommodate ICPD recommendations, there has been little improvement at the local level. They state that most studies indicate a lack of concern for client needs and preferences, and that poor women are particularly disadvantaged within the programme in obtaining an appropriate quality of care. Although direct evidence is lacking, they state: "poor quality of care likely has contributed to high levels of foregone, delayed, or discontinued practice of contraception and consequently to unwanted pregnancy among current or potential clients".

Overall there has been progress in improving the quality of care provided in reproductive health programmes in the Asian and Pacific region. However, this progress has been hampered by a lack of understanding and appreciation of the importance of client preferences and by service delivery systems that are resistant to change (Abdullah 1999). Change in reproductive health programmes has been most apparent in improvement in the quality of services rather than in terms of quality of care. A similar conclusion is also made by Hardee and others (1999), who state that the "reproductive rights aspects of Cairo have received far less attention than the health aspects".

Priority roles for family planning programmes

Much of the region, especially areas of South Asia, remains in a situation where birth rates are high, levels of contraceptive use are low, unmet need for family planning is high and childbirth is accompanied by a high risk of death for both the mother and her new-born infant. In these countries, efforts need to be made to ensure that individuals are provided with the means to achieve their desired family sizes within programmes that provide the highest possible quality of care. In these countries, to the extent practicable, other elements of reproductive health should be integrated with family planning.

There are many other developing countries in the region, however, which have made great strides in increasing contraceptive use, lowering birth rates and improving the health of mothers and children. It is situation in this latter group of countries, particularly with regard to the roles of family planning programmes, that is focused upon below.

Serving vulnerable groups

What are the roles that the family planning programmes of these countries should play? Should the structure and funding patterns of the programmes change? Should the programmes exist at all? These questions are being faced by a number of family planning programmes in South-East and East Asia. Jones and Leete (2002) argue that there are two priorities for family planning programmes of countries in the region where fertility has fallen below replacement level. The first is to turn over more of the provision of contraceptive and other reproductive health services to the private sector. Potts and others (1999) argue that shortfalls in expected international and domestic resources for reproductive health services require that much more emphasis be placed on commercial family planning services in developing countries. The role of the Government in this situation would be to ensure that the quality of services is maintained at a high standard and that services to those segments of the population that cannot afford to pay for them are maintained.

Ensuring that vulnerable groups have access to affordable reproductive health services in a context where many programmes are attempting to broaden user fees is a priority issue for Governments. In countries where high priority is placed on family planning, such as China, this can mean that family planning services remain free to all through the government family planning services. In other areas of reproductive health, such as maternal care, where user fees are required, there is increasing concern that many poorer women do not have access to services (IHS 2002). Although many couples in China could undoubtedly afford to pay for family planning services, and indeed many urban women do so, there remains a need to subsidize access to the full range of reproductive health services for poorer women.

There are other population groups that for one reason or another do not have access to reproductive health services. Lack of access may result from social barriers, lack of information, limited physical access, economic difficulties or even discrimination. These groups, which vary from country to country, can include migrants, particularly international migrants, minority groups and slum dwellers. Programmes need to identify the groups that cannot access services and ensure that appropriate services are provided.

In the Bangladesh family planning programme, the change from a field-based to a fixed-site contraceptive delivery system is based, in part, on a desire to reduce the high cost of the family planning programme. Utilizing a fixed-site system would also allow the programme to promote more effective methods such as the IUD and sterilization. Arends-Kuenning (2002) argues, however, that fieldworkers have been most effective at meeting the family planning needs of poor and uneducated women and that removing fieldworkers completely from the family planning programme could affect the contraceptive choices that these women can make.

The issue of the extent to which national family planning programmes need to play a role in providing affordable contraceptives and other reproductive health services came forcefully to the fore during the recent "economic crisis" that affected South-East Asia and parts of East Asia. The crisis raised fears that large segments of the population might not be able to obtain contraception in those countries, such as Thailand, where increasing proportions of women had begun to access contraception through the private sector. Prachuabmoh and Mithranon (2002) report on the results of a pilot study in Thailand that indicate that although overall the crisis appeared to have little impact on the use of contraception, those women most affected by the crisis were the most likely to report that they would abort if they became pregnant. These results suggest that in a context such as that of Thailand, where low-fertility preferences have become so entrenched, contraceptives are seen as a priority good and will be purchased even in poor personal economic circumstances. The desire to avoid pregnancy in these situations, however, may also lead to higher levels of abortion when contraceptive failure occurs. In order to not place an undue burden on poor couples and provide them with affordable and effective contraception, family planning services are still required for vulnerable groups in societies where fertility has reached low levels.

Some might also argue that family planning programmes may also play a role where the policy objective of a "low-fertility" country is to increase fertility. McDonald (2002) in reviewing public policy options to increasing fertility does not mention a role for family planning programmes, although he does see an active role for policy in this area. Those countries where fertility has declined to such low levels that a policy response to increase fertility has been elicited, have primarily been developed countries where national family planning programmes have not existed. As an increasing number of developing Asian countries reach a point where increasing fertility is seen as an objective, national family planning programmes could play a role through providing fertility services for those who cannot afford to access the private sector and through promoting positive attitudes towards childbearing (see also Harbison and Robinson 2002).

Providing services to the unmarried

The second priority area identified by Jones and Leete (2002) is to ensure that the unmarried have adequate access to reproductive health information and services. Demographic and social transformations in the Asian and Pacific region have led to calls for a greater focus on the reproductive health of adolescents. Adolescents are one of the fastest growing segments of the population. Rising ages of marriage also result in longer periods during which adolescents remain unmarried. This trend, combined with social changes that are weakening social norms against premarital sex, is resulting in higher levels of sexual activity among the unmarried (Mehta and others 1998; Gubhaju 2002).

Increased levels of sexual relations among the young subsequent increases in levels of premarital pregnancy and the spread of sexually transmitted diseases among the young are of concern to many policy makers. Increases in levels of unsafe abortion among the unmarried (Ahman and Shah 2002) and high proportions of adolescents among those persons infected with HIV are further indications of the dire need for reproductive and sexual health services for the unmarried. It should be noted, however, that where adolescents reproductive health services are provided, in the majority of instances, activities have been confined to providing adolescents with "family values education".

The provision of adolescent reproductive health services is constrained by cultural proscriptions about providing sexual information to adolescents, particularly the unmarried, and widespread beliefs that providing information on sexual issues will lead to an increase in premarital sexual behaviour. The result is limited political commitment to establish and/or strengthen adolescent reproductive health programmes.

At a UNFPA-sponsored workshop in 2000 that reviewed the existing situation of adolescent reproductive health in East and South-East Asia and the Pacific island countries, the lack of reproductive and sexual health knowledge of adolescents was highlighted (UNFPA 2000). Many issues raised during the workshop revolved around the greater vulnerability, and the more severe consequences resulting from sexual behaviour, of adolescent girls compared with boys. For both sexes it was noted that parents generally did not discuss sexual issues with their adolescent children, that school-based programmes on sexual education were either non-existent or extremely limited in their approaches and that adolescents lacked resources to access private sector reproductive health services.

The use of public sector services is often restricted for adolescents. Many countries in the region restrict access to publicly funded family planning services to married women of reproductive age. Even in programmes where unmarried persons can theoretically use services, provider's perceptions may hinder their access. Tu and others (2002), in a study of family planning workers' attitudes to providing sexual and reproductive health services to unmarried youth in China, found that many providers expressed reservations about providing services to the unmarried. Tangmunkongvorakul and others (2002) report that providers in both the public and private sectors in northern Thailand were ambivalent about providing reproductive health services to unmarried youth, and tended to view unmarried clients in a negative light. Given the reception that they are likely to receive when seeking reproductive health services, it is not surprising that many unmarried adolescents are hesitant to seek services from the formal health sector.

The proposed "Pattaya Programme of Action on Adolescent Reproductive Health" made recommendations to improve adolescent reproductive health that were aimed at the individual, provider and societal levels (UNFPA, 2000). Concentrated efforts to change some of the underlying societal factors that increase the vulnerability of adolescents in the areas of reproductive health, particularly those factors related to gender inequality, were recommended. These efforts are required to bring about long-term change. However, the removal of barriers to providing friendly and respectful reproductive and sexual services to adolescents should be the immediate programme priority. Preventive programmes that stress abstinence from sexual relations are needed and innovative ways to present information about the benefits of abstinence to youth should be explored. Where abstinence is not possible or is not the choice made by the unmarried, reproductive health services that include the provision of affordable contraception should be made available.

Improving sexual health

In addition to and in some ways crosscutting the two areas discussed above, a further priority area for family planning programmes should be to integrate sexual health services into their services. Although sexual health is included in the definition of reproductive health of the ICPD Programme of Action, there were few recommendations on how the provision of sexual health services should be improved. In assessing how countries in the Asian and Pacific region had adjusted their reproductive health programmes after ICPD, Abdullah (1999) observed that apart from sex education for adolescents, few countries appear to have incorporated aspects of sexuality or sexual health into their programmes.

A major difficulty in attempting to incorporate sexual health into family planning and other aspects of reproductive health is the sensitivity associated with discussing topics related to sex. Even researchers have tended to shy away from directly researching aspects of sexuality. Hawkes, Pachauri and Mane (2002) note information on sexuality in Asia has been limited until recently and it has only been the impact of HIV/AIDS that has spurred efforts to understand more deeply the relationship between sexual and reproductive health.

Dixon-Mueller (1993) argues that family planning providers need to learn about the sexual preferences of their clients in order to provide services that meet their clients' particular needs. For example, the type of contraceptive preferred may relate to how it affects sexual relationships. In providing STI services, it is also important to understand the sexual practices of clients. However, except for NGOs, there have been only sporadic attempts to provide family planning workers with counselling skills in the area of sexuality.

The issue of gender-based power imbalances in sexual relationships is of particular salience for reproductive health. Lack of power takes away the ability to make choices. Where this lack of choice occurs in the context of sexual relations, it can lead to adverse reproductive health outcomes. Such outcomes can include the inability to protect oneself against STIs or unwanted pregnancy, being denied access to reproductive health services or being denied sexual pleasure (Blanc 2001).

Blanc (2001) calls for programme interventions that attempt to ameliorate power imbalances in relationships as a strategy for improving aspects of reproductive health. She notes that improving spousal communication seems to be important "in preventive behaviour for HIV/AIDS and STIs as well as in the prevention of unwanted pregnancies and the improvement of sexual pleasure". A study of married couples in India also found that there was very limited communication among spouses about RTIs and that this lack of communication affected treatment-seeking behaviour (Santhya and Dasvarma 2002).

There is increasing evidence of high levels of non-consensual sex, particularly among adolescents. Gubhaju (2002), in reviewing some of the limited research available on this topic for Asia, notes many young women in relationships are at particular risk of being coerced into sex. Such coercion can also occur in work situations where males have authority over women. Evidence from a study in rural India indicated that a high proportion of abortions among unmarried women resulted from decisions to end unwanted pregnancies that were outcomes of non-consensual sex (Ganatra and Hirve 2002). We have little information in Asia about the males being coerced into sex.

The whole issue of gender-based violence has received scant programme attention and little research attention in Asia. Hardee and others (1999, p. s8) in their review of the post-Cairo progress of eight countries, including Bangladesh, India and Nepal, concluded that "gender-based violence remains outside the scope of most programs".

Family planning in reproductive health programmes

Family planning programmes have several well-documented advantages in providing broader reproductive health services. This includes the presence of a network that in many countries reaches down to the village level. Through this network it is possible to disseminate information and provide basic services to the bulk of the population. Family planning workers are also well versed in dealing with sensitive topics. In many societies, family planning has been considered to be a private matter and it has taken considerable time and effort to enable family planning workers to discuss contraceptive issues. In areas such as the provision of HIV/AIDS services, family planning workers would seem to have an initial advantage in taking on this role. The basis for this new role is that AIDS is primarily a sexually transmitted disease. In the provision of contraceptive services, family planning personnel have shown that it is possible to discuss matters that are sexually related, although much more training is required in this area. Finally, the condom is well known in many countries as a contraceptive method and its use as a dual-protection method could be promoted within this context.

In order to take full advantage of family planning programmes in providing other reproductive health services, there is, however, a need to expand the perceptions of the target populations of clients. Family planning programmes in most countries have been established to target married women of reproductive age. As noted above, this often means that interests of other segments of the population, such as unmarried women, are often ignored. The focus on married women of reproductive age can also result in negative outcomes for this target population. For example, one of the most effective strategies for treating RTIs, including STIs, for women in low resource settings is using the syndromic approach to manage male urethral discharge and genital ulcers. Treatment of males is very effective in reducing transmission of infection to their female partners. Applying the syndromic approach to women is less effective because of the large proportion of women who are asymptomatic, or who may be reinfected by their male partners after their own treatment (Haberland and others 2002). Given the more limited power that women have in influencing the conditions of sexual relations, prevention activities directed at women will be less effective unless their male partners are also included. As family planning programmes evolve into more comprehensive reproductive health programmes, they must actively seek to involve both women and men in their programmes.

In the regional review of progress towards integration of reproductive health services, Walker (1998) concluded that significant progress had been made in integrating services. He notes that further progress requires a better understanding of low gender issues influence the provision and use of reproductive health services. The need to clearly define what services are to be integrated and the resource needs for such integration are also cited as necessary practical elements in taking integration forward. These issues remain central to efforts to integrate family planning with other reproductive health services.

Conclusion

During and following ICPD, concern was expressed that the emphasis on reproductive rights of women would weaken family planning efforts. This concern was rooted in the view that family planning programmes were a key factor in constraining fertility and that reducing the primacy accorded to family planning programmes within the area of reproductive health would be detrimental to long-held societal goals of reducing birth rates. This view is still held by many.

However, the experience accumulated in the eight years since ICPD should help to allay these fears. The integration of family planning into expanded reproductive health programmes that provide women and men with choice in planning their reproductive lives, while still incomplete, has not led to reversals in fertility decline. Couples in very diverse contexts throughout the region have demonstrated that they wish to choose the number of children they have and under what conditions they have those children. At the individual level, this may mean a need for reproductive health services to provide assistance to couples that cannot reach their desired family size. But for the majority of couples it means providing them with choice to limit their fertility while enjoying a healthy life.

What is required is efforts to systematically document and disseminate the efforts that have been made to change the reproductive health services to become more responsive to clients. Through exposure to the successful impacts of changes in policies and programmes, decision makers may be more likely to support the fundamental changes required to implement a reproductive rights-based approach to reproductive health. At the same time, there needs to be continuing research, particularly in the form of evaluation of pilot projects, to address some of the issues that are of conern to policy makers.

The issues from the the Programme of Action where considerable work remains to be undertaken are many. Some of the priority areas are related to difficulties in transforming cultural values that support an environment and that limit the informed choice of individuals belonging to some groups in the population. For example, the development of adolescent reproductive health programmes has been hampered by the widespread belief that unmarried adolescents should not be exposed to information and/or services related to reproductive health. Entrenched systems that support gender inequality also restrict choices available to women while some societies provide legitimation for limited involvement of men in reproductive health.

There is also the need to move forward from considering only ICPD in considering how to improve reproductive health. As noted in this paper, the interrelationships between sexual relationships and reproductive health were not a main focus at ICPD. However, the centrality of sexual relationships to reproductive health cannot be disputed and there is an urgent need for programme interventions aimed at fostering reproductive health through improving the quality of sexual relationships for both men and women. Family planning programmes, while not the only institutions that can be utilized to improve sexual health, are ideally placed to provide such services.

Family planning programmes remain central to reproductive health. In many countries of the region, some of the more traditional roles of family planning programmes, such as the provision of free contraception and efforts made to change family size norms, are of declining programme relevance. In other countries, these activities remain important. In all programmes as one moves forward efforts to foster improvements in reproductive health in the region, further development of family planning services within the context of improving the sexual and reproductive choices of women and men is required. Family planning programmes must ensure that the poor and other vulnerable groups are able to access quality family planning and other reproductive health services.

References

Abdullah, Rashidah (1999). "Overview", in *Taking up the Cairo Challenge* (Kuala Lumpur, Asian-Pacific Resource and Research Centre for Women.), pp. 3-16.

Ahman, Elisabeth and Iqbal Shah (2002). "Unsafe abortion: worldwide estimates for 2000", *Reproductive Health Matters,* vol. 10. No. 19, pp. 13-17.

Arends-Kuenning, Mary (2002). "Reconsidering the doorstep-delivery system in the Bangladesh family planning program", *Studies in Family Planning,* vol. 33, No. 1, pp. 87-102.

Attane, Isabelle (2002). "China's family planning policy: an overview of its past and future", *Studies in Family Planning,* vol. 33, No. 1, pp. 103-113.

Bairagi, Radheshyam (2001). "Effects of sex preference on contraceptive use, abortion and fertility in Matlab, Bangladesh", *International Family Planning Perspectives,* vol. 27, No. 3, pp. 137-143.

Bang, Rani and others (1989) "High prevalence of gynaecological diseases in rural Indian women", *The Lancet,* January, pp. 85-88.

Berer, Marge and T. K. Sundari Ravindran (1999). "Preventing maternal mortality: evidence, resources, leadership, action", in Marge Berer and T. K. Sundari Ravindran, eds., *Safe Motherhood Initiatives: Critical Issues* (Oxford, Blackwell Science).

Bhatia, Jagdish and John Cleland (1995). "Self-reported symptoms of gynecological morbidity and their treatment in South India", *Studies in Family Planning,* vol. 26, No. 4, pp. 203-216.

Blanc, Ann (2001). "The effect of power in sexual relationships on sexual and reproductive health", *Studies in Family Planning, vol. 32, No. 3, pp. 189-213.*

Bruce, Judith (1990). "Fundamental elements of the quality of care: a simple framework", *Studies in Family Planning,* vol. 21, No. 2, pp. 61-91.

Caldwell, John, James Phillips and Barket-e-Khuda (2002). "The future of family planning programs", *Studies in Family Planning,* vol. 33, No. 1, pp. 1-10.

Dixon-Mueller, Ruth (1993). *Population Policy and Women's Rights: Transforming Reproductive Choice* (New York, Praeger).

East West Center (2002). *The Future of Population in Asia* (Honolulu, East-West Center).

ESCAP (1998). *Asia-Pacific Population Policies and Programmes: Future Directions,* Asian Population Studies Series No. 153 (United Nations publication, Sales No. E.99.II.F.4).

Fortney, Judith (1987). "The importance of family planning in reducing maternal mortality", *Studies in Family Planning,* vol. 18, No. 2, pp. 109-114.

Ganatra, Bela and Siddhi Hirve (2002). "Induced abortions among adolescent women in rural Maharashtra", *Reproductive Health Matters,* vol. 10, No. 19, pp. 76-85.

Greenspan, Allison (1993). "Changes in fertility patterns can improve child survival in Southeast Asia", Asia-Pacific Population and Policy Paper No. 27, (Honolulu, East-West Center).

Gu, Baochang, Ruth Simmons and Diana Szatkowski (2002). "Offering a choice of contraceptive methods in Deqing country, China: changing practice in the family planning program since 1995", in Nicole Haberland and Diana Measham, eds., *Responding to Cairo* (New York Population Council), pp. 58-73.

Gubhaju, Bhakta (2002). "Adolescent reproductive health in Asia", paper presented at the IUSSP Conference on Southeast Asia's Population in a Changing Asian Context, Bangkok, 10-13 June.

Haberland, Nicole and others (2002). "Pitfalls and possibilities: managing RTIs in the family planning and general reproductive health services", in Nicole Haberland and Diana Measham, eds., *Responding to Cairo* (New York, Population Council), pp. 99-113.

Harbison, Sarah and Warren Robinson (2002). "Policy implications of the next world demographic transition", *Studies in Family Planning,* vol. 33, No. 1, pp. 37-48.

Hardee, Karen and others (1999). "Reproductive health policies and programs in eight countries: progress since Cairo", *International Family Planning Perspectives,* vol. 25 (Supplement), pp. S2-S9.

Hawkes, Sarah, Saroj Pachauri and Purnima Mane (2002). "Editorial introduction", *Culture, Health & Sexuality,* vol. 4, No. 2, pp. 125-131.

Hull, Terrence (1998), "The challenge of contraceptive implant removals in East Nusa Tenggara, Indonesia", *International Family Planning Perspectives,* vol. 24, No. 4, pp.176-179.

Institute for Health Sciences (IHS) (2002). "Reproductive health and reproductive health services in rural China and Yunnan", unpublished paper

(Kunming Medical College).

Jain, Anrudh and others (2002). "Learning about clients' needs: family planning field workers in the Philippines", in Nicole Haberland and Diana Measham, eds., Responding to Cairo (New York, Population Counil) pp. 99-113.

Johansson, Annika and others (1996). "Abortion in context: women's experience in two villages in Thai Binh province, Vietnam", *International Family Planning Perspectives,* vol. 22, No. 3 pp. 103-107.

Jones, Gavin (1998). "The Bali Declaration and the Programme of Action of the International Conference on Population and Development in the context of the population dynamics of the Asian and Pacific region", in ESCAP, *Asia-Pacific Population Policies and Programmes: Future Directions,* Asian Population Studies Series NO. 153, (United Nations publication, Sales No. E.99.II.F.4), pp. 59-78.

and Richard Leete (2002). "Asia's family planning programmes as low fertility is attained", *Studies in Family Planning,* vol. 33, No. 1, pp. 114-126.

Kaufman, Joan and others (1999). "A study of field-based methods for diagnosing reproductive tract infections in rural Yunnan Province, China", *Studies in Family Planning,* vol. 30, No. 2, pp. 112-119.

Khan, Atiqur Rahman, Tan Boon-Ann and Suman Mehta (1998). "Quality of care and target-free approach for family planning programmes", in ESCAP, *Asia-Pacific Population Policies and Programmes: Future Directions,* Asian Population Studies Series No. 153 (United Nations publication, Sales No. E.99.II.F.4), pp. 145-166.

Knodel, John., Aphichat Chamratrithirong Nibhon Debavalya (1987). *Thailand's Reproductive Revolution* (Madison, University of Wisconsin Press).

Koenig, Michael, Gillian Foo and Ketan Joshi (2000). "Quality of care within the Indian family welfare programme: a review of recent evidence", *Studies in Family Planning,* vol. 31, No. 1, pp. 1-18.

Lien Phan and others (2002). "The prevalence of reproductive tract infection in Hue, Vietnam", *Studies in Family Planning,* vol. 33, No. 3, pp. 217-226.

Luther, N.Y., S. Thapa and S.B. Westley, (1999). "Nepal survey shows that 'family planning saves lives'", Asia-Pacific Population and Policy Paper No. 29 (Honolulu, East-West Center).

McDonald, Peter (2002). "Sustaining fertility through public policy", *Population,* vol. 57, No. 3, pp. 417-446.

Mehta, Suman, Riet Groenen and Francisco Roque (1998). "Adolescents in changing times: Issues and perspectives for adolescent reproductive health in the ESCAP region", in ESCAP, *Asia-Pacific Population Policies and Programmes: Future Directions,* Asian Population Studies Series No. 153 (United Nations publication, Sales No. E.99.II.F.4), pp. 167-194.

Miller, Jane and others (1992). "Birth spacing and child mortality in Bangladesh and the Philippines", Demography, vol. 29, No. 2, pp. 305-318.

Murthy, Nirmala and others (2002). "Dismantling India's contraceptive target system: and overview and three case studies", in Nicole Haberland and Diana Measham, eds., *Responding to Cairo* (New York, PopulationCouncil), pp. 25-57.

Popkin, Barry and others (1993). "Nutrition, lactation and birth spacing in Filipino women", *Demography,* vol. 30, No. 3, pp. 333-352.

Potts, Malcolm and others (1999) "Paying for reproductive health care: what is needed and what is available?" *International Family Planning Perspectives,* vol. 25, (Supplement), pp. S10-S16.

Prachuabmoh, Vipan and Preeya Mithranon (2002). "Below- replacement fertility in Thailand and its policy implications", paper prepared for the Workshop on Fertility Decline, Below Replacement Fertility and the Family in Asia: Prospects, Consequences and Policies, National University of Singapore, 10-12 April.

Ross, John and others (2002). "Contraceptive method choice in developing countries", *International Family Planning Perspectives,* vol. 28, No. 1, pp. 32-40.

Santhya, K.G. and Gour Dasvarma (2002). "Spousal communication on reproductive illness among rural women in southern India", *Culture, Health & Sexuality,* vol. 4, No. 2, pp. 223-236.

Schuler, Sidney Ruth and Zakir Hossain (1998). "Family planning clinics through women's eyes and voices: a case study from rural Bangladesh", *International Family Planning Perspectives,* vol. 24, No. 4, pp. 170-175.

Tangmunkongvorakul, Anurat and others (2002). "Providers' perspectives in addressing sexual and reproductive health needs in northern Thailand", paper presented at the IUSSP Conference on Southeast Asia's Population in a Changing Asian Context, Bangkok, 10-13 June.

Tu, Xiaowen, Nian Cui and Ersheng Gao (2002). "Attitudes of family planning workers on the provision of sexual and reproductive health services to unmarried young adults in China", paper presented at the IUSSP Conference on Southeast Asia's Population in a Changing Asian Context, Bangkok, 10-13 June.

UNFPA (2000). "Report of the UNFPA Intercountry Workshop Adolescent Reproductive Health for East and South-East Asia and the Pacific Island Countries" (Bangkok, UNFPA).

Walker, Godfrey (1998). "Implementation challenges of reproductive health, including family planning and sexual health: issues concerning the integration of reproductive health components", in ESCAP, *Asia-Pacific Population Policies and Programmes: Future Directions,* Asian Population Studies Series No. 153 (United Nations publication, Sales No. E.99.II.f.4), pp. 115-144.

Winckler, Edwin (2002). "Chinese reproductive policy at the turn of the millennium: dynamic stability", *Population and Development Review,* vol. 28, No. 3, pp. 379-418.

WHO (1998). *Unsafe Abortion: Global and Regional Estimates of Incidence of a Mortality due to Unsafe Abortion.* (Geneva, WHO).

13

Adolescent Reproductive Health: Lessons Learned from the Intervention Projects

Adolescents aged between 10 to 19 years, are a large and growing segment of the population. At 1.05 billion, this is the biggest-ever generation of young people and their number is increasing rapidly in many countries (UNFPA, 1998a). The population of adolescents will continue to grow because of the growth momentum of age structure and the high fertility rate in the past. Globally, the largest share of adolescents is and will continue to be in Asia, which has 60 per cent of the world population (UNFPA, 1998b).

In recent years, adolescent reproductive health has become one of the most widely talked about and sensitive health issues among programme planners around the world. "Adolescent sexual and reproductive health refers to the physical and emotional well-being of adolescents and includes their ability to be healthy and remain free from too-early or unwanted pregnancy, unsafe abortion, sexually transmitted diseases (STDs) including HIV/AIDS, and sexual violence or coercion" (Senderowitz, 1995; WHO, 1998). However, in assessing commitments made since the International Conference on Population and Development in Cairo in 1994, adolescent reproductive health rights remain inadequately addressed. The Programme of Action of the Conference called for orgaizations to initiate or strengthen programmes to better meet the reproductive health needs of adolescents (United Nations, 1994). Numerous programmes have been developed to address adolescent reproductive health needs accordingly. Yet, five years later, there exist legal, religious and social barriers which prevent adolescents from receiving the services offered to them and still there is room for policy makers to concentrate their attention on the urgency of the issue (UNFPA, 1998b).

Early marriage and especially childbearing can have a profound and long lasting impact on a woman's well-being, education and ability to contribute to her community (Liskin and others, 1985; McCauley and others, 1995). Teenage childbearing is most common in developing countries, where one quarter to one half of women have their first child by age 18. Although some 10-19 years olds are beginning to experience the changes that come with puberty, many are entering sexual relationships or marriage (Alan Guttmacher Institute, 1998). Each year, about 15 million young women aged 15 to 19 give birth (PATH, Program for Appropriate Technology in Health, 1998). Early childbearing adversely affects the mother and the child. Teenage mothers face a higher-than-average risk of mortality compared with mothers in their 20s and their children have a higher level of morbidity and mortality. Because girls generally continue growing physically during adolescence, pregnancy and childbirth before attaining full growth results in a competition for nutrients between the growing adolescent and the growing foetus (=>foetus) (United Nations, 2000). Childbirth at an early age also has a negative impact in the sociocultural and demographic context. Compared with a woman who delays childbearing until her 20s, the woman who has her first child before age 17 is likely to obtain less education and fewer job opportunities. Moreover, childbearing and child-rearing become a burden when the mother is emotionally or physically immature to do so (Singh, 1998). Yet, complex physical, familial and cultural factors that are often poorly understood determine who will marry when and who will begin childbearing during adolescence. Available data demonstrate that while the needs and experiences of adolscents vary around the world, there are similarities within the cross-national and regional noundaries.

The principal risk factors for adolescent reproductive health can be categorized under two broad names:

Boilogical factors	Social factors
• Incomplete physical Growth • Increased nutritional requirement • Sexual maturity without being prepared for parenthood	• Lack of adequate knowledge about sexuality and reproductive need • Limited access to health and family planning services • Time gap between menarche and marriage • Employment • Poverty • Early marriage • Adolescent fertility

The above two categories of factors simultaneously contribute to one or more of the following consequences:

• Interrupted education and career	• Pregnancy-induced hypertension
• Premarital / unsafe sexual activity	• Difficult delevery (obstructed and prolonged labour)
• Low contraceptive use	• Foetal growth retardation and low-birth-weight baby
• Early and unwanted pregnancy	• Premature birth
• Unsafe and illegal abortion	• High infant mortality

• STD/RTI	• Prenatal mortality
• HIV/AIDS	• Maternal mortality
• Anemia and malnutrition	

Sources : Liskin, L., N. Kak, A. H. Rutledge, L. C. Smit and L. Stewart (1985). "Youth in the 1980s: social and health concerns", Population Reports 13(5), Series M, Number 9; McCauley, A.P.,C. Salter, K. Kiragu and J. Senderowitz (1995). "Meeting the needs of young adults", Population Reports 23(3), Series J, No. 41 (Baltimore, Johns Hopkins School of Public Health, Population Information Program also available online at: www.jhuccp.org/pr/j41edsum.stm) and Senderowitz, J. (1995). "Adolescent health: reassessing the passage to adulthood", World Bank Discussion Paper No. 272.

Note: RTI = reproductive tract infection.

As modernization occurs within the bounds of traditional systems, it is difficult to adopt any change; while young people face challenging lifestyles, the older generations' attitudes remain unchanged. If it is required to promote safer sex, for instance, information on safer sex and contraception should be given, and relevant health services provided. Yet, sex education for adolescents, even social interaction and often dialogue between the sexes, are not acceptable in many cultures.Cultural attitudes in many Asian countries, stemming from the adolescents and their parents, favour norms of premarital chastity. As such, there still exists a disturbing picture of teenage abortion seekers in South Asia and the Pacific region, comprising both married and unmarried girls (Jejeebhoy, 1996a). Adolescents are acutely sensitive about gender discrimination. Owing to a lack of access to education and a lack of exposure, young girls' economic dependency on men has, to a large extent, contributed to their being submissive and not making decisions about their own lives (Mensch and Lloyd, 1998).

Focusing on adolescent reproductive health is a challenge and opportunity for healthcare providers as well. Unlike adults, adolescents often lack basic reproductive health information, skills in negotiating sexual relationships and access to affordable confidential reproductive health and family planning services. Many do not feel comfortable discussing sexuality with parents or other key adults with whom they can talk about their reproductive health concerns (PATH, 1998). Likewise, parents, healthcare workers and educators are frequently unwilling or unable to provide complete, accurate, age-appropriate reproductive health information to young people. This is often due to their own discomfort and the false belief that providing the information will encourage increased sexual activity (Baldo and others, 1993). On the contrary, studies deny the belief that sexual education contributes to earlier or increased sexual activity in youth. Rather, it causes a delay in the onset of sexual activity or a reduction in overall sexual activity (Baldo and others, 1993; Grunseit and Kipax, 1993).

This review attempts to investigate the type of interventions that are being offered by different agencies for improvement of the reproductive health of adolescents in Bangladesh and tries to assess the impact of these programmes in terms of some reproductive health indicators, comparing recent Bangladesh Demographic and Health Survey (BDSH) data, such as the 1996-97 BDHS and 1999-2000 BDHS.

Needs of the adolescents

Roughly, one in five people in the world is an adolescent. Like many other groups, adolescents all over the world have specific concerns and problems. Their circumstances and needs vary tremendously depending on individual characteristics such as age, sexual activity, schooling and employment status, as well as their position within the range of adolescent years. Since adolescence is a period of rapid physical, emotional, social and sexual maturing, adolescents need a full range of quality reproductive health care, as well as information and counselling (Alan Guttmacher Institute, 1998; McCauley and others, 1995).

Today's adolescents are the next generation's parents, workers and leaders. To fill these roles to the best of their ability, they need the guidance and support of their family and community, and the attention of a government committed to their development. As economic modernization, urbanization and mass communication change the expectations and behaviour of adolescents, adaptation to new ways is likely to be inconvenient and at times, painful. But adaptation is inevitable and inescapable (Alan Guttmacher Institute, 1998). Most countries recognize the necessity for and value of education for young women. Education contributes to the health of women's children and families and facilitates her use of information and services (Liskin and others, 1985; McCauley and others, 1995; Senderowitz, 1995; Jejeebhoy, 1996b; Alan Guttmacher Institute, 1998). Government and other social institutions, therefore, must find new ways to enable families to enrol girls in school and to encourage young women to stay in school and complete their basic education.

Young children and teenagers often learn about sexual matters from peers, siblings, parents and the media (Hong and Nam, 1989; Lema, 1990) but the information they obtain through these channels is usually limited and may be erroneous (Ogutu-Ohwayo, 1991; McCauley and others, 1995). Formal instructions tailored to the age and background of the adolescents involved, is an important source of accurate information about sexuality, pregnancy, childbearing, contraception and STD prevention. Comprehensive sex education programmes not only cover biological facts but also provide adolescents with practical information and skills regarding sexual relationships and contraceptive use. Although programmes encounter religious or political opposition, most studies show that they do not encourage sexual activity; rather, they are associated with the postponement of early sex and, among sexually active adolescents, with the use of contraceptives (Baldo and, 1993; Grunseit and Kippax, 1993; Haider and others, 1997).

In addition to STD and pregnancy risks, many young people who are sexually active have been forced into sexual relationships, either through violence or for economic reasons (UNFPA, 1997; Hossain and others, 1998; PATH, 1998; Alan Guttmacher Institute, 1998) and are in need of counselling, information and contraceptive services. Married adolescents who become pregnant may not encounter the same social risks as their unmarried counterparts, but they face the same complications from STDs and the health risks of early pregnancies. Along with increased exposure to STDs and unintended pregnancy, adolescents who engage in sexual activity outside of marriage may face social stigmas, family conflicts, problems with school and the potential need for unsafe abortion (McCauley and others, 1995).

Governments, along with NGOs and even the media, have a role of play in improving the adolescents' ability to protect themselves against unwanted pregnancies and STDs. Special efforts are needed to educate and motivate men to cooperate with their sexual partners in the use of contraceptives to prevent unwanted pregnancies and diagnose and treat STDs. Adolescents women require access to a range of contraceptive services (Liskin and others, 1985; UNFPA, 1997).

• Privacy and confidentiality are important aspects of service provision for adolescents, who may be uncomfortable discussing sexual matters or may fear condemnation from their families or communities if they reveal their sexual activity (McCauley and others, 1995; PATH, 1998). Care provided specifically for adolescents must be sensitive to young women's limited access to transportation and their often-meagre financial resources. The degree to which the service environment welcomes adolescents will determine the extent to which adolescents avail themselves of reproductive health care.

The situation of adolescents in Bangladesh

Adolescents comprise 25 per cent of the total population in Bangladesh, the number being approximately 33 million in the year 2001. Among them, about 48 per cent were females and 52 per cent males. Box 1 shows some selected characteristics of female adolescents in Bangladesh. This large group of adolescents is a major social concern because they will exert a high population momentum effect on the future increment of population in Bangladesh. The annual growth rate of the adolescents population is 4.33 per cent, compared with 1.7 per cent for the total population. The absolute size is expected to rise to 35 million by the year 2010 (Barkat, 2000).[1]

Box 1. Selected socio-economic characteristics of female married adolescents in Bangladesh, 1999-2000

Mean age at marriage (years)	16.9
Rural inhabitants (per cent)	75.6
Islam follower (per cent)	92.3
Not educated (per cent)	27.4
Unemployed (per cent)	88.6
Mass-media exposure (television, radio, newspaper) (per cent)	4.4
Not allowed to go to health facility (per cent)	76.5

Source: Bangladesh Demographic and Health Survey, 1999-2000.

In Bangladesh, social norms and mores strictly

support premarital chastity. Further, sexual encounter is supposed to occur only within marriage. The current section deals with the description of Bangladeshi adolescents reproductive health on the basis of information collected from two nationally representative surveys for married female adolescents. Since adolescents are vulnerable to many reproductive health hazards owing to their physical and mental immaturity, it would have been worthwhile to compare some of the important reproductive health indicators for both married and unmarried adolescents in this section, including their health-seeking behaviour. Since sexual relationships for any unmarried adolescents are socially regarded as promiscuity, any broad-scale study failed to collect such information apart from few small sample quantitative or qualitative studies. These study findings indicate that, though a substantial proportion of adolescents become sexually active before marriage (Haider and others, 1997), they do not admit it for a fear of social harassment and probable obstacles in future marriage (box 2). This section also covers the health-care utilization by the married adolescents in terms of antenatal care, tetanus toxoid coverage, delivery at a health facility and seeking treatment for pregnancy-related complications. Information on health-seeking behaviour for unmarried adolescents is also rare (box 3), as social restrictions hinder them from admitting their sexual activity outside marriage; they also do not feel comfortable seeking family planning or STD services from nearby clinics and pharmacies. They perceive that providers would be judgmental and unfriendly to them (Bhuiya and others, 2000).

Box 2. Premarital sexual behaviour among adolescents

One study in Bangladesh with adolescents from urban and rural areas revealed that nearly one fourth of the unmarried females and 29 per cent of the married females have had any sexual contact by age 19. By contrast, 61 per cent of unmarried and 69 per cent of married male adolescents reported some premarital sexual encounter by age 19, with a mean difference of 6-8 years for urban and 3-4 years for rural areas. For adolescents women, sexual partners before marriage were mostly their "future" husbands (Haider and others, 1997). Another small-scale baseline survey reported that 127 males and only 3 females out of 2,626 unmarried adolescents had premarital sexual exposure, with 15 years as the mean age at first sexual encounter. Of these males, 52 had sex with commercial sex workers and did not use a condom (Population Council, 2001).

Box 3. Health-care utilization by unmarried adolescents

A clinic-based intervention found that a total of 4,580 adolescents, with 94 per cent girls visited the satellite and fixed clinic August 2000 and December 2001. Among those, 57 per cent were unmarried visiting the clinic for immunization, RTI/STI services and very few also came for problems related to menstruation and general health problems. (Population Council, 2002).

Notes: STI = sexually transmitted infection; RTI = reproductive tract infection

Table 1 shows some selected reproductive health indicators of adolescents derived from the 1996-1997 and 1999-2000 BDHS data (Mitra and others, 1997, 2001). We also investigated what changes occurred between the two surveys. The information indicates, that there was little change in terms of fertility, proportion never married, use of contraception and unmet need for contraception. Box 4 provides information on the proportion never married among adolescents in 1999-2000. Similarly, there has not been much change in infant mortality. However, there was a dramatic decline in child mortality, which declined from about 44 per 1,000 births to about 29 per 1,000 births. Surprisingly, the proportion of adolescent mothers who were pregnant increased from 14.7 to 15.9 per cent between the two surveys. About 52 per cent of adolescents were never married at the time of the survey and the percentage who were married by age 15 was 28.5. Because of the censoring effect, the age at marriage for the 15-19 age group could not be estimated, i.e. all of them will not be married by age 19.

The level of HIV/AIDS knowledge has changed significantly since 1996. Knowledge of HIV/AIDS increased from 17 to over 30 per cent among ever-married adolescents between the two surveys. As part of the HIV/AIDS prevention programme, the mass media are playing a greater role to create awareness among the general public. Adolescents reported that television was the most important source of information about HIV/AIDS)20.1 per cent). The other importnat source were radio (10 per cent) and friend/relative (11.5 per cent) (Mitra and others, 2001). The recent BDHS covered some other aspects regarding HIV/AIDS knowledge among adolescents. Relevant information from the table indicates that only about 19 per cent of them did not know any proper way to prevent HIV/AIDS. The distressing situation is that only 8.5 per cent of the married female adolescents were found knowledgeable about sexually transmitted infections.

Table 1. Reproductive health situation of female adolescents in Bangladesh, some selected indicators, Bangladesh Demographic and Health Survey, 1996-1997 and 1999-2000

	Indicator	Situation	
A - Fertility and requlation		1996-1997	1999-2000
1.	Current fertility (births per 1,000 women)	147	144
2.	Child ever born per woman	0.39	0.37

3.	Children living	0.35	0.33
4.	Who have began childbearing (percentage)	35.6	34.7
5.	pregnant at the time of survey (percentage)	14.7	15.9
6.	Percentage never married (15-19 years)	49.8	51.9
7.	Contraceptive prevalance rate	31.0	30.5
8.	Unmet need for family planning (percentage)	19.0	21.0
B.	Infant and child mortality		
1.	perinatal mortality	..	71.6
2.	Neonatal mortality rate	70.2	72.2
3.	Post neonatal mortality rate	35.9	31.4
4.	Infant mortality rate	106.1	103.6
5.	Child mortality rate	43.6	29.2
6.	Under five mortality rate	145	129.5
C.	Maternal and child health		
1.	Recipients oftetanus toxoid (per cent)	79	85.5
2.	Received antenatal check-ups	29.3	39.9
3.	Delivery at health facility (per cent)	3.4	6.7
D.	Nutritional status		
1.	Short stature mothers (per cent) (<145 cm)	19.0	18.4
2.	Acutely malnourished mothers (per cent) (BMI<18.4 per cent)	50	50.5
E.	HIV/AIDS		
1.	Ever heard of HIV/AIDS (per cent)	17.2	30.2
2.	Sources of knowledge - ratio	7.6	11.7
3.	Sources of knowledge - televisions	11.7	20.1
4.	Sources of knowledge - friend/relatives	6.8	11.5
5.	Unknown to any valid way to prevent HIV/AIDS	..	19.3
6.	Perception of HIV/AIDS - a healthy person can have HIV/AIDS	..	66.4
7.	Perception of HIV/AIDS - healthy person cannot have HIV/AIDS	..	13.5
8.	Communicate with spouse about HIV/AIDS prevention	..	18.4
9.	Knowledge of STIs	..	8.5

Note: Two dots (..) indicate that the data are not available.

Box 4. Proportion of never-married adolescents girls in Bangladesh, 1999-2000

Current Age (in years)	Proportion never married
15	70.7
16	58.6
17	46.2
18	40.9
19	30.7

Source: Bangladesh Demographic and Health Survey, 1999-2000.

Information on maternal and child health indicates that the percentage of adolescents who had tetanus toxoid during pregnancy increased between the two surveys. For instance, according to the 1999-2000 BDHS, 85.5 per cent of teenage mothers reported receiving TT, as against 79 per cent in the 1996-1997 BDHS. There was also a 10-percentage point increase in the antenatal check-up recipients between the two survey periods, although no change was found in the delivery of births that took place in the health facility. The proportion of adolescent mothers receiving antenatal care rose from 29.3 per cent in 1996-1997 to about 40.0 per cent in 1999-2000. However, both the surveys reported only about 4 to 7 per cent births that were delivered at health facilities.

The nutritional status of the adolescents did not change at all between the two surveys. Adolescents mothers' nutritional risk was measured in terms of mean height (in cm), which can be used to predict the risk of difficulty in delivering children, given the association between height and size of pelvis. Also, the risk of giving birth to low-weight newborn is highest among women of small stature. The survey data on nutritional status indicate roughly one in five teenage mothers were shorter than the cut-off point of 150 cm. About 50 per cent of teenage mothers are acutely malnourished (body mass index (BMI) <18.5).

Table 2 shows the percentage distribution of teenagers (15-19) who were mothers or pregnant with their first child according to the 1996-1997 and 1999-2000 BDHS. The information reveals that 31 per cent adolescents were mothers in 1996-1997 and another 5 per cent were pregnant with their first child. The comparable figures for the 1999-2000 BDHS were about 30 and 5 per cent respectively. Thirty-five per cent of adolescents have begun child bearing in 1999-2000. In the same period, a small proportion of the adolescents also reported that their last child was mistimed (box 5).

There has been a slight decline in this proportion since the 1996-1997 BDHS, which showed that 36 per cent of women aged 15-19 had begun child-bearing.

Table 2. Adolescent pregnancy and motherhood in Bangladesh, Bangladesh Demographic and Health Survey 1996-1997, 1999-2000

Age	Percentage who are				Percentage who have	
	Mothers		Pregnant with first child		begun childbearing	
	1996-1997	1999-2000	1996-1997	1999-2000	1996-1997	1999-2000
15	8.5	11.6	5.5	4.3	14.1	15.9
16	23.5	22.2	5.2	3.8	28.4	26.0
17	32.6	30.8	3.7	5.7	36.4	36.5
18	43.2	39.0	4.7	6.0	48.0	45.0
19	54.6	52.5	3.1	4.8	57.7	57.3
Total	31.0	29.8	4.6	4.9	35.6	34.7

Box 5. Percentage of female adolescents reporting their last child as mistimed according to current age, Bangladesh, 1999-2000

Current age	percentage
17	1.1
18	0.8
19	1.9

Source: Bangladesh Demographic and Health Survey, 1999-2000.

Box 6. Proportion of adolescents who knew about menstrual regulation and used the procedured by place of residence, Bangladesh Demographic and Health Survey, 1999-2000

Place of residence	Knowledge	Use
Urban	76.5	2.7
Rural	71.1	1.7
Total	72.4	2.0

This section further investigates another reproductive health indicator, such as knowledge and use of menstrual regulation of the married adolescents on the basis of information collected from the BDHS

1999-2000 (box 6). The data suggest that slightly over 72 per cent of adolescents reported knowledge about menstrual regulation (both unprompted and prompted).

Health-care utilization by the adolescents

Pregnancy, particularly in adolescents age, is associated with many life-threatening risks. In the past, these aspects were not studied in any survey. The Bangladesh Maternal Health Services and Maternal Mortality Survey, 2001 shows detailed information on the knowledge of adolescents about these life-threatening issues associated with pregnancy and their health-care utilization. Table 3 shows knowledge of pregnancy or delivery-related complications that might cause death and health-seeking behaviour for those life-threatening conditions of married adolescents (National Institute of Population Research and Training, 2001). Overall knowledge was high but specific knowledge of life-threatening conditions was low. The information suggests that over 43 per cent knew about tetanus a life-threatening conditions during pregnancy or delivery. About 29 per cent of females reported knowledge about retained placenta and above a quarter (27.8 per cent) about obstructed labour. From 10 to 18 per cent of the females knew about prolonged labour, excessive vaginal bleeding, convulsion/eclampsia or bad position of the baby. Only about 5 per cent knew about severe headache/high blood pressure or edema/ pre-eclampsia that might threaten the life of the mother during pregnancy or delivery.

Table 3. Percentage distribution of married females aged less than 20 according to their knowledge of maternal complications and their health-seeking behaviour, 2001

	Indicator	Situation 2001
A.	Knowledge of life-threatening conditions during pregnancy	
1.	Knowledge of any life-threatening conditions during pregnancy/delivery	79.2
2.	Knowledge of severe headache/high blood pressure	5.2
3.	Knowledge of edema pre-eclampsia	5.4
4.	Knowledge of convulsion/eclampsia	17.1
5.	Knowledge of excessive vaginal bleeding	11.6
6.	Knowledge of tetanus	43.3
7.	Knowledge of baby in bad position	18.3
8.	Knowldege of prolonged labour	10.9
9.	Knowledge of obstructed labour	27.8
B.	Type of assistance sought for complications	
1.	Did not seek assistance	45.1
2.	Sought assistance, but not at health facility	30.5
3.	Went to a facility/doctor for assistance	24.4
C.	Type of health facility visited for complications	
1.	Government hospital/Thana Health Center/Maternal and Child Welfare Centre	44.4
2.	Satellite/Expanded Programme for Immunization clinic	5.2
3.	NGO and private health facility	16.2
4.	Private doctor	18.6
5.	Traditional doctor/other	15.5

Source: Bangladesh Maternal Health Services and Maternal Mortality Su`rvey, 2001 (preliminary report).

The health-seeking behaviour of the adolescents who had complications shows somewhat alarming conditions, as nearly half of the adolescents did not seek any type of assistance for maternal complications and another one third opted for some non-facility assistance. Yet, a little less than one fourth of the adolescents went to a facility/doctor for their pregnancy or delivery-related complications. Further, among women who went to a facility for treatment, the most commonly mentioned place was government hospital facilities (44.4 per cent), followed by private doctor (18.6 per cent) and NGOs and private health facility (16.2 per cent). A sizeable proportion of these adolescents also sought assistance from a traditional doctor or other for their complications.

Adolescents programmes and interventions currently in operation in Bangladesh

Since the Declaration of the International Conference on Population and Development in 1994, a good number of NGOs as well as government agencies in Bangladesh have introduced adolescent reproductive health programme in their project activities. The directory published by the Population Council, Dhaka indicates that more than 100 NGOs were working in the area of adolescent reproductive health and their welfare (Hossain and others, 1998). Recently, UNICEF compiled the types of interventions these NGOs are providing (UNICEF, 1999).

The general objectives of these NGO programmes include:

- Illiteracy eradication
- Empowering adolescents
- Promotion of individual development and support for the betterment of future life.
- Exposure to reproductive health matters

The activities taken under the programmes are as follows:

- Group formation
- Skill development training
- Literacy/non-formal education
- Micro-credit/income-generation activities
- Adolescents family life education
- Sex education
- General health education
- Reproductive health services
- Leadership training
- Legal support, e.g. regarding violence and abuse
- Advocacy with families and community members to obtain support for programmes

Concerns about the current reproductive health programmes

Although many interventions have been provided over the last few years, very little is known about the impact of these interventions, it is necessary to assess the correlates of these interventions. The interventions introduced by both the Government and local and international NGO, raise some valid and crucial questions, such as:

Government's programme

Government's intervention	Programme	Programme component	Target group	emarks/ inpacts
Enducation programme	Secondary Education Scholarship Programme	1. Nationwide stipend 2. Book stipend	Girls in Class VI to X in rural area	Increase in female enrolment in shcool
Health programme under the Health and Population	Essential Services Package	1. Health services 2. Health education 3. Health and Hygyenic environment	Students in Class V to X sector programme	
	National Nutrition Project	1. Monitoring girl's height, weight 2. Educationsession on nutrion, personal hygiene and reproductive health care 3. Micronutrient supplements 4. Counselling	Unmarried in-and out of shcool girls	
Directorate of Health and Family Planning	Essential Services Packages	1. Education 2. Nutrition Clinical treatment 4. Behavioural Change Communication (BCC) about reproductive health	BCC for girls aged 12+ and boys aged 13+	

What is the experience from the Government's secondary education sholarship programme and those of various NGOs? Is there any evidence that completion of secondary education increased age at marriage beyond 18 years and, if so, what is the age at marriage of girls who completed secondary education under the project?

How many girls having completed secondary school

are able to continue higher secondary education so that it really has an impact on age at marriage and on reproductive behaviour?

Do the girls who completed secondary education after being enrolled in the Government's secondary education scholarship programme have any means to continue higher education? Do they have access to employment opportunities? If not, what will their parents do in the given cultural setting? One logical option is that they may be married off. It is also expected that education usually expands employment opportunities and educated women may delay marriage and child earing to earn income. Women's education is also associated with better child health. Women with some formal education are more likely to obtain care during pregnancy, immunize their children and take appropriate action when a child becomes ill.

NGO programmes

Name of NGO	Programme area	programme component	Target group	Remarks impacts
Population Council	1. School 2. Community	1. Education Programme 2. Friendly clinical service 3. Inform thought telephone and print media	1. Boys and grils in class VIII and IX in school 2. Out-of-school aged 13-19, working or non-working	1. Improved reproductive health Knowledge 2. Increased clinic visitation by unmarried for counselling 3. Increased antenatal care recipients 4. Positive attitude towards repro-ductive health behaviour
International Center for Diarrhoeal Diseases Research, Bangladesh	School	1. Hooklet 2. Adolescents friendly clinic services	Students of grade VIII, IX and X in school	
	Community	Adolescent Development Package	Adoloscents aged 13-15 and 16-19 years from all	

		1. Health education 2. Health Services 3. Credit and skill training programme	Categories
	Workplace	Peer approach Health Services	Female garment Workers aged 13-19 years
Bangladesh Women's Health Coalition	1. School 2. Community	1. Adolescent Family life education 2. Club based in the community	Girls in grade VIII. and IX in School in urban and rural areas and school Dropout adolescent girls from the community
Bangladesh Rural Advancement Committee	Adolescent reproductive health Education	1. Formal school 2. non-formal school 3. Club and skill Training	Adolescents aged 11 to 14 years
Under-privileged Children's Educational Programmes	Schooling opportunities	Education	Poor urban working/ street girls 10+ and boys 11+
Center for Mass Education in Science	School	Life-oriented non-Formal education	Girls aged 11 to 19 years

What is the experience from the existing health programme of Government and NGOs regarding the reproductive behaviour of the adolescents? Have any specific indicators of adolescents reproductive health been identified at the national level? Does the programme suggest any positive change in the reproductive health indicators of the adolescents? If, so what are those indicators?

The adolescent family life education programmes raise important questions: which curricula are more effective in changing risk-taking behaviours, either by delaying or reducing sexual activity or by increasing the use of protection? What are their characteristics?

What is the impact of additional programme components, such as parent programmes, peer programmes, after-school discussion sessions and individual counselling? Are programmes more or less effective when teachers teach them or peers or outside experts? Are these appropriate and acceptable ways to teach adolescents so that they receive instruction more relevant to their personal experiences?

What is the impact of the programme location (school-based or school-linked) and the location of its sponsor (school, clinic or other community agency)? How can school-based programmes be reinforced by community-wide efforts and vice versa?

On the basis of the review of Bangladesh adolescent programmes, it is not possible to identify successful programmes that can be replicated.

Lessons from programmes of other countries

Experiences from programmes of other countries on adolescents reproductive health suggest that a combination of approaches is often most effective in reaching adolescents, but very few have been rigorously evaluated for impact, making determination of best practices a challenge (PATH, 1998). It is therefore inevitable to assess the nature of these programmes and to ascertain the successful experiences that are feasible and can be replicated in other countries with a similar cultural context.

A wide variety of youth-oriented services and programmes have been found to operate in both developed and developing countries, differing according to the group of adolescents to which they belong. Adolescents in different settings are reachable in a varying manner. For those who are in school, school-based clinics are available in some developed and developing countries. Unlike developed countries, in developing countries school-based services are often limite by restrictive policies, personnel shortages, lack of private areas for counselling and poor links to resources outside the school. Yet, some school-based clinical programmes in some developing countries show some extent of success. The Nepalese school-based AIDS/STD awareness programme by the B.P. Memorial Health Foundation (BPMHF) uses a peer education model (UNFPA, 2000) as its programme tool. In Jamaica, such a programme enabled adolescent girls to continue their schooling during pregnancy; to return to school after the birth of their child; and to avoid another pregnancy during adolescence. The programme also helps adolescents to continue their education and thus to delay first pregnancy, and offers them family planning information and services, skill-building on childcare and other life-planning services (Barnett and others, 1996). An evaluation of the Jamaican programme found that less than 2 per cent adolescents reached by the programme had a second pregnancy before graduating ir starting work (UNFPA, 1997), which shows that providing a supportive environment where pregnant girls can continue their education can make a significant defference in their futures. This programme found the combination of education, information and services to be the key to pregnancy prevention.

In some Western and Latin American countries, youth-oriented clinic services are available to provide a wide range of clinical and social services such as pregnancy and STD prevention, counselling and testing (Pathfinder International, 1998). Such adolescent friendly health clinics are also available in other parts of the world. For example, one intervention programme in Thailand aims to be a friendly one-stop health clinic, which is accessible, convenient, confidential and culturally as well as socially sensitive to youth's sexual and reproductive health problems and needs. The youth-friendly clinic and educational/recreational centre in Belize, called Planet Youth, reaches out to both students and young adults who are no longer in school and uses music and theatre to provide pertinent sexual and reproductive health information in the form of positive entertainment (RHO, Program Examples, 1997-2002). This programme suggests that reproductive and sexual health programmes designed for adolescents, particularly those who are not in school, benefit from meeting youths in their own environment the programme also indicated that commitment from staff, donors, parent and the young people themselves has been the key to programme success.

It is often revealed that owing to adolescents' cultural, social and geographic diversity, reproductive health programmes based in schools and health facilities cannot reach all segments of the adolescents population. Hard-to-reach adolescents such as those not attending school, working or living on the streets, who have been sexually abused or exploited, indigenous groups or newly-wed couples can better be reached under the community-based programmes. Community-based outreach programmes in different countries such as El Salvador, Indonesia, Mexico, Thailand and Viet Nam are especially important for groups such as out-of school youth, "street" youth, and girls who have limited freedom to leave their community. These community-based projects have a variety of formats to reach youth where they congregate for work or play.

Trained peer leaders in a programme in Thailand facilitates young women living in the workplace to learn and practice skills such as negotiating, planning and sexual health, like using a condom (Cash and Anasuchatku, 1995). In Mexico, gang members are trained to reach out-of-school adolescents (PATH,

1998). In El Salvador, the peer education approach for gang adolescents suggests that programmes must provide information appropriate to the level of knowledge and skills of the community, as well as use the language of youth. The El Salvadoran approach also indicates that programmes should target young women emphasizing negotiation skills so that they can say "no" to unprotected sex and reinforce their self-esteem. Moreover, programmes must make condoms available to youth, so that availability is not an excuse for not using a condom during a sexual act. The experience from the Indonesian programme on street outreach workers indicates that involving gay youth in the overall programme builds trust among the gay community, finding the selection, training and supervision of outreach workers to be the key to the programme's success.

Special approaches to reach the adolescents and to meet their needs are also being carried out in some other countries. For example, the Urban Life Network, Life Net program, in Thailand, a new approach to meet youth reproductive health needs, by bringing skills and strengthening relationships, reveals that reproductive health education materials should be adapted into formats that are engaging and entertaining to youth, using language and terminology that youth understand (RHO, Program Examples, 1997-2002). Programmes also involve people other than youths such as parents, religious leaders, health officials, and community members to raise community awareness and advocacy regarding the importance of adolescent educational reproductive health needs.

In Kenya, where the Government restricts discussion regarding reproductive health issues, the Kenya Scouts Association showed that it is possible to reach out-of-school youth with family life skills through scouting programmes, and working with homogeneous groups (either in school or out-of-school) works best. The programme also recommended that involving all stakeholders (parents, teachers, scout leaders and the management) in planning and implementing the project helped to address potential concerns and build support for the project. In Uganda, the media approach to address adolescent concerns about sexual and reproductive health demonstrates that it is possible to openly address sexuality in the African context if the material is tasteful, well-written, scientifically accurate, and based on adolescents' questions (RHO, Program Examples, 1997-2002).

Until now, we have discussed some specific interventions that are in operation around the world. However, the lack of analytical studies to assess the impact of interventions has led to our inability to identify specific successful interventions that could be recommended for replication. One of the weaknesses of these experiences is that it does not tell the sample size and methodology of the data collection. It is important to have a mixed safer-message because adolescents areat different ages and at different points in their sexual development. It is unfair to over-promote condoms to adolescents who want to abstain from sex and, conversely, to over-promote the value of abstinence to adolescents who are already sexually active. There must be a message for every adolescents, where they are not on the safer-sex continuum.

Limitation of study evaluation

Not surprisingly, the quality of the research methods employed and the strength of the resulting evidence for the impact of the programmes vary greatly from study to study. For example, to minimize selection biases, some studies used random assignment of adolescent to the intervention or comparison conditions, whereas others did not. Some studies involved large sample sizes to ensure adequate statistical power in detecting statistically significant results, while others used relatively small samples, reducing the chance of finding programmatically significant differences. Some measured programme effects for only three months, while others measured long-term impacts of up 24 months. And finally, some used more rigorous statistical analyses, while others failed to control statistically for design limitations. Because of those variations in quality, the strength of the evidence from each study should be considered with caution. Additionally, the strengths of any conclusion about the impact of programmes are confined by the limitations of both individual studies and all studies as a group.

Implications and conclusions

Although as many as 100 NGOs are working in Bangladesh for the improvement of adolescent reprodu ctive health, none of these interventions has been tested or evaluated to claim success of the programme. Consequently, none could be recommended for replication. Programmes recognizing that adolescents can engage in healthy, fulfilling sexual relationships, rather than focusing only on the negative outcomes, may go far in reaching young people with important information. Programmes to improve adolescent reproductive health must understand the risks they face and consider the many influences on adolescents' lives. Such factors as whether adolescents have initiated sexual activity, are married, in school or working, are important. The impact of poverty, gender inequities, legal restrictions and various cultural expectations must also be addressed. Adolescent sexuality is a sensitive subject in all cultures. Programmes that offer reproductive health services to adolescents can expect to encounter some resistance from their community.

Among the programmatic challanges for adolescent interventions, the most important is to opt for the appropriate way to reach the huge number of adolescents in Bangladesh and to provide them with reproductive health services. The mechanism and strategy to provide friendly and acceptable services to the vast number of adolescents adding every year to the existing number need to be decided. Moreover, the barriers prevailing in the society make adolescents reluctant to visit the reproductive health service centres. This situation has facial programme planners with the challange of adopting ways to overcome the barriers and thereby create a supportive environment at the community level in which the process of maximizing sexual reproductive health service utilization by the adolescents will be accelerated (Nath and Barkat, 2000).

Rapid population increase and urbanization place pressure on national health, education and social infrastructures, further reducing access to basic needs. On one hand, it necessitates expeditious implementation of an effective programme, and on the other, the traditional and cultural norms prevailing in Bangladesh hindered the acceptability of new ideas and strategies. Strategies like sex education in schools and easy availability of contraceptives still pose a question of acceptability in the socio-cultural setting of Bangladesh. The health-seeking behaviour of adolescents in Bangladesh indicates that they are more likely to consult non-medical persons (kabiraj/ religious and traditional healers/canvasser) for reproductive health illness, owing to their negative attitude towards service providers. Whether education will change adolescents' health-seeking behaviour as well as induce a positive attitude of adolescents towards service providers is another important programme aspect.

Successful programmes provide necessary counselling and clinical services and aim to help adolescents develop skills to make healthy life choices. These programmes respect the needs, concerns and insights of young people by including them in the design and implementation of activities. Working together with parents, community leaders and health professionals can create programmes that address young people's needs and help them to enjoy a healthy adolescence and become healthy and responsible adults (UNICEF, 1998). With the need for adolescent health services growing fast, it is important that new and expanded programmes build upon successful experience.

In order to address young people's reproductive and sexual health concerns, there need to be more researches and age-specific data to highlight the seriousness of youth's unmet needs for reproductive and sexual health information and services. Whenever possible, programmes should be monitored, evaluated and documented to ensure that their challenges are understood and their successes replicated.

In Bangladesh, the annual age-specific fertility rate for adolescents aged 15-19 according to the 1999-2000 BDHS, is 144 per 1,000 females, which accounts for about 22 per cent of the total annual age-specific fertility rates. This implies that at least one fourth annual fertility could be avoided by increasing the female age at first marriage to 20 years and beyond. Whether the current secondary education programme would help to increase the age at first marriage of adolescents beyond 20 years remains to be seen. The future rests heavily on the welfare of adolescent women, on how well they fulfil their roles as mothers, as contributors to the economy, as teachers of the next generations and as sources of strength for their communities and countries.

As they work towards claiming their full and legitimate place in the world, young women face hardship and challanges. But the challanges for communities and countries to give young women the helping hand they need and deserve is even greater.

References

Alan Guttmacher Institute (AGI) (1998). Into a New World: Young Women's Sexual and Reproductive Lives, (New York, Alan Guttmacher Institute).

Baldo, M., P. Aggleton and G. Slutkin (1993). "Does Sex Education lead to Earlier or Increased Sexual Activity in Youth?", poster presentation at the Ninth International Conference on AIDS, Berlin, Germany, Global Programme on AIDS/WHO (unpublished).

Barkat, A. (2000). Adolescent Reproductive Health: A Challenge, (Dhaka, Bangladesh Rural Advancement Committee (BRAC).

Barnett, B., E. Eggleston, J. Jackson and K. Hardee (1996). Case Study of the Women's Center of Jamaica Foundation Program for Adolescent Mothers, (North Carolina, Family Health International).

Bhuiya, I., U. Rob. M.E. Khan and A. Al-Kabir (2000). "Reproductive health services for adolescents: recent experiences from a pilot project in Bangladesh", paper presented at the International Conference on Adolescent Reproductive Health: Evidence and Programme Implications for South Asia, 1-4 November, Mumbai, India.

Cash, K. and B. Anasuchatku (1995). "Experimental educational interventions for AIDS prevention among Northern Thai single female migratory adolescents", Women and AIDS Program Research

Report Series (Washington DC, Internatioal Center for Research on Women).

Grunseit, A. and S. Kippax (1993). Effects of Sex Education on Young People's Sexual Behaviour (Geneva, Global Programme on AIDS, World Health Organization).

Haider, S.J., S.N. Saleh, N. Kamal and A.N. Gray (1997). "Study of adolescents: dynamics of perception, attitudes, knowledge and use of reproductive health care", Project Report, Population Council and Read. Population Council.

Hong, M.S. and J.J. Nam (1989). "Implication for student's sex education in Korea" Journal of Population and Health Studies 9(1):148-181.

Hossain, S.M.I., I. Bhuiya, A.K.U. Rob and R. Anam (1998). "Directory of organizations working with adolescents/youths" (Dhaka, Population Council).

Jejeebhoy, S.J. (1996a). "Adolescents sexual and reproductive behaviour: a review of the evidence from India", Working Paper No. 3 (Washington DC, International Center for Research on Women(ICRW).

1996b. "Women's education, autonomy and reproductive behaviour: assessing what we have learned" (Honolulu, Program on Population, East-West Center).

Lema, V.M. (1990). "Sexual behaviour, contraceptive practice and knowledge of reproductive biology among adolescent secondary school girls in Nairobi, Kenya", East African Medical Journal 67(2):86-94.

Liskin, L., N. Kak, A.H. Rutledge, L.C. Smit and L. Stewart (1985). "Youth in the 1980s: social and health concerns", Population Reports 13(5), Series M, Number 9.

McCauley, A.P., C. Salter, K. Kiragu and J. Senderowitz (1995). "Meeting the needs of young adults", Population Reports 23(3), Series J, No. 41 (Baltimore, Johns Hopkins School of Public Health, Population Information Program also available online at: www.jhuccp.org/pr/j41edsum.stm).

Mensch, B.S. and C.B. Lloyd (1998). "Gender differences in the schooling experiences of adolescents in low-income countries: the case of Kenya", Studies in Family Planning 29(2):167-184.

Mitra, S.N., A. Al-Sabir, A.R. Cross and K. Jamil (1997). Bangladesh Demographic and Health Surveys 1996-1997 (Dhaka, National Institute of Population Research and Training (NIPORT).

Mitra, S.N., A. Al-Sabir, T. Saha and S. Kumar (2001). Bangladesh Demographic and Health Surveys 1999-2000, (Dhaka, National Institute of Population Research and Training (NIPORT).

National Institute of Population Research and Training (NIPORT) (2001). "Bangladesh maternal health services and maternal mortality survey, 2001", preliminary report.

Nath, D.K. and A. Barkat (2000). "Policies, programs and services for young people's reproductive health in Bangladesh", paper presented at the High-Level Policy Makers Seminar on South-to-South Collaboration, Tokyo.

Ogutu-Ohwayo, J. (1991). "Family life education program of Uganda". Comments on Youth

Programs in Uganda (Personal communication).

PATH (Program for Appropriate Technology in Health) (1998). "Adolescent reproductive health: making a difference". Outlook 16(3).

Pathfinder International (1998). "Insights from adolescent project experience: 1992-1997" (Galen, MA, pathfinder).

Population Council "(2001). "Improving adolescents' reproductive health: Bangladesh", Research Update No. 1, January 2001.

(2002). "Improving adolescents' reproductive health: Bangladesh", Research Update No. 2, January 2002.

RHO (1997-2002)."Program Example", this program example was adapted from materials presented in Description of Specific Programs That Were Assessed for Their HIV/AIDS Communication to Adolescents in Malawi, Zambia, Kenya, and Uganda.

Senderowitz, J. (1995). "Adolescent health: ressessing the passage to adulthood", World Bank Discussion Paper No. 272.

Singh, S. (1998). "Adolescent childbearing in developing countries: a global review", Studies in Family Planning 29(2):117-136.

UNFPA (United Nations Population Fund) (1997). "UNFPA and adolescents" (New York, UNFPA).

(1998a). "The state of the world population 1998 report" (New York, UNFPA).

(1998b). "Report on the round table on adolescent sexual and reproductive health and rights: key feature actions" (New York, UNFPA).

(2000). "Communication and advocacy strategies: adolescent reproductive and sexual health; case study: Nepal", National Resource Center for Non-Formal Education, (NRC-NFE) (Nepal, UNFPA).

UNICEF (United Nations Children's Fund) (1999). "A selective review of interventions for adolescents girls in Bangladesh".

United Nations (1994). Programme of Action of the International Conference on Population and Development, help at Cairo, 5-13 September 1994.

(2000). "Fourth report on the world nutrition situation: nutrition throughout the life cycle", Administrative Committee on Coordination sub-Committee on Nutrition.

WHO "(World Health Organization) (1998). The Second Decade: Improving Adolescent Health and Development (Geneva, WHO).

Index

T

Abbreviations

AHRMS	Access to Health and Reproductive Health Services
APC	Asian Population Conference
APPC	Asian & Pacific Population Conference
BDSH	Bangladesh Demographic and Health Survey
BPMHF	BP Memorial Health Foundation
CDR	Crude Death Rate
ECAFE	Economic Commission for Asia and Far East
ESCAP	Economic and Social Commission for Asia & Pacific
FDI	Foreign Direct Investment
GDP	Gross Domestic Product
ICPD	International Conference on Population & Development
IMR	Infant Mortality Rate
NAYA	Nepal Adolescent and Young Adults Survey
ODA	Official Development Assistance
OEDP	Organisation for Economic Corporation & Development
PATH	Programme for Appropriate Technology in Health
RTI	Reproductive Tract Infection
SOLIDN	Society for Local Integrated Development Nepal
STD	Sexually Transmitted Disease
T-BIRD	Thailand Business Initiative for Rural Development
TDRI	Thailand Development Research Institute

TFR	Total Fertility Rate
UNDP	United Nations Development Programme
UNFPA	United Nations Fund for Population Assistance
WPC	World Population Conference